D1641421

EELS

THE FINAL FRONTIER

*I'd like to dedicate this book to Jean,
my wife, for putting up with me and my
fishing for all these years and unconditionally
supporting me when life's been tough.
And to Josie, the best friend and fishing
companion I ever had, who sadly died
on 19th April, 2001*

EELS

THE FINAL FRONTIER

An insight into the world of
eels and eel fishing

Steve Ricketts

2009
THE MEDLAR PRESS
ELLESMERE

Published by the Medlar Press Limited,
The Grange, Ellesmere, Shropshire.
www.medlarpress.com

ISBN 978-1-899600-97-7

The author and publisher would like to thank all those who
have given permission for copyright material to be reproduced
in this book. If any have been inadvertently overlooked they
will be pleased to make the necessary arrangements.

Produced in England by the Medlar Press Limited, Ellesmere.
Designed and typeset in 11 on 13pt Garamond.

FOREWORD

When it comes to fishing for big eels the angler needs to glean as much information as possible to be consistently successful. In this book Steve shares his experiences of a lifetime of eel fishing that can only help other anglers in their mission for a big eel. Steve has never been afraid to research his fishing by asking other anglers, reading books and other literature available, seeking out potential big fish waters, and trying out and experimenting with new ideas, often spending many sessions between bites, on some very hard waters. It's not easy when no one knows where that big eel could come from; it could be anywhere from the smallest farm pond to the largest reservoir or loch. Using the knowledge he's gained to seek out new waters with potential and locate likely swims, Steve has been able to catch many good eels to well over six pounds and I have little doubt that sometime in the future a very big fish will succumb to his baits.

In this book Steve shares his wisdom, which you should find invaluable in your own search for big eels and the tremendous sport they provide. Catching big eels is never going to be easy. Eels by their very nature are often put off from feeding by moon phases, air temperature, water temperature, and clear skies or just simply by being 'not in the mood'. All of us eel anglers have experienced times when, even on prolific waters, we have blanked, because for some reason the eels were just not having it on that night. In my opinion eels are a formidable quarry, the ultimate challenge in freshwater fishing. They hold many mysteries and defy any attempts to establish patterns; their behaviour can vary from water to water making consistent success difficult to achieve. But far from discouraging us these problems excite us to the challenge, so read the information contained in this book and it will take you on a voyage of discovery into the world of big eel fishing. Take note of what some of these great anglers advise and you won't go far wrong in your own search.

Mick Bowles

CONTENTS

Acknowledgements

From the very beginning of my obsession with pursuing big eels and before I had the nous to make my own decisions and choices, two anglers alone have influenced my fishing career. The late John Sidley, a legend to many and someone I never got to know well enough in person, taught me an awful lot through his writings. Mick Bowles, another great eel pioneer, also played a tutorial role and was not even aware that he'd been doing it. Many years ago he inspired a young angler to pursue eels far more energetically than I could ever have anticipated. His perpetual encouragement has kept me passionate about this style of fishing for well over thirty years now. I am very grateful for his valued advice and for granting me permission to use material that was featured in the British Eel Anglers' Club (BEAC) magazines. Cheers mate!

The biggest thanks must surely go to Ivy and Snook, my grandparents, for starting me on a journey that I have never looked back on. I can never thank them enough.

The enthusiastic offers of help from many anglers, with both text contributions and photos, have been a great source of encouragement on a task I have not found easy. And to all those who have helped I am most grateful. I have received particular help from the following: Damian Wood with his brilliant illustrations; Barry McConnell and Brian Crawford for their contributions to 'Some Memorable Sessions'; Mark Duffy for his knowledge on canal fishing and Nick Duffy for his boundless enthusiasm even while supporting a young family - his phone calls are energising to say the least. A big thanks also to the NAC and the ESG for help with my research; to Petra and Ingrid, my good German friends, for helping an Englishman out with his German language difficulties and to Bradley Baits for supplying me with all my bait requirements for as long as I can remember. To the many other people from all over the world who have sent photos and material I am truly grateful; even if I have erroneously failed to mention your names, you have not been forgotten.

And finally thanks to Jean, my wife, for having faith in me when I lacked it and for just being there - I am forever in your debt.

A Time For Reflecting

The lone eel angler sits quietly behind his rods, sipping his tea. It's been another uneventful night as usual; the bobbins have remained motionless ever since he arrived some hours before nightfall. The darkness is receding now, slowly releasing its grip on the world, the ever increasing brightness over the eastern horizon shows where the sun will soon appear, the beginnings of another glorious hot summer's day. Any frustrations the angler may have felt due to the unproductive night have been absorbed by the gentle, relaxing atmosphere of this beautiful July morning. As the countryside becomes more visible, the once silent, tranquil air fills with the sounds of croaking frogs and the songs of birds as they set out in search of breakfast.

The angler watches a kingfisher, perched low in the branches of an ancient oak, awaiting the opportunity to dive for its first fish of the day. There it sits, eyes transfixed on the water, completely motionless, until suddenly it plunges into the lake, a blur of colour, only to reappear seconds later with its victim well and truly caught in its long powerful beak. Mist is rising from the surface of the lake, where small fish can be seen dimpling the surface, almost giving the appearance of rain. Then, without warning, the flat calm is disturbed by a larger fish, porpoising playfully, sending ripples across the water. The angler gazes across the lake, watching the fish activity. Deep in thought, he nostalgically reflects upon his many previous encounters with large eels in the lake, remembering both those he had won and those he had lost.

This is a time for reflecting, it's the time when the memories come flooding back, the good, the bad, happy and sad, and the downright filthy. The angler drinks in the atmosphere, at perfect peace with the world around him. His thoughts are momentarily disturbed by a rustling from the undergrowth and after a few moments a water rat appears, sniffing the air, whiskers twitching, then scampers across the bank and into the water. The angler watches the creature until it swims out of sight. The day is beginning too for the lake's ducks, which set about their new day in the usual raucous fashion. The warming rays of the sun spread across the lake, bringing everything to life. Soon the gentle stillness of the lake will be shattered by the hordes of kids and pleasure anglers converging to enjoy a summer's day by the lake. It's time to pack up and go home; the delightful, majestic half-light of dawn has given way to bright sunshine, making the rest of the day something of an anti-climax.

INTRODUCTION

Have you any idea what a *bundaal* is (German), a *snurring* (Swedish) or *un pipale* (French)? No? Well you would certainly recognise them if you saw them for they are all names for the European eel. This book is about the dedicated pursuit of big eels, not a thought that inspires many anglers to grab their rods and dash to the bankside but for some die-hards it is the ultimate challenge, the last unknown frontier in fishing. Many years of hard fishing may be required to accomplish even a moderate level of consistent success, for a big eel is a powerful, awe-inspiring fish by anyone's standards - thick-set, muscular and mean-looking, it has a reputation for being a nightmare to land and handle. But big eels are so far removed from the line-tangling menace of the little eels most fisherman encounter and curse, it could almost be considered another species. There are many anglers out there who will not even approach a big eel after it has been hooked or landed, choosing to cut the trace line and let the fish go rather than deal with it on the bank. But those anglers who do not specifically fish for them have to admit to being impressed by a big eel's appearance even if only witnessing someone else's capture, or having the good fortune to accidentally hook one themselves (although this may not be perceived as such at the time).

The dedicated Anguilla hunter is commonly imagined with blood-shot, tired eyes peering out from under a woolly hat, tatty clothing covered in eel slime and a face covered in mozzie bites. He carries archaic fishing tackle and is shunned by everyone else on the water. In reality this couldn't be further from the truth, at least for the majority of us. The modern Anguilla hunter has an unrivalled thirst for knowledge, a need to understand the eel's behaviour and without doubt, a great love of catching them. Tackle and rigs are regularly modified and altered, different baits are trialled, and most importantly, we take great care of our captors and release them alive.

I truly believe eels should command the respect of the big fish world as much as any other species of fish but they appear to be seen as an eccentric exploit rather than a serious long-term challenge. I have therefore decided to put pen to paper (very difficult for an eel angler) and have written this book in the hope that it may enlighten a few of you as to why we pursue a fish most anglers seem to loath. I also hope that this book becomes a valued and worthy addition to the ever growing specimen hunter's library and if it tempts a few of you into having a dabble for what I regard as a very formidable opponent it will have done what I most hoped it would achieve. This book may also appeal to those experienced eel anglers who would like to know more about their quarry; or to those anglers just curious as to why people fish for eels in the first place. As most anglers decide to specialise in one species or another at some time during their fishing career, I hope that I can convince them that the catching of big eels is just as much an achievement as catching a specimen of any other species, if not more so.

With the dedicated pursuit of one species comes the urge to increase catches and this soon gets the old grey matter working overtime. 'Chuck it and chance it' fishing is no longer enough and the angler needs to catch those bigger fish, not by luck, but by a determined, well thought out approach. To catch big fish consistently you need to understand as much about the species being sought as possible: their basic habits and behavioural patterns; the way the fish works in regards to finding its food; which areas it prefers to occupy and any little quirks or oddities the fish may have. In fact, ideally, you must know your quarry better than it knows itself. Seeking out big fish of any species, let alone eels, is a serious challenge that requires time, effort and dedication, but you should never lose sight of the fact that fishing should be a pleasure and that there are other things in life. Too many good relationships have gone down the drain due to the absentee specimen hunter neglecting his household responsibilities. Try and take satisfaction and enjoyment from all your fishing, from every fish you catch, irrespective of their size. The catching of big fish is by no means a measure of someone's angling ability, although it does help to keep you motivated, especially if you can sneak the odd specimen out every now and then. There are days when I can only spare a few hours, yet I still enjoy running a stick float down a small stream and catching 4oz dace as much as the long weekend sessions bivvied up after eels. One of the most important ingredients of success is to simply enjoy what you are doing. If the fishing starts to become a chore, take a break and return when the urge takes you. This is sound advice; I have taken breaks and returned with the fire rekindled, raring to go. Burnout does become a problem amongst specialist anglers and many a good friend and fisherman has quit for this very reason.

Searching out those old lakes, hidden away in the wilds and rumoured to contain legendary fish, can, at times, be almost as exciting as trying to catch the monsters. Walking round a new lake and imagining where the big fish are lurking, then deciding on a suitable choice of swim, is all very much an integral part of the process. Big eel fishing should not be taken lightly. The angler, who has a deep knowledge of the fish, understands waters and knows when and where to use the correct tackle will be far more successful in the long run. The angler who uses his initiative rather than blindly following the ideas of other anglers will, in the end, succeed. And success gained this way is by far the most satisfying.

There is a worrying trend amongst modern anglers to follow fashion and eel fishing is definitely not fashionable. It is at the other end of the scale, with eel fishermen being seen as scruffy eccentrics. Yet I would argue that we are pioneers on the final frontier of angling, individualists with free minds who do not follow fashions. If you are sitting down reading this book, there's a good possibility that you feel like this too. Eel fishing is a specialised branch of our sport. It will never attain the following other species have - it's too hard and success can be a long time in coming - but the reasons we go are probably the same as those that drive the rest of the specimen hunting world: we go fishing to enable us to forget the hustle and bustle of everyday life, the stress of work and other worries; we go to lose ourselves in the pleasure of being by the water, to enjoy the peace and quiet and the prospect of catching a whopper by design.

I very much hope that you enjoy reading this book and that it helps you to put some better fish on the bank, or even your first fish, come to that. I have enlisted the help of some of the country's top eel anglers, past and present, in an attempt to provide a thorough and experienced view of this branch of angling. Your early results will not match theirs, given that many of them have been fishing for decades, but with thought, dedication and patience you may one day even surpass their achievements; such is progress. Take pleasure from everything you catch, retain a sense of humour and enjoy what you do; this is really what all fishing should be about.

Tight lines!

CHAPTER ONE

A BRIEF HISTORY

Has the thought ever crossed your mind as to why there are so few serious eel anglers if the fish I speak about is the challenge to end all challenges? I've thought about it and for the life of me cannot come up with a legitimate answer. Most anglers have at some time or other hooked a fish and wondered what the bloody hell they've become attached to as it battles away on the end of the line. They anticipate a fish of four or five pounds, and when finally an eel surfaces of around a pound and a half in weight they're suddenly disappointed that it's 'only an eel'. What do they want from a fish? They've just had a fight pound for pound beyond the capabilities of most other fish and they're miffed they might lose a hook or get their net slimy. Some fishermen just don't want to know about eels, displaying incredible ignorance and sometimes just down-right stupidity: there are a few anglers I know who, with any mention of eels, would be on a soapbox in Hyde Park before you could blink an eye. I've also been told that eel fishermen are too secretive about their quarry.

I hope I can persuade you to at least try eel fishing; meet some of us on the bank and you'll be surprised by how open we can be and how many of us there are tucked away in far-flung corners of quiet little lakes. We have a passion for our fishing matched by very few groups these days. True, many of us have been known to beat around the bush when it comes to discussing the subject of eel fishing, especially when taking part in the lakeside chitchat that is now so commonplace on many of today's syndicate and club waters. But that's not because we have a great secret to hide or even that we dislike the company of other people, indeed nothing could be further from the truth. When confronted by another like-minded angler with a mutual admiration for eels it's a hard job to shut us up - rabbit, rabbit, rabbit, we could talk the hind-legs off a donkey. What really makes us clam up and dodge the subject is those mind-numbingly predictable remarks like 'Why on earth do you wanna catch them?' or 'You've gotta be mad

As a youngster this was my idea of heaven.

fishing for eels' - and those are some of the more pleasant remarks that drive us to fish the unsociable swims. And as for being considered mad for doing so, that's a matter of opinion, although my wife might well agree as her idea of going fishing for the weekend is to disappear inside the bivvy with a bottle of wine and a good book, hic! Maybe she does have a point worth considering.

So, what with the endless taunting by bankside plonkers, the endless blank sessions that are entailed, and the filthy English weather, why, you may well ask, do we still want to fish for eels? It's a question I've put to myself on many a fruitless night and the answer is always the same: fascination, not just with the catching of them but their whole mysterious life cycle. Over the years I've dabbled with all sorts of fishing: match fishing, pursuing big carp and pike, even chasing marlin and sailfish in the Indian Ocean. Yet as soon as my feet are back on English terra firma my thoughts turn straight away towards old slimy. If it were possible to explain this strange affliction I could probably solve all the problems of addiction single-handed and retire a very rich man.

My curiosity with the highly edible, not to say phallically suggestive creature known as the eel started when I was very young, the seeds of fascination being well and truly planted by my grandparents. In 1962 I was born into a family that treated pie and mash and jellied eels as the food of the gods and so have been associated with eels for a very long time - not always in ways that had any regard for their preservation. Life has taught me one simple rule about eels, and that is that people who do not eat them usually despise them, either for what the small ones do to their tackle or for the fact that, in appearance, they resemble that age-old terror, the snake.

My love affair with trying to catch the enigmatic eel with a fishing rod and line started a long, long time ago - a time when an armpit fart was the funniest thing in the world (apart from the real thing of course) and when a tin of Tizer stopped me asking the inevitable question 'are we nearly there yet?'. My grandparents and John and Doll (my uncle and aunt) would regularly take me on holiday. We'd pile into the back of a VW camper-van and head for scary Aunt Daisy's in Aldringham, Suffolk. In theory, I was going along so as to give my parents a rest, but I soon discovered that this was a subtle ploy - adults have an ulterior motive for most things in life and my trips to Suffolk were going to be no exception. The real reason, so it turned out, was that I was to be used to catch dinner. On many occasions, much to my absolute delight, I was left to try and catch eels, sometimes at Thorpness Mere, set adrift in a little leaky old punt, or best of all at a place called the Eels Foot Inn at Lieston. That really is the name of the place (I've got a cloth badge to prove it). Whilst they sat in the pub with cold beers I would be set loose on the other side of the hedge, lowering worms through small gaps in the abundant weed-beds of a narrow two-foot deep drainage channel. Although they very rarely exceeded a pound in weight, I remember them as being huge, slimy monsters.

One encounter I had with them almost scarred me for life. It was a typically warm summer's day in July. My grandparents had left me happily catching small eels from the nearby dykes while they enjoyed the hospitality of the Eels Foot Inn. As I slowly worked my way from weed-bed to weed-bed an eruption of bubbles and bottom debris halted my progress. My curiosity was fully aroused, as I knew from my limited experience that a fish had entered the weed-bed and I had taken fish in similar circumstances by dropping my bait into any available clear spots amongst the weeds. Scampering along to the still bubbling weed-bed, I lowered my worm into a small gap and waited for the float to settle. It always took a bit of jiggling to get it to drop through the surface muck but in the end it usually settled nicely. I was in no way prepared for what happened on this occasion. Instead of settling, the float shot away and the 6-foot glass rod was nearly wrenched from my hands as it took on the most alarming bend I had ever witnessed. As I screamed at the top of my voice, Snook (my grandad), followed by others from the pub, came running to see who was trying to kill me, only to find me hanging on to the rod for dear life. A large black eel, intent on dragging me in, was trying to leave the dyke from the opposite bank. Snook grabbed the rod and hauled back, the rod creaked and bent double. Another good pull and the eel came slithering out of the water on to our side of the bank and just lay there in the grass, unmoving, its eyes fixed on us, or so it appeared. The thing I clearly remember, even now over thirty years on, was the appearance of that fish. It was jet black with a multitude of white scars running over its head, and a large bottom jaw giving it the appearance of a boxer who had suffered a very hard life.

Snook stepped forward saying "Dinner's up, lads" and grabbed the eel, which in turn sank its teeth into his wrist. Arms flailing, Snook flung the eel back in the direction of the dyke, into which it disappeared like a scalded cat and was never seen again. Many times over the years I re-fished that section of dyke and never hooked an eel that remotely approached the size of that one. I feared that fish like I feared the monster under the bed, yet I dreamed of catching it again, seeing it drift out of the mysterious depths of sleep to take my bait. Snook said it was probably around three pounds in weight and still talks of it whenever eels are mentioned in polite conversation. And me, I'd still like to catch it again, although my aspirations are now somewhat higher than a 3-pounder.

Even as I progressed into my early teens I couldn't escape eels. I tried, but the only place that I could fish at the time was choc-a-bloc with them. I spent much of the early Seventies fishing. When I should have been beavering away at school, me and my fishing bud Terry, could be found wetting a line in and around Old Father Thames. During the summer school holidays and on most weekends I could be found fishing the old docks in and around south-east London and the Thames at the back of the council estate where I lived. I have some fond memories of the docks but they are very different places now, having been developed for up-market residential housing, and most of the place names have been changed to make the area sound more attractive to the wealthy occupants. It would be nice to think that some of the old residents are still swimming about in the docks (now quaintly known as 'quays') but as I'll probably never bother to fish there again, I will never really know for sure.

Right: Two 1lb eels from the river Delph in Norfolk 1978.

Below: A typical docklands swim from my early fishing exploits.

I suppose, when it boils down to it, I never set out deliberately to catch eels from the docks - they just happened to come along whilst I was fishing for anything that would pull the lobworm-baited float rig under. Sometimes ignorance is a great asset when you're a youngster; I didn't know eels were predominately bottom feeders and happily float fished for them. How many people now, I wonder, would consider fishing for eels six foot down in forty foot of water during daylight hours? Back then, I didn't know any different and I caught a lot of fish from the docks, not just eels but also roach, bream, carp, trout, rudd and smelts, at a time when most people had written these places off because of the supposedly high levels of pollution.

Now smelts are definitely one of the strangest fish I ever came across when fishing the docks. These are not the salmon fry; they are a species in their own right. When I had the misfortune of encountering a large shoal of these luminescent silvery-green fish I went home stinking not of fish, as you would expect, but cucumber of all things. I often had problems trying to explain to my mum that I had been fishing and not fighting in the local greengrocers. Anyone who has ever caught smelt will know exactly what I mean; on the frozen fish that you buy for pike bait from tackle shops the smell is nowhere near as strong.

At the tender age of fifteen my career prospects had improved and I'd managed to talk my way into a Saturday job in 'Lock, Stock and Barrel', the local tackle shop. This introduced me to new ideas such as using ledger rigs for eels, something I had never previously considered. Working in a tackle shop I got to hear all sorts of tall stories, and even those I suspected as being total fabrication (polite word for bullshit) fired me with enthusiasm to go fishing. The tackle shop also gave me access to the fishing weeklies and monthly magazines, and I would marvel at the fish in them for ages. I started cutting out and collecting information or pictures on eels, and anything else to do with fishing on the Thames, much to the annoyance of my boss as, by the time he got around to reading the papers, they were full of holes. Working in this type of environment, it wasn't long before I had the incentive to start fishing for certain fish by design and one of my hopes was to catch a big eel. With two new Woolworth's carp rods and a pair of Intrepid Black Princes (anyone else remember those?) I started trying to emulate the catches of fish I'd seen in the papers.

Over the next few years, on my faithful Honda SS50 moped, I made trips to several weirs on the Thames, a lake in Suffolk and another small lake in Kent, all of which gave me plenty of fish but not the size of fish I so desperately wanted. So, not getting the success I thought I deserved, and being 'at that age' as they say, my fishing career went on hold for a while as my hormones kicked in and I discovered the scourge of all fishermen, women. However, even with the hormones flooding through my veins I still managed to do some fishing but I must admit it was mostly after carp, pike and tench. Eels didn't feature much more on my wanted list until the exploits of two anglers began to grab my attention: John Sidley and Mick Bowles. One or the other of these two seemed to appear regularly in the angling papers with good fish - fish I wanted to catch.

These anglers rekindled my interest and it wasn't long before I was back into eel fishing, leaving many a girl with broken hearts as I exchanged nights in with them for nights out with a fishing rod. It was also around this time that I became aware of the British Eel Anglers' Club (BEAC), formed in May 1980 by three anglers, Mick Bowles, John Sidley and Gerry Rogers. It wasn't long before I became an enthusiastic member, looking forward each quarter to its regular magazine and bulletin. I never really became an active member of the Club until its latter years when I began to write articles and to attend as many of the Club fish-ins as possible. By then, with a personal best eel of 4lb 2oz, I considered myself on the way to becoming a serious eel angler and was full of enthusiasm. Some of the best years of my eeling were spent on club fish-ins, not because of the great fishing, although there was some of that, but because of the camaraderie and characters that I met on these trips. However, after John Sidley passed away, I seemed to be in a minority as club membership dwindled. For me it was a sad day when the British Eel Anglers' Club (BEAC) finally faded out of existence in the mid to late Nineties. I learnt an awful lot about eels and eel fishing from the Club and, since then, have taken fifty-two fish over five pounds and five just over six. With luck, there will be bigger ones in the future. For this I owe the Club a big debt of thanks.

My eel fishing has progressed a long way from those early days of innocence. I still enjoy catching eels of most sizes but I no longer weigh fish under three pounds nor photograph fish under four. This is not to say I don't respect fish of this size, as any eel over two pounds is a good fish; they are just not the specimen fish I'm after. Having caught hundreds of eels this size I have served my apprenticeship and now the search is for bigger things - the eel angler's dream, maybe that elusive double, or what I regard as the magic figure, eight pounds.

Now, in the twenty-first century, a large proportion of my eeling is concentrated on low population, big fish waters that can be very hard. I have yet to set my hook into that exceptionally big fish but will keep on trying, occasionally dabbling for other species to keep me sane. My upbringing determined that I would fish for eels and I have never been able to shake that off, something I curse my grandparents for after a rough session. Now, where once they were caught for the pot, all the fish go back. It's something my grandparents would curse *me* for but, having hunted and learnt so much about the eel, I would much rather see them swim back to the depths from which they came.

So if it's a challenge you seek, try and catch an 8lb-plus eel by design. There is no harder task in the specimen-hunting world than that. Eels are one of the few fish that have not been artificially fattened up with high protein baits or trout pellets and then stocked in commercial fisheries. (If they are there, they've got there under their own steam and may well have gone undetected for many years.) They are also one of the few fish that have defied all man's attempts to control, breed or domesticate them. Size apart, eels offer a challenge few other fish can match, and that is the challenge of pursuing a truly wild indigenous fish: the last corner of the unknown for British anglers to conquer. I hope I will enjoy many more years hunting one of the most ancient of British fish . . . and with that thought in mind I will get on with the book.

Chapter Two

The Eel's Life Cycle

Most people know something about the strange life cycle of the eel - where it breeds, its journeys to and from the ocean, for instance - but there is far more to the mysterious life of the eel than even the most experienced angler could ever imagine. There are extraordinary features about the lives of many migratory fish, but none perhaps more extraordinary, more startling, than those experienced by the humble eel. In strength, in stamina, in diversity, the eel is the rival of the salmon; in many respects it outshines it. These two species, so different from each other yet so very much alike both journey many miles to spawn and die, a journey that takes them across the world at great peril. So what makes the eel stand out? Well, for a start, many of the facts unearthed by modern science would almost certainly have been considered science fiction were it not for a few pioneering, extremely single-minded men.

So, in the spirit of those who have researched the eel in the past, I will begin simply by introducing you to the eel and its family. I will delve into some of its history, one that is so very much entwined with ours. It is a partnership that has evolved over eons of years to the extent that we have incorporated it into our language ('as slippery as an eel') and have named geographical places after it - Eel Pie Island on the Thames and Ely in Cambridgeshire (said to be so named because rents were paid in eels to the lords of the manor). I will also try to unravel some of the many mysteries surrounding its quite remarkable life cycle as well as taking a look at some of the problems it faces now. Some of these problems are naturally occurring phenomena that most wild creatures have to contend with at one time or another; others are solely caused by man's ignorance of the delicate ecosystem in which he lives. The eel's journey to and from the great oceans is fraught with danger and its long-term survival will depend not only on how it deals with the obstacles in its way but on how man controls his use of the environment.

Anguilla anguilla is the Latin name for the fish we more commonly know as the European or common eel. It is almost certainly one of the most well known and easily recognisable of the fish species we have swimming around our inland waterways and coasts. Over time, in fact many millions of years, eels have adapted so well to their environment and specialised way of life that evolution has had little need to improve on a very successful design. Consequently the eel's appearance has not significantly changed since its ancestors swam the lakes and rivers way back in the Cretaceous era, an era when dinosaurs roamed freely and man had yet to make an appearance. Even today, with the advent of fast food and off-the-shelf dinners, most non-anglers will recognise eels straight away, and the main reason for that is their continued gastronomic and economic importance to us. Throughout man's evolution they have been regarded as an important source of nutrition and today, with a global market in excess of $2 billion dollars, they have become even more popular. In the Orient, they are highly regarded as a prized delicacy, and demand for them in Europe is not that far behind. Therein lies one of the greatest threats to their continued existence.

Describing the European eel to a non eel-angler is a relatively easy task but there are things you probably never knew. For instance the eel's skin is particularly interesting, it is smooth and polished, with a surface that is devoid of roughness, yet embedded in the skin are scales. If you look closely at large specimens you will notice the fish is covered in small oblong patches placed at right-angles to each other forming an intricate mosaic-style pattern. These are very rudimentary scales, rarely bigger than four or five millimetres, and unlike those of other fish, they do not overlap and are attached to the eel's thick, flexible skin. Known as cycloid scales, they form after roughly five or six years of life and are a type of scale that is unique to the anguilliforme species as they are enclosed and not external. Most fish have a garment of scales, which serves to protect the delicate skin underneath. With the eel, the scales are actually lodged into the skin, making the eel the naked fish of the waterways. In addition to these scales, eels protect themselves with a slippery coating of mucous, which, coupled with their undulating suppleness, make them extremely difficult to handle (as anyone who has tried to grasp one will know). So, here we are presented with the first of the eel's mysteries: are these scales regressive or progressive and what function do they serve, as little protection is gained by their size and placement? I have yet to find a reasonable explanation in any of the current research.

A little word of warning here to all those people who have to handle eels, especially those people who cut them into chunks and eat them. Eel's blood is poisonous and if you have a cut or a nasty scrape, the poison could find its way into your system. The first signs of poisoning are inflammation, itchiness of the wound followed by discoloration, discharge and sometimes fluid retention. The toxic substance called *ichthyotoxin* (or fish poison) is found in many species of fish, mostly tropical, but then the eel was conceived in the tropics. The eel's serum is extremely toxic - a few milliletres injected into a rabbit would undoubtedly kill it. Eels can sometimes bleed around the mouth and gills for no apparent reason so people handling eels should take care. This could be a form of self-defence as it seems unlikely they would produce toxic blood for any other purpose. Having said all that, I have never actually heard of anyone being poisoned by an eel but forewarned is forearmed.

Eels have a dorsal fin, starting close to the head and running continuously down the back, and an anal fin, which starts just behind the vent and continues until it joins with the dorsal fin. There is no separate tail fin. The eel is part of a very large family of fish, Anguilliformes, which include approximately four hundred known species. Of these, only fifteen varieties are known to live in freshwater. The species includes some of the ocean's meanest predators, for instance the conger and the voracious moray - fish that can attain lengths of well over three metres (ten feet) and weights of several hundred pounds. However, most species of eel are less than one metre in length. Their natural habitats include lakes, rivers and many of the shallow coastal waters and estuarine systems throughout the world although some species have been found flourishing at depths of over 250 metres (820 feet). The eels that fall into the family of Anguillidae are catadromous, that is they require salt water to spawn but then live out their lives in freshwater lakes, rivers and streams.

Eels have several neat survival tricks tucked up their sleeves and one is a rather special ability that very few other species of fish possess. They have a very dense capillary system close to the surface of their skin which enables them to absorb small amounts of oxygen directly from the surrounding air and they can also hold a small amount of water in the mouth and throat that is used to keep the gills wet. (You may well have noticed this, as eels out of water appear to puff up their heads.) Providing they remain damp, eels can therefore slither out of one stream or lake and travel across land until they arrive at another watercourse, something they do with unerring accuracy. It's also believed that they use their highly developed olfactory senses to locate new areas of water to occupy. There have been many documented instances of eels surviving out of water for more than forty-eight hours in the right conditions.

Once eels enter freshwater they become secretive creatures, feeding principally on bottom dwelling invertebrates. Their intake is largely determined by what is available - live and dead fish being taken occasionally - and most of their feeding activity occurs during the hours of darkness. The eel seeks darkness with as much eagerness as it seeks warmth; on the whole it is to be numbered with all the nocturnal creatures of the water, which become active after the sun has set. It retains the impressions acquired in the depths of the ocean where it was born. On the majority of waters only at night do they move, give chase and eat but there are exceptions. The muddy estuaries and lakes scattered around our country offer eels twenty-four hour feeding as light rarely pierces these environments. Eels possess an extremely acute sense of smell that is of great assistance in the location of its food, a subject I will come back to in the next chapter. Old and decaying food is highly unattractive to the European eel; it very much prefers its meals to be fresh even if they are not alive and kicking.

Hunting for food in cold weather is minimal; eels roll up and bury themselves into silt or weed-beds, almost going into hibernation below temperatures of 10°c, as cold weather can prove lethal. The eel's aversion to the cold is a well-documented fact; there are no species of eels in the arctic regions - none in the rivers of Siberia, the Volga, the Danube or any of its tributaries. Europe has four different species and the further south you travel the more abundant in size and quantity the various species of eel become.

Once they have taken up residence in a lake or river system, larger eels appear to become quite territorial. Researchers have been especially interested in determining whether eels have territories, and if they do, how big they are. It's an important issue for biologists because it impacts on decisions relating to the monitoring and management of eel fisheries. Scientists have found that eels do have territories and that the size of these areas varies according to location and food supply. Eels that inhabit small streams and rivers tend to move around far more than their brethren that inhabit our lakes, pools and canals. These territories are where they will hunt and forage for their food. They are only believed to change these habitats during transitional periods such as spring and autumn, returning each season to the same place. There is some evidence to support this as eels that have been transported, tagged and released have successfully found their way back to their original home waters. Steven Parker, a marine researcher in the state of Maine, USA, attached transmitters to eels before moving them ten to seventeen kilometres away from their home range into waters of different salinity. He found that the eels were not only able to survive this abrupt change in salinity, but were able to make their way unerringly back home to where they were originally captured. It made no difference which direction they were moved in, or into what territory they were placed, they quickly and directly orientated themselves towards their home water.

Extreme measures like blinding the nostalgic little eel doesn't slow it down for one moment. And squirting formaldehyde into its nostrils to kill the epithelium (the thin lining of tissue that contains olfactory sense cells) results only in what has been described as 'a significant loss of orientation ability'. The only way, it seems, to prevent an eel from getting home is to sever its olfactory nerves entirely. Such invasive studies I find extremely distressing; the fact that they were thought to be necessary by the scientific community is a measure of their frustration when faced with behaviour for which they have no easy explanation. Even after all these tests and experiments it still remains unclear what cues eels use to locate an area; olfaction is the most important, but is not the only sense used. It may also be possible that eels possess an inbuilt compass to orientate themselves by using the Earth's magnetic fields, but why it should go to all this bother rather than making its new environment its home is beyond our understanding at the present time.

Eels are also known to be a very slow growing fish, and can attain great age if prevented from migrating or if just left alone undisturbed. One eel known as 'Putte' was caught in 1863 as an elver and was placed in an aquarium at the Museum of Halsingborg, Sweden. She died eighty-five years later in the autumn of 1948, and this is the oldest European eel of which I have any details. I have managed to locate one report of an eel that was supposedly older but this was a New Zealand long-finned eel that was dated at a hundred and six years old!

To find out how old an eel actually is you need to count the rings on the sagittal otolith bone, in much the same way as you would count the rings on a tree. (The otolith is a small part of the organ that controls the eel's sense of balance.) This technique is by far the most accurate means of determining the age of any species of fish and is widely accepted as such. To achieve this, the eel has to be sacrificed and the otoliths removed. The otolith is then burnt and cracked, mounted against a glass slide in silicone rubber and the rings are counted under 100-x magnification. As a rough guideline, female eels will mature anywhere between ten and eighteen years old, at an average weight of between one and three pounds, although they can achieve much greater weights. Males mature much earlier, somewhere between nine and twelve years and only reach half the weight of the females. These are only rough estimates as eels as old as fifty-seven years have been known to set out on the migratory run. W. Russell Poole and Julian D. Reynolds have attempted to prove this in their research on Irish eels. Why there is such vast variation in age and size in these individuals is something we just can't find an answer for at the moment; perhaps sometimes a flood frees fish landlocked for a long time and at other times Nature's trigger does not fire. It's a subject that, again, needs more research.

So now let's join the eel on its journey, starting from British waters. With the coming of autumn the mature eel is driven by incomprehensible urges more mysterious, more impenetrable than our minds can fathom, to make for some particular watery dwelling thousands of miles away. The adult eel, moved by an instinctual force, which outweighs the vast distances involved, is then compelled to leave its safe, comfortable home in the lakes and streams of England. They are driven to make their way towards the sea, gorging themselves with as much food as they can eat in preparation for a journey that over millennia has increased to epic proportions. Around 130 million years ago, when the Atlantic was no wider than the English Channel and most of the world was covered by the Pacific Ocean, the distant relatives of the European eel had only a short hop to spawn in this narrow stretch of sea. Over time, as the Earth's tectonic plates shifted and the continents moved apart, the eel's journey to the spawning grounds has increased to many thousands of miles.

As the eel exits freshwater on the start of its migration and approaches saltwater, their bodies begin to undergo numerous physiological changes. They put on a considerable amount of body fat. Their eyes become larger, almost doubling in size and the retinal pigments that are sensitive to red light in freshwater are replaced by pigments sensitive to the blue light that permeates the ocean environment more easily. This provides them with optimal vision in the sea. Their body coloration then changes to silver and they increase their ability to excrete salts; this is when sea anglers regularly know them as silver eels. The final phase of the of the eel's life sees even more dramatic transformations. Once the eels are at sea the next changes happen to their bodies as they approach the continental shelf. Their stomachs dissolve, rendering them incapable of eating and they spend the next year swimming and drifting with the current. The female eel now directs all her bodily resources to the generation of eggs; her ovaries grow to occupy almost her entire body cavity where she can carry as many as 20 million, when released, free floating eggs. She then spawns somewhere around mid-water (although this has never been actually witnessed). After performing this duty, spent and exhausted, the adult eel disappears and is presumed to die. Much of this part of an eel's life was deduced from size distribution across the Atlantic, and basically speculation, as the spawning of the eel has never been witnessed nor has an adult ready to spawn eel ever been found in that region. We only know about the formation of the eggs from laboratory tests where eels have been given hormone treatments to advance artificial maturation.

Since the 1920s it has been presumed that once the eels arrived at the breeding grounds from their various different continents they engaged in a mating

Top: Image from The Outline of Science (1922) *1. The transparent larva called a Leptocephalus. 2 and 3. The gradual change to a cylindrical shape. The body becomes shorter and loses weight. 4. The young elver, which makes its way from open sea to estuaries and rivers. It is 2-3 inches long. 5. The fully-formed eel.*

Bottom: Close-up of the elver or glass eel stage. These are now recognisable as the fish we catch.

free-for-all, or what is known as a 'panmixia'. However, there is now strong evidence to suggest that this may not always be the case and that eels mate with the eels that have come from the same regions from which they started their own voyage. This may just be down to timing as migrating eels from one area would arrive at different times to those from another and the arriving eels would mate with whoever was around, and this would, most likely, be their travelling companions. Mating in this manner means that information passed on through the genes is not corrupted with new DNA from eels arriving from different parts of the world. Interestingly, there have been several recent breakthroughs in genetic isolation, which have further added to the eel's mystery as they appear to suggest that a tiny eel, at birth, is already programmed with the genetic codes and directions back to the same place from which its parents originated.

After the eggs have drifted around in the swirling Sargasso currents for a while the tiny eels hatch. They bear no resemblance to the adult fish whatsoever; instead they look like tiny, transparent leaves and are called *Leptocephalus brevirostris*, which is Greek for thin head, short nose, a name that was given prior to anyone realising this was the larval stage of the eel.

They drift along at the mercy of the currents, feeding on plankton until approximately three years on when they arrive back at our shores measuring about 45mm, having undergone another metamorphosis. They now resemble tiny eels and are called 'elvers' or 'glass eels'. These new eels, which could have fallen prey to pretty much anything with a mouth on their voyage home, are now capable of becoming predators themselves. They prey on tiny invertebrates as they make their way back to the ancestral haunts in the pools, lakes and rivers their parents left over four years earlier, thus completing the cycle. One of the most famous places to witness this mass arrival was Epney on the river Severn, an event known as the 'eel fare' (the celebration of young eels running back up the rivers). Here they would once appear in their millions but sadly not today, thanks to the reduction in stocks caused by the eel's increasing popularity as a deli food and the need to stock eel farms . There is one old report of almost two and a half tons of elvers being landed in one day on the Great Ouse, but catches such as these are truly a thing of the past and may never be repeated, several pounds being regarded as a good catch by today's standards

Research into the eel's life has gone on for many thousands of years; the Egyptians studied them, as did the Romans, and they were even worshipped as gods by some Indian cultures. One of the earliest people to have a go at solving the riddle of the eel is believed to be the Greek scientist Aristotle, 2,400 years ago. Aristotle was acknowledged as being a pretty smart man who gave a lot of thought to the eel. The Greeks considered eels a great delicacy, regarding them as the king of fish, and, allegedly, Aristotle was not averse to tucking into a plate of eels baked in a coating of asparagus, cabbage and beet whilst pondering the great mysteries of the fish he was devouring. One of the things that troubled the great philosopher was the fact that eels appeared to have no reproductive organs when dissected, no eggs and no sperm, and tiny eels just appeared as if by magic. In fact, he concluded in his great book 'The History of Animals' (*Historia Animalium*) that eels were born from the Earth's guts by spontaneous generation and as such needed no fertilisation.

Almost three hundred years later, the renowned Roman naturalist Pliny the Great proposed another theory that became widely believed. He, too, believed eels self generated but that they did so by rubbing against rocks, and in so doing produced shreds that then became young eels and swam off. At least this idea has some precedent in nature: plants can be propagated from cuttings and Pliny simply applied this principle to eels without further observation. Other early explanations given for the birth of the eel are farcical to say the least. Some believed that eels sprang from rotting vegetation on the bottom of a pond; that they magically emerged from the gills of other fish; that they emerged from dying beetles; that they grew from horses' hairs dropped in water; that they issued from the cool, sweet dews of May mornings; not to mention that old wives' tale passed down from our own area of fenland up near Norfolk. St Dunstan, so the story goes, in a holy rage consigned a group of sinful monks and priests to eternal slippery penance and the eel was born of a curse.

Eels appearing to emerge from a dead beetle from David Cairncross' The Origin of the Silver Eel, *1852.*

In the early eighteenth century the great Linnaeus, in successive editions of his *Systema Naturae: 'Anguilla'*, stated that eels are 'viviparous', that is to say their eggs are fertilised internally and the young are brought forth alive. It was a theory torn apart by Francesco Redi of Pisa, who clearly showed that the young eels taken from inside the adult fish were in fact parasitic worms. It wasn't until 1777 when the renowned Italian scientist, Carlo Mondini, a professor at the University of Bologna, suddenly claimed to have discovered the eel's reproductive organs that eels were deemed acceptable to class as true fish. His *De Anguillie Ovariis* at the time was considered a masterpiece of accurate descriptive writing and by all accounts is still regarded very highly today.

This discovery raised many doubts amongst much of the scientific community, especially one of his fellow countrymen, Spallanzini, another illustrious physiologist and a supporter of Redi's earlier theories. Much bickering and hurling of scientific papers ensued and it wasn't until 1850, long after Mondini's death, that his hypotheses were ratified by Martin Rathke who, in that year, published the definitive guide to the genitalia of *Anguilla anguilla*. Almost all discoveries rely on an element of luck and in 1895, in the Straits of Messina, two Italian scientists, Grassi and Calandruccio were to have theirs. The Straits of Messina are the scene of violent conflicting currents caused by a giant plateau reaching out from great depths of water. Here, creatures normally living in the depths are driven to the surface and in this very place the first real evidence of the eel's origins was discovered. Grassi and Calandruccio, in the course of their research, caught some small clear ribbon-like creatures in a net and placed them in a tank; after some time the new genus they thought they had discovered developed into baby eels.

Johannes Schmidt (1877-1933) Danish oceanographer and biologist; discoverer of the breeding grounds of Anguilla anguilla.

I think it's now time to introduce into this story the adventures of Johannes Schmidt, Danish ichthyologist and oceanographer, a man whose place in anguilla history is forever assured for he is accredited with discovering the migration route of the European eel and its breeding grounds off the coasts of Puerto Rico and Bermuda in the Sargasso Sea. This great sea quest took him from Iceland to the Canary Islands, from North Africa to North America. It was an adventure that would span eighteen years of his life from 1904 to 1922, broken only briefly to allow the Great War to intercede. Johannes Schmidt had raised money for his

The Sargasso Sea

expedition and although it was undoubtedly inadequate for such a voyage, he was not to be put off: true passion cannot be tempered by mere cash flow. The Danish research ship *Thor* was fitted out and his quest began. His first eel, in its larval stage, was captured west of the Faroe Islands and from that point onwards he continued to catch larval eels at different stations right across the Atlantic, plotting a path that would inevitably lead him to the eel's long sought-after birthplace. In 1913, now having the faster schooner *Margreth* at his disposal, he continued to search. At latitudes 20 and 30 degrees north and longitudes 50 and 65 degrees west he came across a vast mysterious region of floating weed and becalmed water known as the Sargasso Sea, an area where the depths plummet away to 5000 metres, almost four miles down. The Sargasso Sea in reality is not really a true sea; it's just a very large area of water formed by currents swirling around in a clockwise direction on the edges of the north Atlantic.

Schmidt had cracked it, after two thousand years of speculation and the assembled evidence of decades of research, everything pointed to this area of the world as the birthplace of the eel. But could it really be the Sargasso Sea, a place many believed to be cursed? All the statistical evidence points to it as the start and finish of one of the most famous biological puzzles of all time but physical evidence is still in short supply. If this is truly the eel's birthplace, as many biologists now accept, the eel's journey is stupendous, surpassing even that of the mighty salmon, but sadly being denied the same celebrity status.

But that is not the end of his story. Schmidt's pioneering research set off a chain reaction. Two of Schmidt's pupils, Ege and Jesperson, set out to catalogue all the varieties of intertropical eels. Another of his pupils, Bruun, was responsible for bringing eels to near sexual maturity through hormone injections, research that may one day impact heavily on eel aquaculture. Many others have followed, using Schmidt's findings as the basis for their own research; it's a powerful legacy to have left and one for which he will always be remembered.

Curiosity will never be satisfied while mysteries remain. We have yet to unravel the riddles of the eel's birth and sex life and the exact nature of how it finds its way around. Perhaps these are things that are destined to remain secrets of the eel for all eternity. But even if we do discover how, when and where, will we ever discover why? Even in the digital era of the twenty-first century, knowledge of the eel's life is limited. Of the fifteen varieties of freshwater eel that exist throughout the world, the breeding grounds of only three are known and details of these are sketchy to say the least. Somewhere out there in the warm waters of the tropics millions upon millions of eels congregate to spawn en masse yet to date this spectacular event has evaded all attempts to have it witnessed by man. In 1993 the German Government sent out a research ship, the *RV Poseidon*, to the Bermudas to learn more about the eel but even with state of the art technology, the world's leading biologists and a multi-million dollar budget, the eel managed to hold on to its secrets.

There are now very strong concerns for the survival of the eel species, as a commercial species that is. Over the last decade or so the arrival of elvers has dropped dramatically - in Germany to one-tenth, and in France to one-seventh, and these are conservative estimates. The ICES (International Council for the Exploration of the Seas) now states that the number of new glass eels returning to Europe is 1% of the levels recorded in the mid Eighties. Almost every other known country that has a glass eel run has shown a marked decline. In Europe, for the first time ever, demand could not be met as we munched through 25 million kilogrammes of eels and the price per kilo for live elvers hit US$1,000 on the open market. This represents a huge amount of eels as one metric tonne equates to around $2^{1}/_{2}$ million elvers. In Japan they consumed 100 million kilos of eel in 1996, almost eating their native eel *Anguilla Japonica* into extinction, and to meet their demand they have now set up high-tech production plants in Europe to harvest the European eel. Now most of Europe's eel harvest goes to the Far East and Asia. The remaining catch is dispersed amongst European eel farms and for restocking attempts in a few northern lakes and rivers; the rest is consumed.

It may help us to more easily understand the eel's current decline if we go back to the beginning of the eel's life to get a better idea of the problems it faces. When the glass eels arrive back at our shores they mass in the mouths of rivers and estuaries awaiting a temperature trigger of around 10-12 degrees before swimming upstream into our lakes and river systems. And while they are waiting for this temperature to be reached they become a target for commercial fishermen. In the 1990s around 1,500 million elvers were taken in estuaries across the length and breadth of Europe. No freshwater eel has ever been bred artificially (as yet no one has discovered a way to match the unique conditions presented by the Sargasso Sea in an aquaculture environment) so eel farms rely on migrating and returning eels to replenish their stock and fulfill demand; in effect they are taking seed stocks. A small percentage of these glass eels do make it through into our lakes and rivers and these eels grow on. But they are still not safe; for the next fifteen or twenty years of their life until they are ready to migrate they are targeted with a multitude of legal and illegal set nets and traps. And when they set off on their journey back down our river systems the silver eels are again trapped and netted in an assortment of traditional small-scale fisheries that still claim around 5,000 tonnes a year across Europe. The final escapees then head off out to sea and are never seen again.

Whatever the true reasons for the decline, netting elvers in their millions as they return to their native rivers and lakes, trapping the mature eels in our inland rivers, lakes and waterways, then netting and trapping those survivors on their migration back to the Sargasso, isn't going to help matters. So we should at least consider the possibility that the shortage might very well be caused by man's own self-indulgence and lack of foresight.

Over fishing is not the only problem affecting eel stocks. There are many others: the destruction of natural habitats, the severance of migratory pathways by dams and other obstructions, pesticides and other industrial pollutants, and oceanic changes due to global warming. They all have an impact. And if that wasn't enough an alien parasite has recently appeared in the European eel's swim bladder. Called a nematode (*Anguillicola crassus*), this parasite inhibits the eel's use of the swim bladder and has an impact on blood chemistry, salt balance control, swimming speed and endurance, as well as buoyancy. It is estimated that it already infects well over 30% of all European eels. This parasite originated in East Asia and is believed to have come into contact with our own European eels through uncontrolled aquaculture shipments. An eel without control of its swim bladder will never hope to complete its 4000-mile journey on muscle power alone - a sad end for such a magnificent fish.

Perhaps it will only be when the eel population is as depleted as the haddock, common skate and cod that people will wake up to their plight. It is only greed and the opportunity to make a quick buck that have so reduced the populations of these fast disappearing species and the wild varieties are now being replaced by farmed fish, perhaps even genetically engineered varieties.

An ever increasing amount of the fish we now purchase comes from fish farms and perhaps it will not be too long before we value wild fish in the same way as we value organic or free-range meat. Fish caught in the wild will become an expensive and scarce commodity. If commercial fishermen had sensible quotas imposed in the first place, and illegal trapping was punished with a realistic penalty, these fisheries wouldn't be in the state they are. Unfortunately, in this day and age, ideas stemming from common sense are usually ignored until it's too late. Until the scientific community knows more about the eel, patience and control must be the main objectives. If not the eel may find itself in some pretty impressive company - like that of the Dodo.

In the early Nineties about 1,000 dip net licences for catching eels were issued in the UK. By 2000 that had risen to 2,500. Approximately 1,000 eel trap licences were issued with an additional 3,700 licences issued to fyke netters. I have been unable to find any current data to check how these figures have changed. These figures came directly from the Environment Agency (EA) eel management document dated March 2000. The EA states that prior to 2002 there was no evidence of a decline in eel stocks (National Eel Fisheries byelaw consultation document – Phase 2) yet I found evidence dating back to 1999 that the International Council for the Exploration of the Seas (ICES) and the United Nations Food and Agriculture Organisation (FAO) had stated that the European eel stocks were outside safe biological limits and that in the present state the fisheries would not be sustainable. Conservationists and fishing groups had also warned that such harvesting could spell doom well before that time, not only for the eels, but also for the wide range of marine and freshwater creatures that rely on them.

The European Union (EU) is placing pressure on the EA to act on the plight of the eel. In December 2008 the EA submitted eleven eel management plans on behalf of England and Wales to the European Union outlining how they will manage eel stocks. These plans and the new regulations will come into force in July 2009, details can be found on the EA website. The EA opened consultations in June 2009 on new national fishing byelaws. In its consultation document it states:

In 2002 we introduced national eel fishing byelaws, replacing a variety of local ones. Since then, the decline in eel stocks has become a major concern right across Europe, and the European Commission has decided that action must be taken.

A commercial eel set-up in Norfolk warning of eel nets laid across the river.

A good 4lb-plus eel from Kent water where the bailiff (Derek Weller)
treats eels with the same respect as any other fish swimming in his lake.

The European Eel Regulation, agreed by 23 separate member states within Europe, sets out what we need to do. A key change is that we need to improve the way we regulate commercial eel and elver fishing. This is not optional and each country will need to put in place actions that will improve and protect their own eel populations. Some of the changes need to be introduced through fisheries byelaws.

The consultation document says its aim is for the changes to be introduced for the 2010/11 fishing seasons. Until adequate controls are put in place the eel is in peril. Further, illegal netting appears to be rife and is almost impossible to

A 5 and two 4s, another good October night on a coastal gravel pit

control, with insufficient manpower to police it. Any improvement in eel stocks may take as long as 15 to 20 years to show on the population so a ban on commercial fishing needs to be implemented now and reviewed at a later date. Pleasure anglers pay £26 per year to fish for fun yet Fyke netters pay £6 a net to fish for financial gain. Commercial licensing is run at a loss: by the EA's own figures in 2000, it cost them about £300,000 to manage yet they only received £70,000 in licence fees!

Under Council Regulation 1100/2007 an Eel Management Plan (EMP) must be prepared by all (European) Member States for implementation from 1st July 2009. The objective of each EMP is to reduce anthropogenic mortalities to achieve a target escapement of adult eels equivalent to 40% of the country's biomass. The UK must report on its own progress against the actions listed in the Eel Management Plans in 2012. They will need to show that any exploitation does not prevent the overall silver eel escapement target of 40% being achieved; otherwise the UK Government may end up breaking the law. This could lead to some or all of the UK eel fisheries being closed.

I cannot see a good reason under the current situation to keep the commercial eel fishery open. You only have to look at Ireland and Norway's recent decisions to see what can be done. Ireland is leading the way in recognising that the eel population is diminishing and has taken direct action to try and protect the species. In 2009 the Irish Government began a 90-year ban on all commercial eel fishing in all of its 26 Irish counties. The ban includes an immediate cessation of all commercial eel fishing and the closure of the market. They are seeking to improve water quality and safe passage in all rivers for migrating eels. The Irish Government also propose to maintain a three-year cyclical evaluation of the eel populace until 2018 to fully monitor their progress and to repeat this every six years after that. The Irish Minister of State Sean Power said that this was necessary to conserve the eel population as the numbers remaining are 'now outside safe biological limits'. At last a government has spoken up about the plight of the eels, reiterating what biologists and eel anglers have known for many years. Maybe they have set a precedent that other countries can follow as Norway has now followed suit.

Norway's fisheries regulators have cut the 2009 catch quota for the European eel by 80% and banned fishing of the eel completely starting in 2010. The Minister of Fisheries and Coastal Affairs, Helga Pedersen, also announced that all recreational fishing of European eels would stop forthwith on 1st July, 2009, as stocks of eels hit historically low levels and continue to decline dramatically. I think Ireland and Norway are making important and brave decisions and showing international leadership in fisheries management and conservation.

Organisations like the British Eel Anglers' Club, the National Anguilla Club and the Eel Study group, to name just a few, had pointed out that there were problems with UK eel stocks many years ago and if someone had taken note maybe action could have been implemented at an earlier stage. Whilst commercial eel fishermen will undoubtedly feel the pinch in their pockets, unless a longer term view is taken the seas, lakes and streams could soon be devoid of any eels at all. It would be a very sad day if this mystical creature should become extinct due to our lack of action. Science has learnt much about the eel, yet its life still remains an enigma. For us to know more we must have a sensible policy for the survival of the eels both for the commercial fishermen and the pleasure anglers. The eel's life story is an amazing one and I, for one, hope it continues. As for you, I hope you have learnt a little something about the eel, its life cycle and its future. Perhaps next time you catch an eel you will view it in a different light and treat it with respect. Treat it the same way you would take care of any other specimen fish for the eel does deserve our admiration. Will the endangered European eel be able to slip through the net of extinction now that two governments have acted? Only time will tell. The European eel is listed as critically endangered in Norway and on the IUCN (International Union for Conservation of Nature) Red List.

CHAPTER THREE

SUPERSENSE

In the previous chapter I talked about the eel's life cycle. In this chapter I will take a more in-depth look at the eel's sensory abilities, in particular olfaction. I will journey deeper into the eel's life and draw on the wealth of scientific knowledge that is freely available in research papers, books and that great modern medium, the Internet.

Many years have passed since I first cut out and saved an article on *Anguilla anguilla*. That early snippet has led me to accumulate a wealth of information, gathered from all over the world, and from my growing pile of scientific literature, angling magazines and books I will try to compile an image of the eel's extraordinary capabilities. I will try to explain scientifically how an eel functions, how it tracks down and locates food and generally how it survives from day to day. I will also put my head on the chopping block and present you with a few of the theories regarding some of their more peculiar and frustrating habits. It will then be up to you to decide whether there is any truth in these tales or if they are purely speculation.

During the battle for survival that goes on every day beneath the surface of our lakes and rivers one fish will not have to try as hard as the other residents to locate its lunch. It may very well have to compete for its food, but it will be one of the first to know if there is a free meal up for grabs. And just how an eel will come to know about the presence of food is by utilising a sense that was developed over four hundred million years ago, in the Devonian period, by its long dead ancestors - a time when fish were the most important and advanced animals living on the planet. Many of these early fish bore a resemblance to the still surviving lampreys and hagfish, although not gifted with such a parasitic nature; they were more likely heavily armoured filter feeders that siphoned tiny food items from the primordial slime of the seabed. Theirs was a world without sight or sound, relying only on direct sensation to survive. Slithering around in the mud they had no sense of smell or taste and relied only on the sensations of making contact with an object. This is how they discovered what was worth eating and what was worth avoiding. These first tentative exploits into the world of sensation were chemical-aided by cells designed to analyse molecules dissolved in the water. But what these early fish really needed was a means to locate food at a distance. This is how the sense of olfaction or smell was developed, the ability to taste from afar. Smell is a long-distance sense, a way of stretching time and finding out in advance what lies ahead. It expands both awareness and opportunity. But it was, in fact, one of those prehistoric fish that made the big leap into the world of senses. So smell, or olfaction, is believed to be the first sense that ever evolved in fishes.

As human beings we are brought up to believe that we have been blessed with five basic senses: vision, hearing, smell, touch and taste. There is also the belief that we may have a sixth sense - an awareness of danger without being able to see or hear it. There are even a few anglers I know who claim to have a sense of style, but I know for a fact that evolution has not been that generous! Joking aside, many people are intrigued by these 'extra' senses. Despite the fact that many of them are well beyond our experience or understanding, we want to know what these other senses are capable of detecting if, indeed, they exist. Which brings us to eels, a fish that is renowned for having astoundingly acute senses, including several that we do not have ourselves.

It is possible that eels may have as many as a dozen different sensory systems at their disposal. These sensory systems all depend on receptor cells that respond to energy or chemicals that have been dispersed in the surrounding environment. They create an electric charge, which in turn, induces a series of events that send signals to the brain. If we were to consider our own sense of smell and taste we would regard these as separate experiences; we smell with our nose and taste with our tongue. Yet both these senses function in precisely the same way: a chemical sample is dissolved in a watery fluid. How tightly this chemical fits into the appropriate receptor dictates the nature of the electrical signal sent to the brain where it can then be interpreted. Since smell and taste are based on the same mechanism, they can be thought of as different versions of the same basic sense, 'chemoreception'. If we were then to group all of our senses - no matter how different they may seem - by fundamental mechanism, we would discover that we do not really have five senses at all. We only have three: photoreception (vision), chemoreception (smell and taste), and mechanoreception (touch and hearing). Similarly, eels do not have a dozen senses, they have four: the three that we have plus electroreception, which is the ability to detect ambient electrical fields and variations in water temperature.

Although we possess some of the same senses as the eel's, theirs have advanced to such a degree of sensitivity they are almost beyond our comprehension and can only really be understood by scientific analysis. The category of senses we do not possess, namely electroreception, is found in many marine and fresh-water fish as well as several species of amphibians. Electroreception is a unique ability that is basically restricted to the aquatic environment as air behaves as an insulator rather than a conductor. This sense works by the eel's lateral line discharging a tiny, continuous electrical current (300 discharges per second), which produces an electrical current in the water around it. This electrical field can be distorted by the presence of any object in the water with a higher or lower conductivity because the lines of the flow of current are changed. Electro sensitivity arises from hair cells located on the skin of certain species of bony and cartilaginous fishes. These cells are mainly located in the area of the lateral line and have lost their cilia, becoming modified for the detection of electric currents in the water (Randall et al, 1997). Electroreception is an additional supersense complementing the eel's hearing and vision.

I know I refer to eels as being able to smell phenomenally well, and this is true but not in the same way that you and I can perceive smells. What they can do is sense extremely minute quantities of dissolved chemical from a great distance, 1000 feet or more. For this to happen a tiny sample of that chemical must interact with receptor neurons that are contained within a specialised, chemically sensitive tissue known as olfactory epithelium. These receptor neurons then send impulses via 'axons' (nerve fibres) to the olfactory bulb.

In eels the chemical-sensitive tissue of the olfactory rosette is located just behind the nostrils or nares. And somewhere in the narrow space between the nostrils there was room for nature to position a co-ordinator: a place where information about smells could be analysed and acted upon, the olfactory bulb. In nearly all other varieties of coarse fish the nostrils of each nasal cavity lie close to one another and the olfactory rosette is virtually round or forms only a slightly elongated oval. In the eel, the nostrils are much further apart; this is due to the fact that an eel's olfactory rosette is considerably wider and more complex. The eel's nostrils are also permanently open to allow the flow of scent-bearing water to pass through the olfactory epithelium. This material, which is composed of a series of closely spaced plates called olfactory folds, serves to greatly increase the surface area of chemically sensitive tissue within a relatively small, compact space.

Let me try to simplify this a bit as even I find this topic heavy going. The olfactory rosette that contains the sensitive epithelium is, as I have said, made up from a number of olfactory folds. The greater the amount of folds, the greater the sense of smell the fish is believed to possess. For example, we credit the carp with a very good sense of smell and they have approximately 30 olfactory folds, however at the lower end of the scale the rainbow trout, which hunts mostly by sight, has roughly 15 olfactory folds. The eel has between 50-70 olfactory folds as standard and in some examples they have been found to have as many as 100. As the water flows through the nostrils and over the olfactory epithelium it brings with it minute samples of dissolved chemical that comes into direct contact with its surface. Within this organ a variety of chemically sensitive receptor cells respond to a wide range of dissolved chemicals, but each functions in essentially the same way. Each chemical has its own distinctive shape that fits snugly into the appropriate receptor cell. This, in turn, stimulates an electrical change in the receptor cell. The more tightly the sample of dissolved chemical fits into the receptor cell, the stronger its electrical response. Information is then processed by the neurons contained within the olfactory bulb and sent to higher brain centres via the spinal chord and the central nervous system. On reaching the brain the signal is then interpreted as a 'smell'. This is all done faster than you can blink an eye.

After much research scientists have learnt to determine how well a fish can smell (maybe detect scents sounds better) by counting the amount of olfactory cells in its nose, but to do this you will need to be equipped with an electron microscope (it will give you something to do when you're not getting runs). A human being has about 5 million olfactory cells covering 5cm^2 of sensory epithelium (sensitive tissue). The humble goldfish, however, has some 270 million olfactory cells packed into 170cm^2 of involuted olfactory labyrinth. With a calculator and a quick bit of mathematics you can work out that a goldfish's sense of smell is approximately 54 times greater than yours or mine. However, in nature things are not always that simple and for various complicated reasons to do with the way neuro pathways send incoming information into the network of cells for analysis, the goldfish's sense of smell is actually calculated to be approximately 2 million times greater than that of a human being. To achieve these results, experiments were undertaken that involved placing a minute earthing electrode into the body of a fish and then connecting a micro, or nano electrode, which can be a thousand times smaller than a pin, to a nerve cell in a sense organ or to the brain's sensory lobes. The tiny electrical currents passing along the nerve were then amplified and the fluctuations in the electrical current were tracked and monitored using an oscilloscope to show any reaction to a scent molecule. This is how the figure of a goldfish's sense of smell being 2 million times greater than that of humans was arrived at. Picking on the humble goldfish again (and in reality this could apply to any other member of the carp family), you might like to know that it is capable of detecting shrimp extract diluted to one nanogram per litre. That equates to nearly a thousand millionth of a gram of shrimp extract dissolved in 1 litre of water and that is by no means an exceptional feat in the aquatic world.

There are two fish that fall into the supersense category - these being the eel and the Wels catfish. The Wels catfish (*Siluris glanis*) has 310 million olfactory cells in its snout, 140 million on its whiskers and a further 90 million spread all over its body. But the eel's statistics are even more impressive; eels can detect an extract of shrimp diluted to one part shrimp, per 3 million million million parts of water, which makes its sense of smell almost 100 million times more sensitive than yours or mine. The eel's almost unbelievable sense of smell also extends to its ability to differentiate between various different odours and scents at miniscule levels. In one experiment carried out by scientists it was proved that an eel could perceive the scent of B-phenyl ethyl alcohol (rose scent) when just a few molecules at a time were present at concentrations as low as one part in [10.sup.18]. This represents the sort of dilution you would get by tipping a spoonful of scent into a body of water 58 times that of Lake Constance, a vast amount of water by anyone's standards. These tests were done under controlled laboratory conditions using pure water and, alas, out on the lake this feat would

Close-up showing the nares and nostrils that equip this fish with its supersenses.

not be possible due to the myriad of other scents and smells that occupy a lake but, even so, it's still a feat that takes one's breath away.

So we know the eel's sense of smell is pretty hot to say the least, how then, does it put to use this amazing ability when trying to locate its food? Living in a habitat where sight is often of little use and sound cannot be localised, only smell can pick up traces that provide the eel with the necessary information that it needs for hunting. But smell on its own is not enough. There has to be a way of telling where a smell is coming from. To achieve this, eels put themselves into what we refer to as an 'odour corridor'. When an eel latches on to an attractive scent it will perform several basic movements. The first will be to turn in the direction from which the smell was sensed, and then to sample the water with their two external 'nares', or nostrils. In a river this will generally mean that they face upstream into the flow but in a lake they will normally face in the direction of the undertow or along a thermocline. A chemical odourant (scent or smell) dissipates very rapidly in freshwater, and even at a short distance from their source they can be extremely diluted making them incredibly difficult to detect. By turning in the general direction of the scent, eels are capable of practising 'stereo smell' - an ability that improves the further apart the nostrils are positioned. The wider the head, the better the chance of smelling in stereo. Having turned into the direction of the smell the eel can then move towards its source. The sensitivity of eels to water-borne chemicals is often so acute that they can actually distinguish which side of their body is receiving the strongest whiff! So by comparing the strength of a chemical signal between its two nostrils, eels can home in on the source of a scent in pretty much a direct line. Most other fish species have to perform a zigzag back-and-forth manoeuvre to arrive at the same place.

It would seem that smell leads these predators to their prey from a distance, but the final move, the kill, may be triggered by another sense. This may be a pressure wave detected by sensory cells along the flank or a weak electrical field produced by a distressed fish. And all these signals seem to be enhanced by smell; possibly linked to it in a way that, as yet, we cannot comprehend.

The eel's olfactory senses are even believed to give it the ability to smell water and to distinguish between the individual scents of each lake or watercourse. The ability to do this is not unheard of in the fish world, as it has been proved that salmon can locate the very same river they were born in after many years at sea. (In experiments, salmon have had their nasal passages blocked and as a result have been unable to find their birth streams - Wisby and Hasler, 1954.) I know there is also a theory that the Earth's magnetic fields are used for navigation by migrational fish, and this may well be true, but in the final stages of their journey the watercourse they are searching for will have flavoured the sea with the unique combination of scent molecules found only in that watershed. These odours will have been dispersed over many miles enabling the returning fish to home in on its scent. It is very hard to imagine just how young eels manage this, relying on just a few special molecules to make decisions on which the very survival of their species is at stake.

Another important thing that was unearthed during experiments was that as the water temperature decreased so did the eel's ability to detect smells at such small concentrations, and, in tests, the strength of scent used had to be increased to compensate for the reduction in temperature. Now maybe here is something we anglers should take note of. During the summer months, when the water temperature is high, the worms and deadbaits we use are excellent baits for attracting eels but can they be improved? As water temperatures drop, cutting deadbaits in half and nicking the tails off the lobworms can maintain catch rates. But as water temperatures drop further and bites dry up, do we then add concentrated flavours to the baits? No we go pike and chub fishing. Sea baits such as herring and mackerel come into their own during winter fishing simply because they have a very high oil content. It's worth a thought or two.

A great deal of the information we have available about the eel's olfactory senses and its life cycle has come to light through purely commercial interest. So the people we blame for the eel's present situation are also those responsible for helping us understand much of what we know about eels. The tests on the eel's olfactory abilities were introduced when commercial eel netters noticed serious declines in their catches after using brand new nets or having their existing nets treated with modern chemical preservatives. Thorough investigations ensued and it was found that certain chemicals used in the construction of the nets and the preservatives were acting as a deterrent to the eels, thus scaring them away from the areas where the nets had been set and resulting in a sharp decline in catches. A list was published stating which chemicals should be avoided when targeting eels. The list is detailed and long but the only ones that should concern us as rod and line anglers are as follows: petrol, diesel, oil, carbolineum, ammonia and tobacco smoke. These chemicals all acted as repellents in very small quantities. The research into chemical analysis also found substances that acted as attractants to eels though none were proved to be commercially viable so no long-term field tests were carried out on them. However the Japanese have carried out far more in-depth research into eel attractors, mainly with amino acids and the bio-chemical breakdown of the mussel. But even their studies concluded that no one substance was particularly attractive. What they did find was that when certain amino acids were mixed together in certain combinations they acted as a feeding trigger.

Will this research lead to the discovery of a wonder bait for eels? I doubt it. It is more likely to lead to the production of paste or pellet type bait for eels kept and grown on in captivity. There may be some possibility for its application as bait for rod and line fishing but I should think large quantities would have to be introduced to wean the fish on to them in much the same way that other fish have been weaned on to boilies. Traditional baits may still prove the most consistent when tackling a truly wild fish. If you fancy having a go at making a paste or boilie type bait, the amino acids the Japanese found in their experiments to be attractants are as follows: taurine, asparagine acid, threonine, serine, glutamic acid, glycine and alanine. However, the combinations that proved to be the most effective were not disclosed so if there is, indeed, a successful combination it will only be found by trial and error on the bankside.

There can now be little doubt about the eel's ability to locate food by means of its olfactory abilities. For rod and line anglers the benefits of this are fairly obvious but are there disadvantages when we set out to catch one? During the warm months of summer the moment your deadbait, worm or special settles

The business end of a big anguilla. (Slava Stochl)

on the bottom every eel within the locality must know of its presence within a very short space of time. The higher the water temperature, the faster and further the scent molecules will travel through the water. Now just because eels are aware of the presence of bait, this doesn't mean they will automatically be attracted to them, for if this was the case we could quickly catch every fish in the area we were fishing. Given that this does not occur we have to consider why it doesn't. Have the bigger eels become selective in their choice of bait or have they smartened up to the way we fish it? The bigger eels often choose to ignore the hook bait yet readily opt for similar food items close by, a trick that carp are renowned for performing too.

If we were to look at the advances in carp fishing over the last few years perhaps we could learn something from them. Large carp were once believed to be uncatchable and many anglers even disputed their existence (does something sound familiar here?) until a few pioneering anglers set out to prove otherwise. These anglers from the golden era of specimen hunting caught many carp and rewrote the record books; but the carp were learning and it wasn't long before they became extremely difficult to catch again. The introduction of the hair rig and the use of high protein, boiled baits set carp fishing alight and the fish started coming out again. Now hardly a year goes by without a new rig or bait coming on to the market. As the fish wise up to one bait or method, anglers then have to change tactics to keep their catch rates going but even so, some of the country's biggest carp still go uncaught for ages. So, if we acknowledge that carp can learn, couldn't we consider that big eels can too? I'm not trying to credit any fish with high levels of intelligence but I do believe that all fish, as they get older, learn by association; they know from experience that certain baits or objects represent danger or at the least a rather unpleasant trip to the world above (from the fish's point of view that is). Most anglers are aware of waters where, during the close season, they can virtually feed the fish from their hands yet, come June 16th, these same fish disappear; evidence, if it's needed, that fish learn and, moreover, that their memory lasts longer than the several days that most people seem to believe.

Close your eyes and let's imagine a scenario that could well be played out countless times every day on our lakes and rivers. A big old eel is swimming along the bottom of the lake in search of food and happens across your nice fresh deadbait or bunch of worms. It swims over and stops next to the bait. The eel is aware something is not quite right yet it's hungry; it receives conflicting information from its senses. Instinct tells it to eat but experience has taught it to be far more cautious. The bait is grabbed but not swallowed and the eel feels something unnatural. This could be the hook or even your trace material but the result is the same - the bait is ejected. This may well be the end of the matter but sometimes the eel will return to the bait, taking hold of it lightly, and in a different area. The first indication of the eel's interest that the poor old eel angler on the bank gets is his bite-alarm bursting into life, no bleeps, no warning. The angler strikes and may have momentary contact with the fish but, more often than not, the strike connects with nothing more than thin air. The hook was never near the eel's mouth and maybe the eel never had any intention of actually swallowing the bait; it's similar to the way a cat plays with a mouse, purely instinctive behaviour. This is possibly one of the reasons for the eel angler's biggest curse; missed or aborted runs. You will find on waters where eels have not received a great deal of angling pressure that your strike rate is far higher than fishing more heavily pressured venues, and the instances of dropped runs will be much less frequent. It's a factor worth considering if you want to improve catch rates.

You could well take this scenario one step further and say that on some waters eels will not touch a bait of any sort with a hook in it. This is not as daft as it sounds, there are waters all over the country that hold substantial populations of big eels that are rarely if ever captured on rod and line. Perhaps these fish, over many years, have learnt to recognise the smell or maybe even to sense the metal hook buried within the bait, thus avoiding them completely; or maybe the bigger fish have come to regard the proximity of lead weights or nylon line as the danger signals. Evidence of this comes from the experiences of commercial longliners when they have pursued eels (a tale worth repeating here although it's been much-quoted by others).

In Holland it was traditional for longliners to use large rocks to weigh down their fishing lines but these were bulky and took up too much room in the boat. Large lead weights began to take their place and shortly afterwards a decline in catches became very noticeable. Some of the longliners then reverted to using rocks and, lo and behold, the catches became normal again. They also found that if the rocks had been sourced from a different location this also resulted in reduced catches. The longliners believed that the eels could detect the lead weights and that, for whatever reason, they had become wary of them.

Such experiences with eels are by no means unusual and have been repeated on many different occasions throughout the world. Given the eel's sensing capabilities, it seems well within its realm of abilities to differentiate between items that have come from different lakes or rivers. As for lead, the only time an eel will probably experience that scent is in a situation not conducive to its longevity. When talking about a fish's ability to associate objects with danger I'm only referring to the biggest and oldest fish as their smaller brethren do not appear to be so discerning. Small fish of all species can be ridiculously easy to catch, but the smart ones soon learn and they are the ones that survive and grow big. A good comparison could be ourselves: we have smart and not so smart anglers and the smart ones catch fish whilst the others continue using the same baits and tackle year in, year out and wonder why their catches fail to improve.

Maybe the eel's ability to associate foreign objects within its own environment could also help to explain one of the other odd behavioural problems they have and that's their habit of abandoning waters after receiving fishing pressure directed solely at them either commercially or through rod and line. This is another one of those well-documented phenomena that happens too frequently to be pure coincidence and there is a wealth of theory and speculation as to why it occurs. I will run through a couple of the relevant theories but it will be up to you to decide which one to believe, if any; and if you have been pursuing eels for any length of time already you may well have formed your own ideas on this subject. The first, and quite a common belief, is that areas that have been eel fished over a period of time suffer a small percentage of eel deaths. Even if it appears that the fish have swum off strongly after catching, they may succumb at a later date due to infection or deep hooking. These lie on the bottom and start to decompose and this is believed to act as a major repellent to other eels. It can of course be argued that eel section is a very good bait for catching large eels on waters where small eels are a problem; but only in its fresh state is eel section a good bait. I cannot imagine that anyone using a foul-smelling piece of eel would seriously expect to catch fish on it. With the eel's sense of smell being millions of times stronger than humans', can you possibly imagine what a dead eel would smell like to another eel? It's possible, however, that it may not even have to be a dead eel that is repellent to its brothers and sisters. Eels, when scared or struggling, release chemicals like ammonia into the bloodstream, which is not as far-fetched as it sounds as some table fish have to be bled to stop the ammonia from spoiling the taste of the flesh. And as I mentioned earlier, ammonia in tiny quantities has been proven to repel eels. Eels may also release pheromones during the course of a struggle in a similar way you and I would sweat or give off body odour, possibly even the scent of fear. Other eels could well be capable of detecting any of these scents and it's a very reasonable assumption that danger signals could be relayed in this manner.

John Sidley, one of the most well respected eel anglers, adamantly believed eels could communicate with each other; it's a theory worth considering. Dogs, cats and many other animals mark their territories by urinating or rubbing scent glands on prominent objects. This leaves their own particular scent which other animals of the same species recognise and understand. It seems possible then that eels might communicate danger in pheromonal discharges and that it wouldn't just be a dead eel that would be off-putting to other eels but a struggling fish, or one just kept in a keepnet; and this might be enough to discourage eels from visiting the area. Fish, like perch, if caught and released while you are still fishing kill the swim stone dead. If the lake is regularly fished for eels more and more areas would become pheromonally marked as danger areas and the eels would have little alternative but to leave the lake. This exodus of eels from a water has been witnessed on numerous occasions by reliable anglers, and with the eel's ability to travel across land on damp nights and smell water, even land-locked lakes are not exempt.

The final theory for why eels vacate a water is the only one that has some scientific basis yet it is almost certainly the simplest. This suggests that something has triggered their migratory instincts.

Whatever mysterious event sets these wheels into motion, it is a common occurrence for eels of all sizes and ages to vacate a water en masse leaving it almost devoid of any eels. These events are widely acknowledged as taking place but as yet there are no firm conclusions about why they happen. What I have said in the last few pages has been derived mainly from observations made by eel anglers, their theories and ideas and some scientific fact but new information regularly appears on the Web if you want to pursue this line of research. Part of the fascination with eel fishing is that the more questions we answer, the more are posed. Why is it, for example, that when fishing a water that has thrown up numerous big fish in nettings and the like, they cannot be caught on rod and line or very rarely? Experiences such as these are common and yet we are a long way away from explaining them factually.

There are undoubtedly many more big eels swimming in our lakes and rivers than we realise, and many fishing clubs have been shocked by the presence of large eels when their waters have been drained or netted for maintenance work. The only answer I have found to catching these big fish is time and patience, no magic formula. If some of what I have written is correct and the big fish have learned to associate baits with danger, or to discriminate between baits that have lines attached to them and those that do not, then waiting for one to slip up may very well be a long process until we can figure a way round it. The underwater world is full of mysteries, with even the simplest of its creatures having the capacity to surprise us when we think boldly enough to research the right kinds of questions. And answers to its riddles are never going to be easy without the gift of hindsight.

Chapter Four

Location

Locating eels is not a problem for they are as much at home in the salt pools and lagoons of our coasts as in the pure mountain lakes and streams of the high country. They are found in stagnant pools and clear running streams, and in this respect the eel is like no other fish as it seems to cope with foul conditions as easily as the good. So, locating them is pretty easy even if they are seldom, if ever, seen. But we are not just searching for eels we are trying to locate the big ones and they are as different to the bootlace variety as a dog to a wolf or a horse to a donkey. Yet there are a few of us who claim to be experienced in the search for big eels (and I use the term 'experienced' loosely). An experienced angler will have to call upon all his accumulated knowledge, all his deductive powers, news clippings from the weeklies, rumours from that little club down the road and all the little snippets of gossip from local anglers. A few, supposedly, rely on instincts buried deep after years of suburban life and there are some amongst us who claim to just 'know' where the fish are - a sort of sixth sense.

For us mere mortals who are not psychic, who cannot see portents in the sky or have the gypsy's ability to discern the future in wet tea leaves, we have to rely on more conventional means and in the next few pages I hope to run through as much as I can to help the would-be eel angler achieve his or her goals. First of all, let me stress that the time and effort spent looking for that one special water, for they do exist, will reap the greatest results if you ever hope to put that really big fish on the bank.

Location is an issue that needs far more deliberation than baits, tackle, rigs or anything else you can think of. If you cannot find a water that contains big eels in the first place, you will not catch them; it's as simple as that. Yet 99% of all the waters you come across will contain eels to some degree or another, so how do you choose between them? How do you find the waters that contain the biggies? The waters that may have the potential to produce really big eels on a consistent basis are not as few and far between as we'd like to kid ourselves; they just require more time and effort to locate. We have clues - a few good ideas and an inkling of the habitats big eels prefer - and an extensive knowledge of watercraft and yet they can still remain an enigma confounding any would-be expert. Your search is therefore going to be a slow process of elimination. Sorting the duff waters from the good ones will take time. Persevere and that one venue - that's all you want, just that one venue to start with - will give you all the rewards your efforts deserve.

There may well be many suitable waters in the area you intend to fish but there will also be a few you should try to avoid. These, by and large, are the waters that have a reputation for producing large quantities of small fish; catching these can become very monotonous when you're after something much bigger. You can also get through huge amounts of hooklengths as small eels have the most amazing ability to tie knots that a boy scout would be proud of. The main problem with waters that have a large bootlace population is that the smaller fish will beat the bigger fish to the bait almost every time. A general rule can be applied here, and that is, on the whole, the more numerous eels are in a given water, the less chance there is that there will be a truly exceptional fish in the same place. But this is only a general rule; I am aware of several waters with large eel populations that have produced fish to 9lb-plus.

In an ideal world we should therefore be searching for waters that are rumoured to contain big fish, specimens of 4lb and upwards. On some of these big fish venues the fishing can be very hard indeed and the beginner can find himself totally out of his league so be realistic in your approach. Make a shortlist of what you want from the venue. You may be after your first 3-, 4- or 5-pounder, or even your first fish, but remember big eel fishing has very few shortcuts. Have sensible aims and set out to catch eels of any size and be happy with just one to start with. Achieve success here and as you gain experience the bigger eels will come your way along with bigger catches. All specimen hunting has a gradual learning curve and it takes time and patience to become truly successful.

If this is your first venture into the world of eel fishing and you are, as yet, unaware of a water with big fish potential I will run through some of the ways I go about tracking down and finding a suitable venue worth fishing. One of the easiest ways to start, other than by simply asking someone else who fishes for eels, is to arm yourself with an Ordnance Survey map of the area you intend to fish. Then set about marking off, preferably with a highlighter pen, any blue areas on the map that look a tad bigger than your average-sized swimming pool. In the search for big eels, that age-old adage 'size doesn't matter' couldn't be more apt as they can live anywhere providing they have food, cover and peace.

A small farm pond covered in duckweed or two hundred acres of wind-torn reservoir may contain what you seek, so rule out nothing at this stage. Take extra interest if there is a lake or such-like that has streams, rivers or even drainage channels that enter or flow close by as this gives the eels easy access to the water. This type of venue, irrespective of size, can often contain a large head of eels in varying sizes so is definitely worth investigating. There is an old theory still floating about amongst many die-hard eel anglers that only lakes that have no access in and out via an obvious watercourse can produce big fish. This 'prison water' theory, as it was known, has proved false on numerous occasions and some very big fish have been taken from coastal lakes, rivers and canals. The British record eel of 11lb 2oz came from Kingfisher Lake, a water that has an inflow and outflow providing eels with access to come and go as they please. Therefore, lakes do not have to be landlocked to have the potential for holding very big fish.

When looking for a new venue it's also worth checking out the local library as they often carry old or out of date maps. Comparing an old map with a new one will soon show whether any of the waters you've earmarked for investigation are new. New waters, say less than ten years old, would be eliminated as possible candidates for producing big eels. Maps can help with the past history of a lake but are not always fully up to date so, once you've selected your water, I would strongly advise a recce just to see if it still exists; you may find it was used as a landfill site last year and that it's no longer there. The recce is also useful in determining who owns the fishing rights on the venue; if you cannot see anyone fishing to ask, there will normally be a board or notice nailed up somewhere in the surrounding area.

Once a suitable-looking water has been found it must meet certain criteria. One of these is age (although it doesn't have to be as old as was once thought), and another is neglect. You would be lucky to find a neglected water in this day and age as it's like finding the proverbial needle in a haystack but a water where eels have never been fished for would fit the bill nicely. On many of our waters, eels are not specifically targeted and as a result they are only ever caught by accident. This may well be the closest any of us ever get to fishing a neglected water. Eels in this situation may very well grow big but they will be cautious, wily old fish, having encountered fishing tackle on numerous occasions. I believe that big eels will thrive on neglect no matter where they reside; like nearly all species of fish they will flourish if left well alone.

As I've advised you to eliminate waters newer than ten tears old, we need to establish at what age a water becomes of interest to the eel angler. We are fishing for what is generally regarded as a slow growing fish so by fishing somewhere that has become established, and has at least got some age to it, we will increase our chances of locating big fish in greater quantities. A benchmark of around twenty years old should be regarded as the minimum age worth considering. A lake of twenty years old will have allowed ample time for eels to enter and become settled in their new environment. This is not to say that younger venues will definitely not contain big eels, as they may well have entered at a large weight after vacating another body of water close by, but in choosing an older lake you are increasing the odds of a big eel being present so my advice is to start there.

Once you've located what you regard as a suitable lake and have gained permission to fish it, ingratiate yourself to the local bailiff and a few of the regulars just to see what they know about the resident eel population. If you are told there are no eels in the lake yet it fulfils all the necessary criteria that we've mentioned, don't be disheartened. Fish it for one season; you may well be surprised by what it contains. On the other hand, if you are told the water is stacked with big eels that plague the poor old carp anglers take the information with rather a large pinch of salt unless it is backed up with photographic or reliable witness evidence. If I had a pound for the amount of times I've had my hopes built up about fishing a new water after hearing stories of monster eels smashing angler's tackle up I would be a rich man. Having fished many of these so-called monster eel waters, I have spent night after night hammering the boot-lace population with only the occasional fish scraping the 3lb barrier. When the locals were shown one of these scraper 3s, the 'monsters' were unmasked: "Cor mate, never seen an eel that big before," and "Look at the bloody size of that thing!" Try it yourself; show a reasonable sized eel to someone who does not specifically fish for eels and it will nearly always be over-estimated in weight. This makes the task of locating big fish waters by word of mouth infuriatingly difficult.

Another question you should remember to ask is 'Has the water ever been netted for eels?' If the answer to this question is yes, and it was netted in the not too distant past, the likelihood of you locating a big fish, which is never going to be easy in the first place, will be reduced by such a margin that you may as well forget the water for many, many years to come. There may well have been the odd fish that escaped the nets, and these may occasionally be caught, but I have seen how effective netting a lake for eels is and experienced the devastating effects it has on the fishing. In all honesty, life is too short to waste it pursuing the few survivors. And lastly, you need to find out if the water has suffered any kind of pollution in the recent past; even low oxygen levels can have an effect. Incidents like these may not always kill the eels but they could very well cause them to abandon the lake so you can save an awful lot of wasted time by doing your research properly.

Finding a virgin water has to be the eel angler's ultimate dream, somewhere with very difficult access so that no one bothers to fish for anything, let alone eels. Even an older water that has only just been opened up for fishing would fit the bill nicely. Waters such as these must offer the best chance of an exceptional eel and you also have the added excitement of fishing somewhere new and as yet untried. That feeling of expectancy you get when casting into unknown territory is a feeling we eel anglers live for. Sadly, virgin waters are few and far between so if you know of such a water I'd certainly recommend that you try to be one of the first anglers on it.

Some of the locations you should be considering as possible candidates are lakes in the grounds of stately homes or private parks, and old castle moats as well as reservoirs. I know of two waters in this category which supposedly contain big fish - Hever Castle Moat and the lakes in the grounds of Leeds Castle in Kent. These are probably home to eels of a size we only dream about and if you could get permission to fish waters like these I am sure you would be well rewarded. There is never any harm in asking for permission; the worst that can possibly happen is you get a refusal.

Other possibilities are waters where night fishing has previously been banned but is now being allowed for the first time. Even some heavily fished commercial fisheries, stuffed with small carp for match anglers, contain some surprising fish when night fished for eels. Old bomb pits, disused quarry pools, gravel pits (one I know that is still being worked contains some exceptional fish), small lakes and ponds that have become local rubbish dumps, mill pools and basins are all worth trying. Disused canals, even used canals like the Grand Union and Leeds-Liverpool, also produce some big fish but tend to be hard places to crack. Canals in the centre of towns can produce surprisingly good results; the canal at the back of Paddington Station in central London produced two 6s and a 7 for one lucky angler; it's not the place I'd choose to fish at night but it shows the fish are there. Disused commercial docks usually contain lots of eels but, given my experiences fishing them as a teenager, I'd speculate that they are not the size of fish we are looking for. That doesn't mean there isn't a biggie out there somewhere; it just means I never caught one. You should also consider trout lakes. We all know what they did for pike fishing, so who knows what size eels could be lurking on the bottom of one of these. Mick Bowles' 8lb eel came from Weirwood Reservoir, a trout water, on the first night it was ever night fished and several other very big fish were lost on the following trips. Big eels turn up in the most unlikely places but the ones I have described are known haunts so fishing areas like these might well improve the likelihood of catching. However, in the end trial and error and, of course, luck will play an important part too.

Scanning the fishing weeklies for big eel photos is another excellent means of identifying locations. If the photo is an accidental capture and not one taken by a serious eel angler, the captor will normally have given away the name of the water from which it was caught, and it's then up to you to find it. Many of these captures come from day-ticket carp fisheries, or waters very similar in nature, and will present the eel angler with a challenge if he decides to pursue it. The sheer number of anglers fishing these types of venue result in the eels having a permanent and readily available food source which requires little exertion on their part. Any eels that are present may very well have been weaned off their natural diet and on to a concoction of maggots, trout pellets and boilies, to list just a few of their options. Such high protein baits may fatten the fish up faster than is natural and may explain why big eels are often taken on carp waters. This can, and will, make it difficult to target the eels specifically as the baits they have become used to will also attract many other species of fish. The same scenario of food abundance can also apply to certain naturally rich waters where, during the height of summer, a profusion of food items will make the catching of eels rather like a lucky dip. The vast amount of natural food at their disposal means that the eels will need to expend very little energy to obtain their daily requirements. These two types of water are best left to later in the year when the natural food levels start to die off and the amount of freebies dropped into the water by visiting anglers also decreases. The following is an article written by my good friend Mick Bowles for the British Eel Anglers' Club (BEAC) magazine, issue 23, 1987. It gives his thoughts on, and insights into, the subject of location.

I have felt rather honoured since my good fortune in catching my eight-pound eel in receiving letters from anglers seeking advice in the quest for big eels, especially the very big fish. I certainly cannot confess to being an expert overnight, if so I doubt whether it would have taken me so long to have caught my eight-pound eel in the first place. However since catching my fish I have been able to sit down and think about why exactly it did take me so long to catch it, and also examine my tactics. As for tactics I felt very confident, indeed I used precisely the same tactics and rigs as John Sidley, and look how successful he has been. Indeed most of what I've learned about eel angling, I learned from John and I honestly put my success down to his valuable and unselfish help over the years.

Without any doubt I am firmly convinced the root of all my problems has simply got to be waters, and the fact that I have not really fished the right ones, in the case of catching big eels. My ambitions were to catch a six-pound eel, and still are, however I don't think, being realistic, I put myself out enough to fish the waters I should have done to get eels of this size. I spent seven years fishing Johnsons Lakes hard in the knowledge that six-pound eels had been caught there before. A logical thing to do, however I didn't fish the lake which had produced more big eels than any of the others for the simple reason I could also catch two's and three's while eeling from the other lakes on the complex, whereas the lake of the big fish produced hardly any eels at all (that's what put me off) but if one was caught, it was generally a large one, usually taken by accident.

One of the very first things that attracted me to eeling was when I first started to eel fish seriously I never blanked, or very rarely, and it was great chucking out worms and deadbaits every night and getting loads of runs. However, I can see now, a very distinct decline in my catch rate since those early years. I could kick myself now for not moving on to Sittingbourne Lakes at the time when the big eel stories were at their peak. I did fish it a few times but was put off by the weed; now the weed has gone and so, it would appear, have the big eels. So how does this help you? Well, what I am trying to say is, if you want to catch the real big ones I think a lot of research and investigations into waters must take priority and depending upon what particular aims you have, try and establish what waters you think will hold the size of eels you require.

*Mick Bowles, Secretary of the British Eel Anglers' Club
with a 4lb 3oz Ardingly eel. (Photo courtesy of BEAC.)*

Now I have come to the conclusion that the heavily fished waters in Kent where I live simply do not any longer hold the big eels in any way like the numbers they did in say the early Seventies. Indeed, looking back through my lists and records of big eels caught in Kent there has been one hell of a decline in the amount of big eels being reported, the numbers have also dropped remarkably and most noticeably since 1976.

Further investigations showed me that of the big eels (4lb-plus) that were in the news, most came from waters with a number of things in common: they had only just opened up to fishing, or night fishing was now being allowed and, again, another interesting thing is the fact that quantity and size of the fish drops away quite remarkably after only a short time of being eel fished. Indeed if I was to look at Leisure Sports Larkfield Number Two lake, this would have given me all the answers. Its eeling quality had declined ever since night fishing had been first allowed. Again the first few seasons peaking for the bigger fish, then when I first fished it I did well for two's and three's, but now I have not had an eel for two seasons. Have the eel numbers declined or have they grown more wary? Big eels still exist as accidental catches, though rare, prove.

It appears to be always the way that I am never in the club which has the big eel reputations. I know one, a village club, where unless you live in it you cannot fish it. What happens is they allow night fishing for two hours after sunset and anglers start getting smashed up or cutting lines to so called monster eels. Now I know of a few waters which hold monster eels, two of which I know are 100% legitimate claims, but these waters do not allow fishing (legally anyway) and one is in a position to be too risky to fish. And I know I am not alone in knowing of waters like these; a few other anglers have told me similar stories of waters they know which hold huge eels but fishing is not allowed or if only I could get on it. For some poor lads, they are fishing club waters, either which in nettings or electro fishing parties etc., huge eels have been seen or actually taken, and yet no night fishing is allowed. What I have written is a result of the conclusions I have come to, as to why I have not caught the numbers of eels 4lb-plus that I should have done in the time I've spent going after them; it may help, it may not, but I think it's worth thinking about. I would still advise anglers new to eel angling to start off on an easier water to gain experience, before venturing after the bigger fish, because you need every ounce of confidence in your tactics and methods, your tackle and bait, timing strikes etc. because when you do start after the biggies, you want everything to go just right for you when it matters.

When the local river floods the excess water is channeled into this large reservoir.
A perfect entry point but no exits. Only a handful of eels have ever
been caught and then accidentally.

Overhanging trees, an island, everything growing wild, the perfect habitat for those big eels.

A very hard water to locate fish on, permanently exposed to strong winds and with very little cover around the banks. It receives little fishing pressure due to the inhospitable environment yet many eels have been electrofished.

A textbook water, over forty years old, access very difficult and only lightly fished due to the permanently waterlogged banks. It is an extremely rich water with a large head of small fish.

As we can see from this, even the best of us cannot hope to get it right all of the time. By doing your homework and asking the right questions you will improve your chances of locating the right fishery, at the right time. No matter how much information about a water you can gather, you will never know, until you actually start fishing, what to expect but you should have gathered a good idea of the main obstacles involved, ie, angling pressure, snags, low density of fish etc. Another good point worth mentioning is that it's sometimes worthwhile seeking out those small local angling clubs, or even match clubs, as they can often have some pretty little waters hidden away in the wilds somewhere. As I've often discovered, if you can join them and find your own, quiet little pool with a handful of big fish, it can all be very worthwhile.

We have now covered quite a bit of ground on how to locate a water that contains the eels we seek but how we go about locating the fish on our chosen water can be just as problematic as finding a water that contains them in the first place. So let's start off with location on a lake, as that is normally the first choice of venue for the angler seeking those big snakes.

Lakes

The eel, unlike most other fish, will very rarely be seen swimming around the lake unless it's in distress of some kind, so visual location of feeding eels is all but impossible. Homing in on them will therefore depend on the knowledge you have gleaned from the locals and your own watercraft abilities. A good idea would be to take an early morning trip to your chosen lake, preferably towards the middle of summer. At this time of year the lake will be displayed in its full glory so make sure your tackle is left at home. You are here on a recce and, talking from experience, if you take your fishing tackle then the temptation to wet a line in the first juicy swim will be irresistible and the lake will not get fully explored.

Observation is the key to being successful; you must learn to read a water, for nothing happens without reason. Fry do not collect along weed-fringed margins just for the sake of it, nor do fish bubble away in certain areas of a lake just to cloud the water. These events happen for a reason, so watch and take in all you see. Keep your eyes peeled as you walk round the lake; for example, look for small fish topping, probably this year's fry, and make a mental note of any areas where they seem to congregate. This could be anything from small, shallow bays to gaps in the reed-beds or where overhanging trees trail their branches in the water. Usually anything offering shelter or cover from predators will be a good place for fry to hole up during the day. Eels will not be far away from situations such as these. Identifying areas where small fish congregate is vital in finding areas attractive to predators and there are many ways to skin this particular cat. Large open pits can be scanned using a pair of Polaroids. It's amazing how much difference they can make whilst fish spotting and will show fish not visible to the naked eye due to glare or ripple. Another way to identify the location of small fish, even without the aid of Polaroids, is to watch for one member of the local wildfowl community, the great crested grebe. These birds will spend a lot of their time diving in pursuit of small fish so keep an eye on them; watch to see if they continually dive in the same area and come to the surface with fish in their beaks. They cannot swallow fish underwater without drowning so they are a good means of locating areas where small fish congregate further out into the lake than you could normally see. These are all areas that will attract eels at some point in time.

Weed-beds, especially if they lie close to deep water, have to be one of the best spots to locate eels. They seem to love being holed up in them and it's one of the few places I would feel confident fishing for them during the day. Finding small holes in the weed-bed and dropping through a small deadbait or worm is a very effective method. It's important to have the correct tackle and the correct rig and not to be put off by trying to present baits in conditions most anglers would avoid like the plague. If you stand back a moment and give it some thought, you will realise that most of the lake's little creatures will be hiding in the weeds to avoid being eaten. Water snails, dragonfly larvae and freshwater shrimps; all sorts of little critters, even the tiniest of fish, will use it for cover. Raking a swim will uncover this harvest; look closely at the weeds you've pulled in. It positively crawls with bugs and things (I am definitely no entomologist) so is it any wonder why nearly all fish love grubbing around in it? As a result of this veritable feast eels will be in there too, searching out their prey, feeling confident with a thick bed of weed over their heads, even in broad daylight. Thus, a perfect habitat is created for the eel as all she has to do is lie up, out of sight, and ambush food as it crawls or swims by, expending as little energy as possible. As I've said before, location is paramount to catching big eels. If they're in a thick weed-bed then it's no good fishing the open water hoping one will swim out and take your bait. Take the initiative and put baits where the fish are. You'll get snagged, caught up, spend ages pulling weed off the line, and may even get smashed as a fish surges through the weeds, but you will catch fish, fish that you may otherwise not have caught if you had continued fishing the comfy swims.

Reed-beds too may offer the same kind of protection to insect life and small fish but do not offer the eel the same degree of cover as the weed-bed. Reed-beds tend to be located in shallow water or close to the bankside, usually much closer in than the favoured weed-bed. Although this may discourage eels during the

Fishing close to marginal reeds can become very productive, especially at night.

day due to disturbance, during the night it will certainly become a hotspot. Baits dropped inches away from reed-beds and in very shallow water account for some excellent fish. I have taken fish from areas such as this when there has been barely enough water to cover their backs and the resulting fight has been quite spectacular.

Islands seem to attract fish like magnets and eels are no exception to this rule. On some waters, apart from the margins, the only attractive feature around which eels can make their homes is an island. But unlike carp, which tend to prefer the point of an island, eels, I have found, much prefer the sides, especially if the bank is undercut and shady. They can lie up there, away from any bankside disturbance, waiting for the sun to go down before moving out to feed. Undercut banks, not just on islands but around the lake itself, are also very good fishing areas but you need to be able to cast to them rather than fish directly off one. Any disturbance would easily spook the fish so it's easier to drop your bait close in and then sit back, well away from the water's edge or, alternatively, cast to it from another swim. Another point to bear in mind is that standing on top of an undercut bank in the middle of the night is not the smartest thing to do as the resulting splash (from falling in) tends to scare the fish!

Freshwater eels behave much like their deep-sea brother, the conger, in choosing for their lairs very snaggy and difficult areas in which to present a bait. Tree roots stretching out into the lake, old cars dumped in the margins, dead trees that have fallen in during winter storms - all make excellent homes for a big eel to hide in. And like the congers on the wrecks, the biggest fish may be nigh on impossible to extract from their holes without using brutish tackle.

As well as the snaggy areas, they also use the features you cannot see: the gullies, gravel bars and deep channels - areas that, from the bank, appear to be no more than barren expanses of open water. Lakes will have a few of these features but nowhere near as many as gravel pits. In most natural lakes the bottom is predominantly smooth and silty with most of the fish-holding areas being found near islands or the margins. Gravel pits are man-made for the purposes of removing as much aggregate as possible, purely for profit. Because of this, the excavator will follow the thickest seams, creating underwater mountains and valleys almost everywhere.

These features are rarely visible from the bank so time spent mapping out the underwater terrain is time well spent. My personal preference for this job is my trusty little inflatable boat coupled with a depth sounder, but barring that (as many places have now banned the use of boats), a lead weight and a large float can be used. This is called plumbing and is simply a matter of passing your line through the swivel on the weight and tying on the float. Chuck the lot into the pit and wind the line tight until you feel the weight move, then pay out line one foot at a time until the float appears on the surface. This gives a pretty accurate measurement of depth.

Once I am familiar with the underwater terrain, be it a lake or gravel pit, the first place I would start fishing is in areas of shallow water dropping away to deep water. Plumbing the lake will easily locate areas such as gravel bars or shallow plateaus and the exact position of all should be noted. During the day I would fish baits in the deepest area of water on the chance of picking up the odd fish but as the night sets in I would then position baits in the shallow water and on the edge of the drop-off itself. Once night has fully closed in, take your torch and shine it into the margins. Insects are everywhere and little fish will be seen darting back into deeper water. I believe this also happens on the bars and plateaus further out, creating a natural feeding area away from the banks. Eels will move out of the deeper water surrounding these areas and feed in the shallower water that has been warmed by the sun's rays during the day.

The margins around the lake are also hotspots and many a big eel has fallen to a bait presented right under the rod tip. Many specimen hunters have cut their cloth by taking fish of all species from the margins so it's a method that shouldn't be underestimated; in fact, it can be a lethal one under the right conditions and in the right hands. Most evenings, after the pleasure anglers and match anglers have finished tiddler bashing, their left-over bait is chucked into the lake. With easy pickings like this available it isn't long before the resident eel population, as well as many other fish, quickly recognise this as an easy and regular food source. If most of the fishing occurs at weekends then mid-week is the time to fish as by then most, if not all, of the free offerings will have been eaten and the fish will still be in the area expecting to find food. Stick to smallish baits when fishing lakes such as this as the eels will have gorged themselves earlier in the week, making large baits mostly a waste of time. When tackling a water like this my baits would be spread out over a large area as the eels tend to be more nomadic and will cover a fair old distance in their nocturnal forays.

For similar reasons, margin fishing on quiet, secluded waters like the Shropshire meres can also be very effective. Insects from overhanging trees will fall into the water and during wet weather conditions the rain washes food items like worms and slugs off the banks into the lake. I have also found, when fishing these quieter lakes, that the margin fishing is very dependent on wind direction especially if you have a prevailing wind. This has the effect of carrying any food

D - is where I would fish for eels with some confidence during the day
N - is where I would position baits during the night
D N - is where you have the possibility to catch eels twenty-four hours a day

items on to one bank and if any of these items are dead animals or fish, the undercurrent created by the wind will carry the smells back along the lake in the opposite direction to which the wind is blowing. Any eel in the vicinity will be aware of the scent trail in no time at all, thereby creating a natural hotspot. On more heavily fished waters, wind direction has nowhere near the same effect on fishing and doesn't create the same sort of hotspots as food items tend to be widespread.

It's also worth locating the spawning areas, although bear in mind that you will need to find them at the beginning of the fishing season when the fish are spawning (obviously). These areas create one of nature's natural hotspots and the eels can sometimes become so preoccupied with them that the rest of the lake is left devoid of eels. On one lake that I fish, the spawning areas for the resident bream shoals are out of bounds and when they have spawned in June/July the eels do not leave these areas for what seems like ages.

It is not until the middle of August that I start getting runs on the bank I am allowed to fish. This is where knowledge of a water, that only comes after fishing it for several seasons (in this case ten), pays off for now I only fish the water between the end of August and the beginning of November, and tend to do a lot better. Even so, this is a very hard water. If there was to be a general rule for eel fishing it would be to fish the shallow areas during hot, humid weather at the beginning of the season where fish may have spawned. Then fish the middle to deep water as the season progresses and as the water temperature drops going into autumn. If you use this as a rule of thumb you can't go too far wrong.

All of the above generally covers what to look for when fishing a lake and should stand people in good stead. But there is something I've missed; something that throws a spanner into all the research and planning we do, and that's the eel's annoying habit of favouring one bank in preference to all others. Eels will be caught all around the lake but one bank will consistently throw up the most or the biggest eels. There seems to be no rhyme or reason for it. For instance, one lake John Sidley used to fish called Westwood Park is a textbook example. The lake was covered in eely-looking features but nearly all the big fish (5lb-plus) came from a few swims on the dam wall area. Several water authorities have also noted these phenomena when conducting netting sorties on lakes, rivers and canals. One bank tends to produce not just the most but also the largest eels. Fyke nets laid in a lake will also show the same results; some nets will be full whilst others will be empty. This is just one of those little quirks of nature that seems to have no justification that we know of other than to try our patience. There is also nothing I can say or do to help you determine which bank you should choose to fish; it may often be the bank that you least suspect. Only trial, error and many rod hours will put this problem to bed.

At the beginning of this chapter I said that the size of water was irrelevant, and it is when you are looking for waters that hold eels. However, when you actually come to putting baits in the water there are other issues to consider. On big waters the choice of swims available is substantial so it may take the eels years to wise up to your tactics and baits. That's depending on how often the place is eel fished of course. Small waters, on the other hand, can effectively blow after only a few trips. Therefore with the smaller venues it's much better to fish 'smash and grab' style; by this I mean hitting it hard for maybe one or two weekends a year

A 7lb 4oz caught by the aptly named Martin Eels. (Photo courtesy of BEAC.)

and no more. This is also worth considering when fishing a known eel water as the pressure it has received in the past may also make it a very hard place to come to terms with. That's why you should always endeavour to find a venue that has seen the minimum amount of pressure. The first eel angler on a new water will catch the most and, usually, the best fish in a very short space of time. Seriously, the effort you put into locating a new, un-eel-fished venue will be far better than flogging yourself to death on a water that has produced big fish in the past.

Now let's move away from lakes and have a look at locating eels in your local river or canal system. This is not a subject I can profess to be an expert in as I have only fished the Thames, Medway and Royal Military Canal in my younger days and then with somewhat limited success. Fishing such a diverse range of venues will teach the angler much more about the eel and its habits than concentrating all efforts on one venue. I rarely now fish these types of water. They require a far more mobile approach and I have become, with age, too lazy, much preferring to bivvy up for several days beside a picturesque lake. I have therefore enlisted the help of anglers far more knowledgeable in this department than myself and who regularly fish canals and rivers. Their more experienced input will give a greater understanding of the problems involved than I could ever hope to relay but I will put pen to paper with what I know before handing over to them.

Rivers

As far as eels are concerned, rivers are the fishy equivalent of our own motorway system. They are the veins of the land, providing eels access to nearly every corner of the country with very few waters escaping their incursions. Fish migrating to the sea will leave the lakes and ponds via drainage channels, dykes or any watercourse they can find. If there is no direct escape from their home water they will travel across land to find one. At the same time, elvers and small eels will be travelling to the lakes and ponds. It's a never-ending cycle of renewal unless man interferes. All this movement means there will be a huge fluctuation in the size of eels you will encounter on rivers, but they will be the easiest to catch by far. The bigger eels do not usually give themselves up easily as the swarms of smaller eels invariably descend on the bait first, but all rivers will contain a few big resident fish; you just have to wade through the countless bootlace eels to get to one. Although there are big eels to be had, rivers do not normally contain many fish over the 5lb mark and there is a very believable theory to explain this. River eels, so the theory goes, are forever competing with the current so burn more energy in just swimming up and down; in lake eels these calories are turned into body fat. It's the simplest and most plausible theory I've come across to explain the size variations between the two types of venue.

In regards to locating eels on a river system much of what I have already said about location on lakes can be applied to rivers; you just have to appreciate the fact that you are fishing moving water instead of still. So where would you actually start when viewing a river for the first time? You should start looking for any bends where the current may have undercut the bank or scoured out a deep hole on the riverbed; even long straight sections with reasonable depths and a muddy bottom will hold fish. If there are any marinas on the river it's a safe bet that eels will not be too far away. Food will get thrown off the boats, propeller action will stir up the bottom and this will attract many fish once night has fallen and the marina's residents have gone to bed. Keep in mind bridges, the new piled ones I'd bypass (a pun there I think) but the old brick built ones are superb lairs; eels just love lying up amongst the old brickwork awaiting nightfall before venturing out to feed. Speaking from my own experience, weir pools and their respective run-offs must offer the best chance to encounter that bigger than average eel. I regard them as excellent places to start fishing as they have a wealth of potential that goes largely untapped by eel specialists. Teddington Weir on the Thames was where I snared my first ever fish over four pounds and many smaller fish kept the bait runners spinning all through the night. The weirs' attraction for fish lies in the eddies and back currents that are continually swirling around over a bottom of rock and gravel, stirring up insect life and supplying the droves of

Teddington Weir.
(Photo courtesy of Mike Ricard, licensed under the Creative Commons Attribution 2.0 License)

small fish with a constant supply of food. Furthermore, fish coming over the weir and getting injured or killed on the rocks will attract many types of predator, not just the eels. If the river you've decided to fish has a weir then I recommend it as a good a place to start as any.

The next piece was an article written by Kevin Richmond for the British Eel Anglers' Club (BEAC) in 1987, reproduced with their kind permission. Kevin is a very well known and respected eel angler with many big fish to his credit. His insights on river eeling are invaluable.

Tidal River Eeling
Kevin Richmond

Tidal river eeling has always been looked upon as an obscure branch of our sport; a backwater for close season 'escapes'. The vast majority of eel anglers fish almost entirely on stillwaters without giving a second glance at any other venue. It's easy to see why. Almost all eels over six pounds are taken from stillwaters or canals. Tidal river anglers take very few really large Anguillas. The largest I know of weighed a fraction over six pounds. My best 'tidal' went 5lb 7¾oz and was taken during an intensive campaign during 1979 when she was part of 101 eels taken from 17 consecutive night sessions. This eel was a Devon record until some guy fishing for flounders pulled in a 5lb 15oz silver eel.

The average river eel tends to fall into the 1½ to 2lb weight range. If an eel angler is prepared to have a break from those elusive 8lb-plus snakes and lower his sights for a while then a great deal of fun can be obtained by fishing these almost forgotten waters. One great advantage is that tidal rivers are not bound by close season restrictions. Such areas are looked upon as common land and therefore fall outside the jurisdiction of the water authorities. This means that close season eeling can be undertaken though I must add that such places are not the easiest of waters to fish. During the period 1973-1982 I caught 805 eels to 5lb 7oz from 257 sessions covering 5,539 rod hours from tidal rivers The weight ranges broke down as follows:

0-1lb   307 eels
1-2lb   302 eels
2-3lb   143 eels (average rod hours for 2lb eel approx 30)
3-4lb   42 eels (average rod hours for 3lb eel approx 100)
4-5l   8 eels (average rod hours for 4lb eel approx 500)
5-6lb   3 eels (average rod hours for 5lb eel approx 1,850)

The first and most obvious thing to remember is the tides (if there were no tides it wouldn't be a tidal river). Some can be quite extreme, rises and falls as great as 25 feet on some south-west rivers have been experienced so forget about using ½oz bombs and slow sinking ledgers; at times I have had 2oz leads skipping on the surface due to the tidal flow. If you can get situated on the inside of a bend then margin baits can just about be fished, that is if the resulting backwater does not fill up with floating weed, driftwood, dead animals etc. As shown in the following diagrams the eels' feeding patterns seem to remain constant along the following lines; it must be remembered that this is based on the tide occurring just before or after dark. Obviously there is the chance of picking up a fish at any stage of the tide. I once caught a 3lb eel while my lead was bouncing along the bottom, landing it over 150 yards from where I was fishing, however the periods illustrated below do tend to give the most activity.

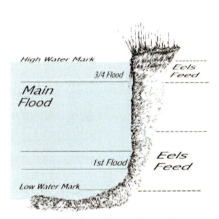

Tide Coming in

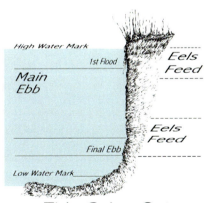

Tide Going Out

Fourteen eels between 3lb and 5lb.

Apart from the tidal flow there are other unwelcome factors; one of the most annoying is the sheer density of bootlaces. If one is to fish successfully then you must of course get bites, convert, and land fish. This means it is impossible not to catch small eels. It is worth noting that when the larger eels move over a baited area they tend to push out their smaller brethren. Whilst deadbaits are excellent in producing a stamp of eels in the 1-3lb brackets, they are not the major food of the larger eels.

In fact the most effective baits for the larger eels are those that are most appetising to the bootlaces! I remember landing a 4lb 5oz eel that spewed up a number of caddis grubs and other small food items. The problem of presenting such desirable baits in a swim long enough for a big eel to take them is something I have yet to solve. Most anglers would, in fisheries with exceptionally large bootlace populations, resort to using eel steaks. I have had much success with this bait on tidal rivers, apart from the fact that I'm never really happy chopping up small eels. Runs are forthcoming, yet seem to go on . . . and on . . . and on . . . And missed! As the aim of the game is to catch as many eels as is possible in order to (a) get maximum fun value and (b) catch the large 4lb-plus eels simply by the law of averages, then medium sized deadbaits fit the bill.

I have caught on a wide variety of baits when fishing tidal rivers. These include lampreys (excellent), slugs (good), snails (non-selective), caddis grubs (non-selective), prawns (need baiting up), paste mixes (need extensive baiting up), liver (good), mackerel sprats (tend to be too soft and last about two minutes when bootlaces home in on them). Finally I will give a brief extract from one of my angling diaries for a night when everything went right.

'Upon arriving at the swim I groundbaited with approximately 20-30 chopped trout, laid over an area of 10-15 foot, to which an additive had been added (glycine). Rods were set up, terminal rigs put on and hooks sharpened. I cast out at 8.30 and had my first run at 9.45, which I missed. Due to the very high tide, the fishing at this period was very difficult; during one stage it was impossible due to the extreme tidal flow and coupled with the level rising over the banks to a depth of 12 inches. I did not land my first eel until 10.50. It weighed 1lb 6oz. Three more eels came up till midnight weighing 11oz 6oz and 2lb 6oz, then sport died until 3.15am when I landed an eel of 1lb 9oz.

'At 3.30am I had a run, which was no different to any of the others - until I hit it! The 1½ lb t.c. rod slammed over and line was rapidly taken. The fish kept pulling over and virtually reached the far bank snags before I stopped it. It was three or four yards away when the line went slack as the

Eric Boyles with a 6lb 3oz eel taken on a club trip to a small Sussex resovoir.

Ardingly Bailiff, Wes Horton, with a 7lb 12oz eel netted from the same venue.

eel belted past me and went through the other two lines, tangling one. By now I was wondering just what the hell I had hooked! Constant pressure brought the eel to within netting distance.

'My main worry at this stage was that the tangled line would in some way foul the bottom or the landing-net, and the sodding thing slid over the net cord and belted off again! It was with great relief that I netted the fish. I bit off the tangled line and carried the eel up the bank into the field, just to be safe. Even at this stage the eel looked big. When the torch was shone on to the net I realised the eel was bloody enormous. With the weigh net included, the eel weighed 5lb 7¾oz, a Devon best! It was in superb condition, measuring 40½ inches with almost a constant 9-inch girth throughout. After all the excitement, I had a brew up. Whilst drinking the coffee, the one remaining rod went off and I hooked into another good eel. This one weighed 3lb 12oz and rounded off an exceptional session.'

Scott Dove with an Essex-caught monster weighing 9lb 2oz. (Photo courtesy of BEAC.)

If you ever get fed up with sitting around ponds blanking, why not give running water a try? Do not expect to catch monsters; such eels are simply not there. I will always have a soft spot for tidal waters. They produced my first 3, 4 and 5lb eels. Come April I will be making the 160 mile round trip to fish them again, simply in order to fish somewhere that never sees another angler, is free and full of eels.

Canals

It was once thought that canals, normally long straight featureless stretches of water that go on mile after mile, held little interest to the specimen hunter. They were more normally the haunts of the match angler seeking to catch bream and roach, with the occasional tench, to win the club's weekly pools money. Then word got round on the angling grapevine that big eels were being caught: 6lb and 7lb fish, and possibly much bigger, lost due to inadequate landing-nets. Since then a small band of devoted eel anglers have tried to unlock the unexploited potential of these canals, keeping their catches quiet until they hit the jackpot.

From my own experience, canals can be bleak places to fish so watercraft will play a big part in finding locations. In the absence of obvious fish-holding areas, anything that breaks the uniformity of the canal should be considered - slight bends, bushes, rubbish dumped in the margins. You may have to walk many miles to find half a dozen likely swims like this. Of course some canals are better than others for locating holding areas and when I do venture on to a canal I usually start by trying to locate lock gates, the older the better and preferably in a state of disuse. Cuttings too; these quiet, out of the way places often have piles of old rubbish on the bottom. Old tyres, shopping trolleys, piles of bricks and old masonry are also good places for a big eel to seek refuge during the day. Occasionally you will come across bridges that cut across the canal and although I have fished alongside a few of these and, surprisingly, caught nothing, I know of a few anglers who rate these areas very highly.

The local match stretch is another area that would automatically make you think of eels. After the weigh-in at the end of a match, many small fish, damaged and dying, plus the clouds of scraped off scales from keepnets, should constitute an easy and regular food source for the canal eels. There is one solitary angler I know who fishes canals almost exclusively. He has discovered that the further away he fishes from the more heavily fished areas, like the match sections, the bigger and more abundant the eels become. He regularly walks over a mile from the nearest access point to his fishing positions and has landed some very big fish. This is contrary to what you would expect as the match sections do represent easy pickings for the eels, a fact that applies to lake eels too. Maybe it's a combination of shallow water and regular bankside traffic, even boating activities, that drives the bigger fish to much quieter areas, but I'm only speculating.

Occasionally, when walking the canal, you come across areas on the far bank where the wash from the boats has eroded the bank. These sections have often been built with wood which has rotted away with time and created areas almost like mini wrecks. Behind the rotting wood, in the shallow water, small fish and insect life abounds. Even though these places can be ridiculously shallow, inches at times, they can become eel strongholds when all is dark and quiet. Canal eels are also supposed to be territorial, wandering long distances under the cover of darkness in their endless search for food, and are believed to travel in groups of several fish at a time. This is thought to explain why an angler can have hours of inactivity, then, out of the blue, have several runs in a very short space of time, sometimes simultaneously on different rods fishing baits in the same area. Bear this in mind if you get a run and miss it; get a bait back in the water as soon as possible and you may be in for another take in double quick time. This is

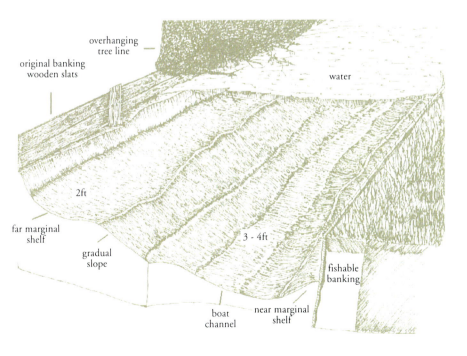

Typical cross-section of a canal.

about as far as my knowledge of canals stretches so from this point on I hand the subject over to Nick and Mark Duffy, brothers who are very successful canal specialists with a string of big fish behind them. As their joint experience of canal fishing is far more extensive than mine their views are greatly appreciated.

Many of the canal systems in and around England are at least a hundred years old, so for the angler in search of big eels there is little doubt that canals are capable of supporting some very big fish. On many of the canals I fish the banks are natural, presenting big fish the opportunity to thrive. Ancient trees, over-grown bushes with their branches trailing in the water, old barges, some derelict and waterlogged, lie against the dense undergrowth. Long tunnels, bridges, deep-water channels and old lock gates, all of these areas can accommodate big eels. Many of these old waterways now support an amazing variety of water life. From fish to small invertebrates and insects, all manner of life flourishes along many of these forgotten waterways. Swan mussels in many places line the bottom and on warm wet nights, untold quantities of worms cover the banks with many finding their way into the canal. This entire fauna represents a rich source of food to the large canal eels. I'd like to share with you my thoughts on the many areas that I like to fish on my local canals and state why I think eels find these particular places attractive.

Bridge swims - Many of the old brick bridges have over the years suffered from severe water erosion caused by barges and pleasure craft. This has resulted in patches of brickwork coming loose and in some places, holes below the water line have occurred. As the brickwork has corroded away and the infill dirt behind it washed out, these holes have been filled by large eels as they are ideal places to ambush any passing small fish. Bridges that have recently been repaired can also still offer the eel a home as much of the old brickwork is slung in the water during the repair work.

Lock gates - The oldest lock gates you can find the better when it comes to locating eels near them. Much of the old timber and brickwork is damp, covered in moss and weedy; this represents the ideal habitat for millions of insects, which in turn attracts many small fish. This is an easy food source the eels will not be unaware of and there may be many fish holed up in the vicinity. One of the problems of fishing around lock gates is they are popular dumping grounds for the general public so be prepared to encounter old bikes, car tyres and discarded clothing so expect to lose some tackle. When fishing these areas I prefer to plumb the depths and look for where the water shallows up just before or after the lock gates, I then position my baits in the middle of the slope. This is an excellent spot to intercept those eels as they leave the safety of the bottom debris in the search for food. One word of caution when fishing around lock gates, many of these areas are high above the water so exercise care when fishing them at night.

Wide bends - Few and far between but another good feature to fish to especially if the far bank is well overgrown, in fact any areas that offer far bank cover I would consider ideal places to position my baits. Disturbances on the towpath negates fishing the inside line and there tends to be little if any cover. The far bank offers an abundance of cover, although it may be much shallower than the nearside bank. The trees and bushes make these areas a lot darker and on occasion eels can be caught during daylight hours. Another area that can produce a few eels during daylight hours is alongside a moored up or derelict barge. But really and truly, fishing alongside a barge is far more productive at night. The same applies to marinas; the odd fish can be taken during daylight but during the night many eels visit these areas in the search for food.

These are the places I would regularly fish but there are places I would avoid like the plague. Places where steel shuttering has been installed to shore-up the bankside are the kiss of death to eel fishing. Okay, you may catch the odd fish if it was installed many years ago but the fish tend to be small and you may have to put many rod hours in to catch one. My advice would be to steer well clear of these areas. And any self-respecting fish will move to cleaner, quieter places.

Mark Duffy with his two best canal eels weighing 6lb 6oz and 6lb 5oz.

Right: Damian Wood with a hard won 6lb canal fish.

Below: Steve Pitts with a fabulous 7lb canal eel.

One last thing on fishing canals is baits. All my best fish have come to fish baits. My two best eels of 6lb 5oz and 6lb 6oz were caught on deadbait and livebait respectively. Worms can be used; the canals I fish crawl with tench and bream and these beat any eels to the bait in double quick time so you're far better off using fish baits. I hope what I have written inspires some of you to give canal eeling a go. There are some very big eels out there to be caught so the best of luck if you decide to give it a bash.

And, finally, one last topic on the subject of locating eels. Are they territorial, do they have patrol routes or do they just wander around on the bottom of the lake moving from area to area? I actually think they do all three but size does greatly influence this behaviour. Small eels can become a right nuisance as many a match angler has found out to his cost. The regular feeding of worms and maggots into the swim will slowly but surely draw in eels, and these are nearly always small, the bootlace variety. One of the lakes I fish contains a large head of eels, all of varying shapes, colours and sizes. On a normal one-night trip during the summer, maybe half a dozen to a dozen fish are on the cards, with a few pushing the 3lb mark. And there are usually more than a few missed runs to keep you busy through the night. For the first time this year I decided to pre-bait an area with a rubby-dubby bag (see Chapter 9 on pre-baiting). By morning I was bug eyed, covered in slime and must have used half the lake's roach population as bait. The culprits proved to be eels in the 1lb to 1lb 8oz bracket. As fast as I could put baits out they were being taken, sometimes before I had even opened the bale-arm. This was manic and as far as specimen eel hunting goes, a waste of time, as not one eel over two pounds was caught. These eels were not territorial, they were simply drawn to the swim as a direct result of the pre-baiting methods. These smaller eels, the 1- to 2-pounders are the ones I believe just mooch around the bottom looking for easy meals; they have no territory but they do appear to have patrol routes. With these eels many can be taken from around one feature without a noticeable drop in catches.

Territorial eels; now these are the ones that intrigue me. The biggest eels are definitely territorial and will have a specific home range. I know this through my own experiences with electro-fishing and from stories I have been told by divers. It has also been the subject of quite a lot of scientific study so, in my eyes, it's fairly well proven. The lake I am fishing at present has been electro-fished several times and one particular fish of abnormal proportions has turned up in exactly the same spot each time. Just coincidence? Divers have told me they quite often see big eels occupying the same place that they were in the last time they dived. These fish never move far from their homes and some are almost regarded as pets; they have become used to being hand-fed by the divers, yet they will not be tempted out of their lairs by more than a few feet. Food left more than a body length away from their refuge is ignored and often taken by other more mobile fish passing through. This has led me to conclude that there is actually a pecking order of some sort. The biggest fish may well occupy the safest and most inaccessible feeding areas. Moving out from here the fish will gradually get smaller until you get to the bootlace eels which are homeless and wander the lake. Do consider this when pursuing big eels. If you are being plagued by bootlaces it may be worth moving swims. If you are fishing a snaggy area and catching nothing bear in mind that your bait could be only feet away from a very big fish. Don't quit these swims until a bait has been fished in nearly every square foot of water no matter how horrendous the snags are. Just use tackle that will be appropriate for extracting them and there shouldn't be a problem (who am I kidding?).

My final comment is that you should always approach a new water with an open mind. Take the time to stop and ponder all the options before starting to fish no matter how obscure or trivial they seem. And if they say "There's no eels in there mate," you can bet yourself a tenner there is. There is no greater sense of achievement than to unravel the mysteries of a particular water and to have your choice of venue/swim vindicated by the capture of a big fish.

CHAPTER FIVE

TACKLE AND EQUIPMENT

In a swim strewn with snags even a medium sized eel can surprise us at times with its power and dirty fighting. Consequently, to land the bigger fish in these situations you will need strong tackle. You do not necessarily need the most expensive equipment on the market but what you do need is tackle of good quality - there is a difference. Big eels will fight hard for their freedom - size for size they fight as hard if not harder than most other species of fish - but there will be none of those long screaming runs associated with fish like carp, except maybe for the initial take.

What you will get is a tug of war, plain and simple. When the strike is made and the hook is set, the eel's reaction is to try and back up, resisting all attempts to drag it forward and often creating a huge vortex on the surface before the fish is seen. With a big fish you may well be held at stalemate for what seems like an eternity before gaining any line. Failing that, the eel may bolt either straight at you, deceiving you into thinking that it's escaped, or it may shoot off to either side. Its intentions will become blatantly obvious though - to bury itself and your line into a nightmare of snags from which you will never pull it free. And for those very reasons, the tackle needed to perform this task has to be strong.

The standard eeling tackle used by many of today's specialist anglers is only suitable for subduing big fish in open, snag-free water. Where there are serious obstructions, snags or weed-beds, I think many such anglers are pushing their luck just a bit: 8lb line and 2lb test curve rods, or even lighter, will not stop a big eel from finding the sanctuary of the nearest immovable object. Using 3lb test curve rods and 15lb line or 30lb braid, as I do, may sound over the top yet when that big one finally comes along, your tackle should be powerful enough to see you in charge, and not the fish. This is a contentious argument with many anglers disagreeing with me, believing that light tackle is the way forward with big eels. I do not hold with this way of thinking. So what if the fight I receive from a 2 or 3lb eel is insignificant? I am not targeting fish of this size and would much rather they didn't take my baits. I am pursuing big eels, and would be absolutely gutted at losing a monster in a weed-bed or other such snag, especially with a hook and wire trace stuck in its mouth. And all because my tackle was not adequate enough to stop the fish from gaining sanctuary, I'd rather not go down that road.

Many eel anglers I have spoken to claim to have hooked fish they couldn't stop or control and have come off the worse, but with stronger tackle this might not have been the case. Of course there is a fine line between going over the top and fishing with balanced tackle. So what tackle is needed to take on a big eel? And just as important, if like me you have grown to like your creature comforts, which items will be required to keep you warm and comfortable in the many days and nights that will be needed to put that big fish on the bank? I have suggestions and will try as much as I can to be impartial in my choice of equipment, as this chapter is not meant to be an advert for any one particular company. I will only comment on tackle that I think is good enough to warrant you spending your hard-earned cash on. As eel anglers we expect a lot from our tackle and it follows it will not always come cheap. Weigh up your own circumstances before embarking on a spending spree at the local tackle shop. Eel angling tackle is specialised but not specific; very little is designed especially for eel fishing, so much of what we use has to be adapted for our own cause.

Rods

The choice of quality rods available to the specialist angler today is truly staggering. Gone are the days of the glass fibre PK3, an exceptional rod whose heyday is well and truly in the distant past (unless of course, you love fishing with what now would be regarded as vintage tackle). Boron, Kevlar, Aramide wraps and a host of other space-age materials rule the banks with many of today's modern specimen hunters. Most manufacturers have to update their rod ranges yearly to keep up with the voracious appetite for designer tackle from the crazy world of carp fishing, so buy a bargain and get last year's model.

Big eel fishing is not about keeping up with designer trends although all anglers love new gadgets to tinker with. It's about hooking and successfully landing one of the hardest species in the specimen hunting world. Therefore designer names are not a necessity. Use whatever rod you like, providing it has sufficient backbone to do the job; the specifications and 'feel' will be the most important factors. When choosing a rod, your first consideration will be the types of areas you intend to fish - are they snaggy or clear of obstructions, do the fish come at long range or are they to be found patrolling the margins?

This will influence the action of the rod and the test curve you will require.

For the beginner, let me give a brief explanation of what we mean by the test curve. The test curve of a rod is the amount of weight required to compress the rod into a 90° angle from a vertical position and the action of a rod is where it starts to bend from to achieve this angle. So ideally, a good all-round eel rod will have a nice through-action, with a test curve somewhere between $2^1/_2$ and 3lb. This is an ideal tool and should cover the large majority of the situations ever encountered. As I said earlier, some anglers will consider this overkill on a fish that you may never see, let alone catch at double figures. But fish of this size certainly exist, and much bigger, and you need the power these rods afford to stop a big eel in its tracks. Wimpy tackle will just end in heartbreak if you are fortunate enough to hook one. Having a strong through-action rod will go some way to help preventing the hook from tearing out when the fish is in close, as the softer action of the rod absorbs much of the stress placed on the end tackle.

Long distance casting rods are of little or no use in eel fishing. Being very stiff, they destroy baits on the cast and rip the hooks out of the eel's mouth at close range. Given a choice, I would steer well clear of them. The ideal length is 12 foot but 13 footers can be used to help cope with longer casting or to overcome marginal weed. The price is what you can afford but £100 will normally buy you as good a rod as you will ever need. For many years I used four ancient $2^3/_4$lb t.c. through-action Armalites that served me well, and only recently changed my rods for a new set of 3lb t.c. $12^1/_2$ footers, which I hope will do the same. Lighter rods can be used as long as the area you are fishing is snag free. Personally, I want the odds in my favour and, given the eel's ability to hook its tail around any object in range and leave you snagged up, I'll stick with the rods that I know can stop a fish before it gets the chance. A good tackle shop should be able to help. Tell them the price you are willing to pay, the test curve and action of the rod you require, and they should be able to offer you several choices within your budget.

Reels

The technology used in the manufacture of modern fishing reels has also greatly advanced, with reels now being made from machined alloys and graphite. They are much lighter than their predecessors and a great deal smoother due to the use of bearings instead of the old brass bushes. Mitchell's famous 300, responsible for the British record eel and numerous other specimen fish, a reel once synonymous with specimen hunting, has now been replaced with reels like Shimano's baitrunner series. These reels are about as good as you can buy in the UK and have many features that are advantageous to the eel angler. My favourite feature is the baitrunner system itself. This is a device that, once engaged, puts the reel into free spool without altering the drag settings; the adjustment of bobbins is then a doddle. More importantly, if fishing in windy or rough conditions the reel can be left in free spool to allow a fish to take line when it runs; this does away with the bobbin and open bale-arm which in bad weather causes endless false takes. Using the baitrunner system is not the ideal way to fish but in atrocious weather it means you can still continue to fish and control the resistance a taking fish feels. This reel has been doing the rounds for a good few years now in various guises and my only complaint is that it suffers badly from line twist, and although this is curable with an item called a spin doctor it is an inconvenience. Still, I would probably rate the Shimano baitrunner series as the best reel available in 2009 that can be adapted for eel fishing, and the new XTE 1000 model is a major improvement on the older ones. Before you go out and buy a reel have a close look too at the Quantum Energy BCS 750. It's a bit on the large size but if you like fishing with the bigger type pit reels this could be what you've been looking for and is very reasonably priced.

On one particular pit I fish the eels tend to come at long range and, because of this, I have a preference for using a pair of big pit reels. Some people have accused me of posing, claiming big pit reels are too heavy and cumbersome and not practicable when pursuing eels. I disagree (not about the posing) for the following reasons. Casting out over a hundred yards with a conventional type reel that has a narrow spool is not only difficult but you have to cast much harder to achieve any sort of distance. This places a lot of stress on the bait, often ripping it from the hook. Line is also drastically reduced on the spool and the line that is left is often embedded on itself or has become crinkly. When fishing at range you need to reduce resistance as much as possible; the sheer amount of line in the water will create enough resistance of its own. So, if you have crinkly line and a half empty spool you may as well not bother, just drop your bait in the margins and keep your fingers crossed. With the pit reels, I use the Daiwa 500 Tournaments, which have a long, coned, polished alloy spool and are not that much bigger than my baitrunners so balance perfectly with most modern rods. The level of line on the spool hardly decreases at distances approaching a hundred yards so you don't get sticking on the spool either, and for me this is where their greatest advantage lies. These reels are only used for long-range fishing but they do have a niche in the eel fisherman's armoury. They hold around four hundred yards of 12lb line but are very expensive so unless you have a water that requires long-range fishing on a regular basis I would consider them a luxury item; baitrunners will suffice for most, if not all, the situations you will ever encounter.

Summing up the ideal reel for eel fishing is, therefore, a little difficult. It must hold over 250 yards of line and have an excellent line lay system. The drag is of little importance providing it does work (the two reels I have mentioned both have faultless drags) as the drag on most occasions will be locked up tight. It should be well made, preferably with an alloy-coned spool and I do like the free spool systems. But ultimately you must use the tackle you have faith in and of course the tackle you can afford.

Bite indicators

There are so many different methods of bite detection; a book could be written on that subject alone. So many things have changed since the late John Sidley used a penny balanced on the edge of his spool with a metal Morris Minor hubcap underneath to signal the start of a take. Electronic bite indicators have swept the markets over the last few decades with many weird and wonderful designs, but I rue the day I sold my original Delkim optonics as I feel nothing available today is as good for eel fishing as they were, or maybe I'm just being sentimental. A bite indicator's function is to perform one basic task - to detect the movement of line, everything else is superfluous. This can be achieved with the most sophisticated of bite-alarms or simply with a piece of cooking foil placed on the line and the angler making full use of his eyes.

The majority of electronic bite-alarms on the market today operate by means of magnets fixed to the end of a wheel, and this is where, for the eel angler, the problem lies, for when fishing with open bale-arms a free running line often fails to rotate this wheel. You can make alterations to the wheels, like treating them with a thin coat of silicone sealer - something I object to doing when paying near the £100 mark for bite-alarms - but it does go some way to solving the problem. When using monkey climbers or swingers in conjunction with these magnetic alarms, they give no problems whatsoever because there is a continuous weight on the line at all times. Monkeys or swingers bouncing up and down on the line as an eel takes can contribute to dropped runs so you have to come up with an alternative solution for keeping the line under tension with as little resistance as possible. A small piece of sponge placed in your first rod eye does the job yet this will still add resistance when our main task is to eliminate it. I very much doubt that you can still get hold of the original Delkim optonics unless you can find some in the 'For Sale' columns of the fishing weeklies; they have been out of production for many years now. If you do manage to locate yourself a set they are definitely a good buy. The optonic is the next best thing but even these seem to be disappearing from the shelves. Optonics work on a different principle in that there are no magnets hence no

John Sidley ready to strike. Notice the hubcap into which the coin drops to signal a run.
Bite indication has moved on a lot since then, yet the aims still remain the same. (Photo courtesy of BEAC.)

resistance. They have a small wheel attached to a paddle which breaks a beam of light inside the indicator. The wheel offers no resistance and a free running line turns it without any problems. They are, in my opinion, one of the best bite indicators available for eel fishing.

Another well-liked method of open bale-arm bite detection is the backbite indicators, although more popular with pike anglers than eelers. These indicators work by being clipped to the rod rest behind the reel. The bale arm is then opened, the arm of the backbite indicator raised up level with the spool, and the line is then clipped into it. When a fish takes, line is pulled from the clip and the arm drops down or the fish swims towards you and the arm drops down, both signalling a take. Backbite alarms come as electronic and sound when the arm moves either way or as clip on indicators that are just visual. They are a little bit dated but still a firm favourite with pike anglers and some eelers.

Technological advancement in fishing can be a good thing but items like electronic indicators should be used as an aid to bite detection and not a replacement for the angler sitting behind his rods and paying attention to his fishing. I have seen numerous so-called anglers, at the onset of darkness, cast their baits into the distance and disappear into their bivvies for the night, relying on the noise of the buzzer to wake them when a run occurs. By doing this they are not putting 100% into their fishing and will be rewarded as such. Mosquito's aside, lakes become magical places once the sun has set, and if an angler sleeps in his bivvy he misses out on the atmosphere of fishing after dark - those twitchy takes that only give a few solitary bleeps - and, in effect, he becomes an armchair angler.

Washing-up bottle tops. How long have these been around? I still favour the use of these between the reel and first rod eye as a visual means of bite indication to complement the electronics rather than using monkey climbers. They are light enough to offer only minimal resistance to a taking fish yet have enough weight to hold the line lightly on the spool when fishing with open bale-arms; just remember not to clip the bottle top shut as sometimes they can twist around the line and jam in the rod eye during a fast take. The idea is that they should fall off when a run occurs, so just hang them on by the little cap. The addition of an isotope also makes them easily visible at night. Bottle tops (they have to come from old bottles of Fairy washing-up liquid to qualify for ultra cult status) may be regarded as old fashioned considering the range of indicators on the market - swingers, hangers, quivers, monkey climbers and so on - but they offer something most of the other methods can't match: they weigh virtually nothing, fall off when you get a take and cost pennies, plus the wife gets to contribute to the enjoyment of your fishing by using the contents of the bottle. How can you beat that? (She's gonna kill me.)

Foul weather conditions will require an alternative to bottle tops as these will not stay on the line in high winds. This is where the old monkey climbers come into their own. They can be weighted to stop them moving about and the tip of the rod can be submerged preventing wave action causing false takes. Even with the rod being at such a steep angle, the line can be held comfortably on the spool by using monkey climbers. I do not use the standard monkeys, much preferring to use the flip top variety above all others; they are difficult to obtain but do release the line much more easily when a strike is made. They are also set up slightly differently to the way in which a carp angler would use them. A carp angler will have them between the first rod eye and the reel, with the metal pole almost touching the rod, whereas an eel angler will have them closer to the reel with the steel rod below the lip of the spool. The idea is that when the monkey reaches the top of the pole, the line comes free from the monkey, allowing line to be taken off the reel with the bale-arm open. I have also been experimenting with using monkey climbers with a rod pod, where they are used almost horizontally and give even less resistance to a taking fish. Fishing with bite indicators this sensitive is only really feasible on waters where you do not get plagued with nuisance fish, otherwise you will be up and down all night replacing the line back in the monkeys. See illustration overleaf.

There has also been a free-spool indicator introduced to the market recently called a rollover indicator. This is the first bite indicator specifically designed for eel fishing by one of the top UK eel anglers, Barry McConnell. It's a brilliant little device that can be seen working on his website before you buy - *www.zandavan.co.uk*. It will probably be the indicator of choice for eel anglers for a long time to come.

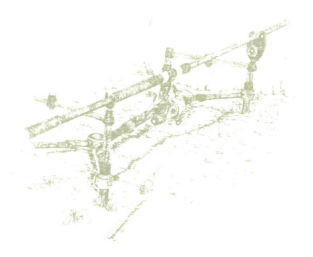

An ideal set-up when conditions allow.

Lines

Again, lines have improved dramatically over the past few years. They are thinner, have greater abrasion resistance and better knot strength than ever before. A few years ago the only lines I considered good enough for eeling were Sylcast and Maxima. Now I have a much wider choice at my disposal, using Fox Steel, Insight GR60 and Shimano's excellent Technum Line. Using them in 12 and 15lb breaking strain, I have had little or no complaints. There are plenty of other good lines available, as well as some right crap that's only fit for holding up runner beans in the back garden. Beware, even some of the most expensive branded lines are sometimes useless, having very little knot strength. A sensible means of deciding which line to use is to pick the brains of anglers who already pursue specimen fish, of whatever species. They will already have done the groundwork and will be using lines that are good quality and that they have confidence in. Also, make sure the line you have purchased is new; lines that have been in the storeroom for donkeys' years or line that has just been sitting on a shop shelf will have possibly deteriorated either due to age or UV exposure. These lines will break on you at the most inopportune moment. It would be handy if manufacturers printed the date of manufacture on the line so we could tell how old it was. Now wouldn't that be nice? Lines breaking when casting, or when applying pressure when snagged or even when tying knots, these are all symptoms of old or poor quality line so get rid of it. A good quality line, with regular use, should last at least one good season before it requires changing.

To err on the side of safety, I renew all my lines over the winter when I have a break from serious eel fishing. With the various different situations you will encounter when hunting eels, the breaking strains of the lines will also need to be varied so it's handy to have a few spare pre-loaded spools. For snaggy or weedy areas I would recommend lines of around 15lb b.s. or in some circumstances 20lb (I have also used braid up to 65lb). With clean-bottomed lakes, 10 or 12lb b.s. should be more than adequate. I would never advise using lines any lighter than this.

What about braids? They are new on the scene but do they have a place in eel fishing other than as hooklengths? I am very gradually being convinced and I think that's because it's hard to teach an old dog new tricks. They have remarkable strength to diameter ratios, excellent knot strength and almost zero stretch when compared with mono but remember that stretch can be a safety factor when playing a fish in close. This is something to bear in mind if you find yourself in a situation where a big fish needs to be bullied; the lack of stretch may well tear the hook free if it doesn't have a secure hold. Having experimented with these lines over the past few years I have identified problems that I do not experience with mono. One issue is that they are so thin and light they slide over the wheel of the bite-alarm without turning it, just like using bite-alarms with magnetic wheels. This doesn't matter if you are sitting over the rods as you respond to the first bleep or movement of the bobbin but when you are in the bivvy because it's chucking it down with rain that's not so funny. I awoke one morning after a wet run-less night to find I had indeed had a run: the fish had taken over fifty yards of braid and tied me to every snag in the lake before escaping. I know this because the lake has an average depth of around two feet and I was able to wade out and retrieve my tackle. The end rig was just a ball of nasty white slime. Braid's greatest attraction is its lack of stretch and tiny diameter but there is a price you have to pay for this. At range, the slightest movement of the bait is detected enabling a fast strike. At distance, the fish is safe as the rod acts as a shock absorber - the closer the fish gets, the less shock is absorbed by the rod and braid so you have to fight the fish much more gently unless you have added a mono shock leader to the line. One area in which I found braids did excel was with the use of off-bottom rigs. Using a floating braid, rig and bait presentation were much improved; as the braid floats it keeps the off-bottom rig in line with the surface, whereas mono sinks and drags the rig down. Braids may very well be the way of the future for lines but, for the time being, I think I'll keep both mono and braids in my armoury. That's a personal choice and I will still keep an open mind on the subject and continue to play around with braids as they improve.

Landing-nets

The landing-net is the one piece of equipment that decides whether you have a personal best eel on the bank or an empty hook dangling from your rod. Many good eels are lost at the net due to anglers believing a 42-inch net is more than adequate. Believe me, 48-50 inches is not overdoing it, I have had my own 60-inch net custom built as I wanted a net that was long without the width of a lot of the shop bought nets. Big eels can have a nasty habit of hooking their tails over the cord of the net and hauling themselves back into the lake, so a good sized net is a must. The best place to find a net that is suitable is to search through the catfish magazines, as they also require big nets. Tackle shops rarely stock nets that are suitable for serious big eel anglers.

This picture shows the difference between a standard 42-inch net and the 60-inch net I had custom built.

Hooks

Hooks, the final connection between you and the fish. Any tackle shop will normally have one wall dedicated solely to hooks with hundreds of patterns, of which only a few are useful to us. Again we are indebted to the carp world for the quality of hooks available, as the manufacture of these items has come a long way with very few of the hooks produced now being of poor quality. Most are high quality, forged and chemically sharpened, so hooks pulling straight or needing regular sharpening should be a thing of the past. Just stay away from the cheapo bucket, and it won't be the hook that lets you down. One more thing to add on the subject of hooks, should it be 'barbed or barbless'? I'm not going to get involved in this argument as I think it's a matter of personal choice. I use barbless on waters I have to and micro barbed everywhere else. The best advice is probably just to use what you believe in and not what someone else does. After that statement here are some of the hooks I have found up to the job.

Z10s : This hook is made by Partridges of Redditch and is an excellent dead-and livebait hook, made from strong Sheffield steel. The shanks are long and the eye of the hook is completely closed: there's no small gap between the eye-hole and the shank of the hook, as with a lot of other patterns, so there is no chance of the line or wire slipping through the gap in the eye. They also have a smallish barb that makes the unhooking of fish that much easier. This hook is highly recommended. Partridge also developed a bait holder hook in conjunction with John Sidley.

THE Z6 : This hook has small barbs up the shank, designed specifically for eel fishing. This is one of the best worm hooks around and is called the Sidley bait holder hook. Fox manufacture a hook called the specialist carp hook series 4 and this is a very good hook for use with small deadbaits and worms. It has a long shank and small barb so unhooking of fish is relatively easy if they are not too deeply hooked.

THE RAPTOR G4 : This hook, made by ESP, is a favourite of mine in the smaller sizes and is extremely sharp. It's best with small worms and specials. Owner Cutting Point hooks and the Penetrator 1 from Gold Label Tackle are both excellent deadbait hooks. The Owners are incredibly sharp having the ability to cut through flesh and bone if the hook becomes buried in the bait whereas the Penetrator has a wide gape that keeps the hook point away from the bait's body. Sizes from 1, 2, 4, 6 should cover every eventuality that arises.

There are many other good brands of hook on the market; these are just a few of the ones I choose to use. In the end it will all come down to personal preference and what you feel confident in using. One type of hook you should never consider using is the stainless steel variety, with a gut hooked fish and a normal hook you can cut the line close to the eel's mouth and the eel will either regurgitate the hook, or its stomach acids will dissolve it in a very short space of time. Stainless steel, however, will not dissolve and the fish has much greater difficulty in disposing of it, with the result that a large percentage of deep hooked eels could die.

In several places in this book I have mentioned items I am experimenting with and I think this next item could be the answer to a problem that has plagued eel anglers for as long as I can remember. Deep hooking of eels is something that has been nigh on impossible to prevent but I have now reduced the amount of deep hooked fish I catch by a significant amount. There have been numerous attempts at resolving this problem but most have either been hit and miss affairs or have affected catch rates too significantly. So I have taken a leaf out of the commercial longliners' book and started experimenting with circle hooks. Commercial catch rates have improved by 80% when compared with using traditional 'J' hooks and the amounts of fish surviving have also increased significantly. And remember, eels are sold alive, not dead. Looking at the circle hooks it's hard to believe they could catch anything. A hook that circles around on itself with the point pointing at the hook's shank looks suspect to say the least. So how do they work? Well, for starters, they are designed to be self-hooking; strike and you will actually miss the take. The principle is that the eel takes the bait and hook fully into its mouth and then, as the fish moves off, the hook is pulled out of the eel's stomach/throat via the trace/line travelling over the scissors of the jaw. On reaching the scissors of the jaw, the bend of the hook locks around the hinge section of the jaw and the point of the hook pulls into the flesh at the scissors. The whole principle relies on the fact that the hook will not snag on any part of the eel internally so it can be swallowed as far down as the stomach without ill effect. As the line tightens, the hook is drawn back past the vulnerable areas and lodges in the corner of the mouth - one hooked fish.

If you use circle hooks the main adjustment you have to make to your fishing style is not to strike. You can only tighten up on the fish and let the hook do what it's designed to do. As we tend to fish with open bale-arms, this method works well with our style of fishing as we can actually allow a run to continue much longer than we ever thought possible without serious consequences to the fish. Baits can be rigged in a number of ways; worms can be hooked as normal and livebaits can be lip hooked. Deadbaits are a different matter; you can lip hook or bridle the hook but on no account threadle it through the fish, it will not work. And use a larger size hook than you would normally use; these hooks are very size dependent, ie, a small hook is unlikely to find a hook hold in a big fish. In the future, if these trials continue to be successful, wire traces may not even be necessary any more as the line will not be in the eel's mouth during the fight. These hooks could become one of our biggest aids in a conservation-oriented catch and release sport.

Care of hooks may sound unnecessary but is important. Many of today's mass-produced lines have the odd faulty hook in the batch. This can be anything from an eye that is not fully closed to a barb that is too deeply cut. Take no chances if the hook looks even remotely dodgy, be thorough and chuck it away; you may end up in tears if you don't. When fishing a water that is known to contain big fish I have got into the habit of changing the hook and trace after every eel, lost or landed. This is my safeguard; eels put an enormous amount of stress on a hook so changing them regularly eliminates any chance of the hook failing due to the previous encounter. Nearly all my hooklengths are prepared in the comfort of my own home and packed individually into a rig wallet. This way I am totally confident in their construction. Another common error is to use rusty hooks, either ones that have got wet in the packet from previous trips or where the rods have been left assembled in a rod sleeve with the end tackle still attached. Inspect and change them if even the smallest rust spot has appeared. The last thing you want is for a couple of bobs worth of hook to let you down on that one occasion when you manage to hook into a really big fish.

Now, weights. A good selection of various sized leads is what tends to give my rucksack its 'Strewth, this weighs a ton' weight. I fish a lot of my rigs into weed-beds and around nasty looking snags and am always losing leads so tend to take a lot of spares. For most of my fishing I use 1oz and 3oz but will use heavier or lighter weights as circumstances dictate. Nowadays most of the leads I use are treated with a plastic powder coating, which you can obtain from tackle shops. I prefer to do my own rather than purchase the ready-coated leads. I'm a fussy sod when it comes to camouflaging my rigs but whether this makes the blindest bit of difference to my catch results I haven't the foggiest. Keeping my rigs as discrete as possible keeps me happy. The Richworth flavour capsule weights are my favourites, where a small dissolvable capsule fits either side of a lead held in place by a rubber band. The capsule can then be injected with fish oils or any other flavours of your choice. Weights designed to plane off the bottom are also handy in snaggy situations.

Other items

The other items I would include in my tackle box are a good selection of swivels ranging from size 3 to 12, and a good variety of snap links. Berkeley make some of the best swivels but whoever's you buy, make sure they are good quality. I also have a good selection of the previously mentioned bobbins; a soft cloth tape for measuring and recording the length and girth of the eels (that is if you remember to use it before you release the fish); and a couple of decent syringes for air injecting baits. I carry two types of syringe. Firstly, the small insulin pins that have needles like hairs which are excellent for injecting air into worms. They leave the tiniest hole from which the air does not leak back. Secondly, the standard syringe which is used for injecting baits with fish oils, flavours etc. All these syringes can be bought from the chemist and work out a lot cheaper than buying them from the tackle shop. I'd also take a good selection of various sized swimfeeders and a packet of tampax if you've got the bottle (I'll explain later); otherwise a small packet of cotton wool will do. I always have a selection of small hooks to nylon and some delicate little floats for bait snatching (and for using these it's handy to have an old whip in the rod bag for convenience) and a couple of different sized forceps. I will not use disgorgers; if I can't see the hook I will snip the trace off as close to the eel's mouth as possible so a decent set of wire cutters are also needed. Kryson's superb meltex PVA bags in various sizes are useful, especially for heavily weeded swims; and I take spare batteries for the optonics, a torch, spare pre-loaded spools of line and loads of other bits and bobs. Many of the items that fill my box to overflowing never get used but I'm loathe to leave anything behind. Always be prepared as they say, 'Dib Dib'.

Some typical eel angler's kit.

Bivvies

For the long stay or 'session' angler a good quality shelter is a must. It becomes a home from home so has to be warm in the cold weather, well ventilated for the heat of the summer and spacious enough to contain all the paraphernalia the long stay angler will ever need. Knowing how unpredictable the British weather can be, we need to ensure all our kit stays as dry as possible and, of course, that we are kept dry and comfortable too. So what should we be looking for in a fishing shelter? Water resistance, speed of erection, the ability to withstand gale force winds? The areas you are fishing will basically dictate your requirements. When I first started to stay out overnight in the search for eels, it was in an old canvas tarpaulin slung over the top of a 50-inch brolly held down with 6-inch nails and bricks. However, following many complaints from fishery owners that my fishing area looked remarkably like a gypsies' camp, I decided to invest in a proper bivvy. I scanned the angling weeklies and eventually came across an advert from Bob Frost Tackle in which he advertised a camouflage throw-over bivvy. Having purchased it I was most impressed and wondered how I had ever got on without one. For almost ten years it served me well before giving up the ghost in storm force winds only a few years ago.

Today's more modern bivvies are a major improvement on the old throw-overs, having the ability to withstand gales and remain waterproof (sometimes). Just check what other anglers think of a particular bivvy before you buy one as this is a far better way to make the right choice than believing all the hype that's spun in the adverts. For eeling there tends to be three main types we generally use but this is not gospel: the basic brolly type shelter, the throw-over or wrap-around bivvy (which may have its own frame or it may just fit over the top of a 50-inch umbrella), and the dedicated long stay bivvy. Some of these dedicated bivvies have removable groundsheets; these are fine but give me a bivvy dome any day. They have sewn-in groundsheets, which keep the bugs and mozzies at bay. Most are very warm, being twin skinned, but this does have its downside; if you do get water inside or spill the teapot, it has nowhere to go, so you need to be prepared to do a bit of housekeeping (horrible word). They also take longer to erect but when you're there for several days does an extra ten minutes really matter? Just beware, some bivvies are simply dome tents made out of cheap green material and marketed for fishing, and although they may appear fine, foul weather normally highlights the weak points. Even some of the best fishing shelters I've used in the past few years have given problems in bad weather. One claimed to be 100% waterproof but a very heavy downpour soon proved otherwise. As the rain beat down a very fine spray of water entered through the nylon cloth making everything damp. Another claimed the same

A good quality well designed bivvy capable of withstanding the worst of conditions.

A good quality bedchair and a warm sleeping bag helps make those long cold nights of autumn more bearable.

degree of waterproofness, which was justified sure enough, but condensation made it just as wet as if it had rained.

So is there any such thing as the perfect fishing shelter? Not really, different fishing environments will require the use of a different shelter. For short overnight sessions a decent umbrella with side infills is fine but even better is the Nash Hurricane, a profile type shelter that is lightweight, simple to erect and good quality. Next would be a throw-over type bivvy for when you need more shelter from wind and rain. In this situation shelters like the Fox Evolution brolly over-wrap are ideal. Again lightweight and a doddle to assemble, these are perfect where you need more shelter from the elements but are still fishing a short session or have a limited amount of space. And lastly, for the long session angler, there are the bivvy domes. These should be able to withstand extreme weather conditions, especially gale force winds. In the areas I am fishing at the moment, wind is the biggest problem and it drives me crazy to have bits of bivvy flapping about in the wind. I also had one bivvy that, during a gale, got totally squidged with me inside; I didn't get much sleep that night. Minor adventures such as these drove me to have a shelter built to my own spec. but there are now some very good ones on the market. Just think before you buy. All single skin shelters will suffer from condensation in cold weather whatever the manufacturer claims. Twin skinned shelters require more space to erect and more patience. Therefore consider where you are fishing and how long you intend to fish into the colder months. If I were to go out and purchase one of the 'off the shelf' bivvies it would probably be a Kevin Nash Viper bivvy fitted with one of the extreme weather outer skins; not cheap but stable, warm and with plenty of room. Or I'd go for the Trokker Armo.

Internals

A good quality, stable bedchair is also a must to go along with the bivvy and nowadays you have a lot of choice. My preference tends to be the three-legged variety as these are the most stable, especially if, like me, you are a little on the large side. These are ideal if you intend to remain in the same swim for days on end. For shorter trips or sessions where you are more mobile the bedchairs with two legs are more functional as many of these can also double up as normal chairs. They are also lighter and much less bulky to carry.

To accompany the bedchair you will also require a good quality sleeping bag and for this you need to consider how much time you will be fishing in cold weather; you could manage perfectly well with a nice thick blanket. But if you do go for a sleeping bag, make sure you can exit from it quickly; I've had some right good laughs watching people hop from their bivvies to strike a run with their sleeping bag still wrapped round their legs because they couldn't get the zipper undone in time. Sleeping bags are rated by the season, the more seasons the bag is stated as having, the warmer the bag is going to be.

There are many other items you can take: cookers, chairs, bivvy tables etc. And most importantly don't ever forget the kettle. Tea making has an uncanny knack of stirring the fish into action and you may well get the only run of the night when you're in the middle of filling the mug.

How much equipment you take depends on how long you intend staying. You can take as much as you like or just the bare essentials for one overnight trip. It all depends on the venue, time of year and how much you want to carry, so what I've tried to do is guide you through the main items to make long stays more comfortable and enjoyable and to suggest tackle options that may help you to put a personal best eel on the bank rather than suffer another lost fish.

CHAPTER SIX

HOW AND WHEN

By this time you should have gained some ideas on where to find and fish for eels. Finding your big eel location is the first step on the road to success and will require a fair amount of effort on your part, but when you actually set out to try and catch them, this is when something else will be needed - patience and a great deal of it. Specimen eel fishing is accepted as hard, there is never going to be any such thing as an easy big eel water so to be consistently successful you need to acquire a very deep understanding of their habits. You may of course be lucky and it may just be a case of being in the right swim at the right time. Luck, as we very well know, is never predictable and by increasing your knowledge of all aspects of your quarry you can certainly increase your chances of making those once in a blue moon captures. The more time you spend pursuing eels, the more you come to understand their behaviour. I can't say that I have become an expert, I have just become experienced and know what to do under certain conditions.

In the previous chapters we talked about finding a venue to fish, location and tackle, but what we now need to know is how to set out our pitch and go about catching them. So from here onwards I will try to advise you on the best way to use your tackle and when to fish for eels to give you the greatest chance of success. Whether you have chosen to fish lakes, rivers or canals, most of the methods applied to catching big eels can be put to use in all three situations. Here I will not delve too deeply into the use of end tackle, nor baits, as these will be covered in far more detail in the following two chapters. Needless to say, ledgering, free lining and off-bottom rigs, and sometimes even float fishing (very much underrated), will be the means of attack on the business end as far as rigs go. But it's just as important to get it right at the other end, the angler's end.

Having decided on your choice of swim, or more likely if you are restricted to weekend excursions, the best choice of swim that has been left to you, you need to get set up. So you make a quick dash back to the car to get the tackle out of the boot before someone else turns up and tries to nick your likely looking spot. A few years ago I could just about manage all my gear in one trip - those were the days. Now it's a minimum of two trips with the trolley. Cart all this paraphernalia back to the swim and don't clatter about like a bull in a china shop, keep disturbance to a minimum and unload with a bit of common sense. The fewer disturbances you make, the more chance you will have of catching fish. There's normally never any need to rush unless it's chucking it down; eels will not usually feed until the evening starts to set in. So if you've arrived with plenty of time to set up before nightfall this shouldn't present a problem.

The layout of the swim will obviously dictate where everything goes but, ideally, I would prefer to set up my bivvy first, and then arrange my tackle and everything else around that. If there is sufficient space available, the bivvy or whatever choice of shelter I have chosen, will be erected as far back from the water's edge as is practicable. And unless the wind is blowing a hooley straight into the swim I will set up with the entrance facing the water. From this position I can observe my rods even snuggled up from inside my sleeping bag. Having a shelter erected close to the water's edge may restrict casting in a tight swim but the biggest disadvantage is that you may very well spook fish that have moved into the shallow marginal areas to feed during the night. These fish are able to detect the angler's presence through vibration created by walking about on the bank; they may not be able to see the angler but they will know he is there. With the bivvy now erected and fixed in the correct position, bedchair in place, sleeping bag un-zipped, cooker fired up and the kettle on, we're ready to prepare for the evening's fun and games, touch wood.

Don't be in a hurry to push in your rod rests; there are a few things to do before you can decide where your rods are to be positioned. Have you fished this swim before? If not, you need to plumb it. By having a cast around with a plain lead you should be able to locate all the underwater features. Even if the swim *has* been fished before, you should still have a plumb around. Gravel bars and gullies will not change position but weed-beds will and this can lead to major seasonal changes in a swim's characteristics which, in turn, can change the feeding patterns of the fish. If you know all about the topography in front of you, it's so much easier than taking an educated guess as to the whereabouts of the underwater features. Cast the lead out and keep the line taut; if you can feel the lead hit bottom then the area is relatively free from weed. It's also possible to determine the make up of the lakebed by the way the lead feels when it thumps down, especially when fishing with braided lines. A solid bang on the rod indicates a bottom make up of something hard, like gravel, whereas a gentler thump may indicate silt or clay. If there is no sensation of the weight hitting bottom and you can feel resistance when pulling on the rod, it's more than likely that you're fishing a weeded area. By locating these areas I can find places where the weed thins out and where the bars begin to shelve off. Once I've placed baits in the chosen spots I mark the line with a power gum stop knot; I can then relax and fish in total confidence knowing that I'm fishing in the right position and not hung up in a weed-bed or buried under a load of silt. When I need to recast, the stop knot lets me know I'm back in the correct position even in the pitch black.

There are other features such as the margins and islands but these are obvious fish holding areas and only a little knowledge of watercraft and some common sense will tell you that. Some of the best anglers I've had the pleasure of fishing with have never been in a hurry to get their rods out; they spend time walking around, plumbing likely areas and generally observing the water, just having a good look. There's been a few times in the past when I should have taken a leaf out of their book instead of wasting time fishing a swim that produced big fish to some other jammy so and so. Think about what you are doing and look for features that will attract eels. Put yourself in the eel's world and try to imagine where you would feed or shelter. I'd like to think that doing this creates a better, more thoughtful angler and certainly it produces a more successful one.

For many of today's specimen hunters time is at a premium so it's important to make the most of every single session. Taking the time to locate all possible feeding areas in your swim helps to get it right and maximises the fishing time that is available. If, after plumbing the water in front of you, the swim appears devoid of any features, you still have the possibility of taking fish that pass through during the night. You will just need to fan your rods out so as to cover the swim as best as possible. But let's hope you have some features in the swim. If you have done your homework prior to the trip and visited the water in advance you should have selected a swim offering at least some features and avoided this problem in the first place.

Position the front rod rests first, the ones with the buzzers on, and push or screw them into the bank; never bang them in. It sends shudders through me when I hear the noise of some plonker banging in their bank sticks with a mallet and can well imagine the fish scattering away from him in all directions. All the same, make sure the rod rests are set firmly in the ground.

Take the time to have a practice cast to the end tackle's final destination and position the rear rod rest so that the rod and line are pointing directly towards the rig's resting place. Ideally this is why each rod should be set up on its own individual bank stick, and by doing this you can really spread the rods out and cover 100% of the swim's features. This may not look the most ultracult set up in the world but it is definitely one of the most effective and is slowly becoming more popular as anglers come to realise its benefits. Isn't it better to catch fish than look cool?

On the rare occasions when the weather in this country allows me to fish exactly how I like, I prefer to have the rods set up quite high, near waist height, angled slightly downwards towards the water. Avoid having the rods positioned at too much of an angle as it then becomes difficult to keep the line on the spool, unless monkey climbers are used as bite indicators. With your rods set up high like this a running eel is capable of taking line in a straight line through the rod to the reel so resistance is kept to an absolute minimum. I can thoroughly recommend using this arrangement; it's one of the most successful in reducing dropped runs. The use of multiple rod buzzer bars and rod pods have their place but should only be considered as a second choice, ie, where you have restricted fishing space so there is no other option. When using several rods on one pod it is not uncommon to see the line going into the water at right-angles from the rod tips. When an eel moves off with the bait, friction is caused by the angle between the line and the rod's line guides. An easy way to see for yourself how much resistance is created is to pull the line through the rod by hand, varying the angle from straight to 45°. When straight, the rod will hardly move but as the angle is increased, the tip of the rod will bounce around very noticeably, even with the bale-arm open and a free running line. Eels will almost certainly feel this added resistance and, in all probability, eject the bait.

The worst state of affairs is to use a battery of rods on one set up, suicide if you do manage to hook a decent fish and the fish is hooked on the middle rod. The result is a nightmare, lines are tangled, rods are in the way when you try to net the fish, all for the sake of keeping everything looking neat and tidy. The advantages of having each rod on its own bank stick then becomes obvious as each individual rod can be pointed in the direction the terminal tackle has been cast to without interfering with each other. They can also be spaced out sufficiently to allow relatively easy netting of fish between the rods. Sometimes, though, there are times when the use of rod pods cannot be avoided, for instance when fishing from dam walls made out of concrete or wooden stagings. Here you will have little choice but to use a rod pod, as there is no other stable means of positioning your rods. If you do intend to fish from a dam wall or similar construction, purchase the buzzer bars that are extendable so that you can fan the rods out a little bit, and only use a maximum of two rods on one pod or just try to keep your casting angles to a minimum. As I keep reiterating, always try and maintain that straight line between hook and rod tip.

With the rods now in place and cast precisely to the areas we've earmarked as having potential, the final checks can be made. For starters, which visual means of bite indication should you use to accompany the electronics? This all depends on what range you intend to fish at, the weather conditions and the presence, or not, of bait-robbing tiddlers, especially if worm is the bait. For margin fishing I would use my trusty lightweight bottle tops, or lightweight monkeys if the wind were too strong. Mid range I would stick with the monkeys, and long range I would just fish straight off the bait runners as I found that constant resistance did not result in as many dropped runs as I thought. Changes in resistance or something bouncing on the line was the biggest culprit. Or even 'clip up', as it's called - no visual indicator. I prefer not to use the shop bought ready made clips; I simply pass a loop of line through an elastic band placed on the rod in front of the reel. This acts as a gentle type of line clip: the more line you pull through the band, the tighter it will hold. It's quite possible that I'd have a different type of visual indicator on each rod; believe it or not they don't all have to match. With the bobbins in place, you can now switch the buzzers on (hands up all those anglers who have forgotten to do this in the past) and check that the line is running freely on the buzzers' wheel and isn't caught up anywhere. Turn the buzzers down low and get the chair out. Before parking yourself down, position the chair not too close to the water, but close enough to watch any movement of those bobbins.

Now sort out the remainder of your equipment. Place the landing-net in close proximity to the rods, preferably somewhere free from brambles and where you don't have to fumble around for it while holding on to a rod connected to a big angry eel. Place the unhooking mat in a clear area if possible; if an eel gets a chance, once unhooked it will take off and I have spent a few worrying moments trying to hack down bushes into which they've escaped. Top the bait bucket up with clean water and have a few freshly dispatched baits at the ready. Move the remainder of your gear either inside the bivvy or to one side of the swim - but keep it visible as there are plenty of tackle thieves about who will appreciate a careless angler. Now, take one last look around the swim so that you are completely comfortable with the layout; this avoids the A over T situation when you dash from the bivvy to hit a run. All checks done, sit down with a cup of tea and watch the light slowly fade away; it won't be long now before those eels slide out of their daytime haunts and go on the prowl for food.

When that screaming run finally happens, the best way to deal with it is to pick the rod up and assist the line coming off the spool by hand. By doing this you ensure that line comes off the spool smoothly, with no deviation in its true course. There will always be that odd occasion when some of the coils of line become stuck but by assisting the fish to take line with your hand any possibility of the line sticking on the spool would have been removed long before the fish ever came to feel it. Brand new lines can eliminate sticking but can cause their own problems when a run occurs. For instance, line can pour off the spool uncontrollably when the weight of the bobbin has gone. This is often caused by over zealous filling with line, but not always; there are some lines knocking about that seem to have a mind of their own. At the same time that the run is happening and you are assisting the free flow of line, keep the rod pointed in the direction that the fish is travelling. This also helps to reduce resistance. Try not to lift the rod in the air or hold it sideways on as this will affect the straight running of the line and create friction on the line guides, which in turn adds resistance to a running fish. This can, and does, contribute to dropped runs.

One of the commonest mistakes made by eel anglers, as well as quite a few other night anglers, is to leave rods on the rests when they get a run. Leaving a running fish to fend for itself with the buzzers screaming and line tearing off the spool is asking for trouble. The only thing this will achieve is to tell everyone on the lake that you have a bite; it does nothing to aid the capture of the fish. In fact it is a positive disadvantage. When fishing with an open bale-arm, line can get caught on the spool, around the reel or bale-arm or in grass and brambles that cover the bankside. If you are not there holding the rod when this happens, or in a position to free it, you can kiss goodbye to that eel, as it will drop your bait the moment it feels that avoidable resistance. By holding the rod you maintain control of the situation. Although dropped runs seem unavoidable, we can reduce their likelihood by fishing with as little resistance as possible, and trying to present the bait in a way that eels will naturally be used to finding it. I cannot over emphasise the importance of resistance free fishing yet there will be times when using a fixed rig or fishing with bait runners will work, however it's very venue specific. If I take one of the large coastal pits I fish as an example, the takes from the bigger fish in this lake are easily distinguishable from the takes of the smaller fish. The biggies move off at a very rapid pace, the line whipping through the rod eyes. The smaller fish give short, stop-start runs - four or five foot of line, stop, then the same again. Sometimes you wind in to find one of these little pests has just sat there and swallowed the bait, the hook almost being passed through its backside, to be polite. Resistance means little to these fish providing it's constant; they will happily spin reel handles or pull line from a bait runner. And given the usual weather conditions at this venue, you often have little option but to fish in this manner. This water has a large head of eels so I think they compete heavily for the available food. The fish pick up the bait and charge off to eat it at their leisure away from the other fish.

So fixed rigs will work but they also have many disadvantages especially when using soft baits like worm; they allow little nuisance fish to whittle away your bait without you knowing, so you can be fishing baitless for hours unless you regularly wind in and check. With resistance free fishing you are usually fully aware of what's going on with your bait whilst it is under the water. Small, regular bleeps tend to indicate the presence of small fish activity. When these stop it's a good guess, if you've been using worm, that all your bait has been removed from the hook. Fixed rigs do not allow this degree of sensitivity yet if the eels are being finicky, and only giving short lifts of the bobbins, small baits

A new PB of 6lb 13oz.

and fixed rigs may put one or two fish on the bank you otherwise might not have caught.

Whack! You've successfully struck that run, the rod powers over and the fish is on. The tell-tale thumping of the rod and the zig-zagging of the line tells you that it's a big eel.

On the majority of occasions you will know that an eel is on the end of your line within seconds of the strike being made. Their fight is instantaneously recognisable. But with very big eels this is not always the case, sometimes they can run, stripping line off the reel in short powerful bursts or kite slowly sideways. Other times they can behave just like a dead weight, hugging the bottom and giving few clues as to what you have become attached to. When that big eel comes along you are on your own, nothing can predict how that fish is going to fight or what it is going to do. Smaller fish are much more predictable and can normally be expected to fight it out in a straight line, making them easier to extract. Sometimes the bigger fish will also follow this rule, but not always. Be warned, eels are far stronger than their weight suggests. A hard fighting big eel is a handful, both in and out of the water, for even the most experienced of eel anglers.

This is how it should be done. Steve Markwell releasing a 4lb eel back into the lake, unharmed and in good condition. (Photo courtesy of BEAC.)

The utmost care must be taken with a big 'un when it comes within range of the landing-net, even more so when attempting this trick on a dark moonless night. They can shake their heads from side to side with frightening ferocity, seemingly hell bent on trying to back paddle into the safety of hidden snags to mock the angler's so-called expertise. No line can be given at this point unless the water is known to be snag free; this is undoubtedly when most big fish are lost. Carefully draw the eel over the net as near the V in the spreader block as possible. Before attempting to lift the net make sure the eel is well and truly engulfed in it. A big eel can easily flip itself back into the water if any part of its body is not fully in the net. The bigger the net, the easier this task becomes. Trying to coax over $3^1/_2$ foot of solid, angry muscle into a standard size land-ing-net presents a daunting prospect in daylight hours let alone by yourself in the middle of the night. That's why I would always advise the use of the largest net you can lay your hands on.

When attempting to land a big eel, take your time, mistakes will happen if you panic and try to rush the netting. If the hook hold has held to this point then nothing but rotten bad luck will stop you getting it safely on the bank. Once the eel has been successfully netted, carry the eel while it is still in the net away from the water's edge and place it on a suitable unhooking mat or soft area of grass and let the fish calm down for a few minutes by covering its eyes with wet netting. This will do the fish no harm providing it is kept damp and allows you time to make sure that everything that you require to unhook the fish is at hand.

The general handling of eels even by some specialists still leaves a lot to be desired. This is mainly down to ignorance rather than a deliberate attempt to inflict harm on the fish. A little bit of thought in the preparation of an unhook-ing area saves an awful lot of grief. There is nothing worse than having to hunt around for your forceps or cutters while the eel tries to wrap itself around every-thing within range. Again, take your time. When handling eels, be gentle and the eel should remain passive. The battle is often fought more on the bank, to get the hooks out, than in the water and if you have difficulty doing this in daylight then imagine how well you will cope in the dark.

Now the eel has had a few minutes to quieten down and you have everything ready, uncover the eel's head and see where the hook is. If it's visible, ie, lip hooked, try and unhook the fish in the folds of the net; I have found eels will remain much calmer with the damp netting material draped over them, especially if the eyes are covered. If the hook is way out of sight the best thing to do is to cut the trace and leave well alone. This way the eel stands a far higher chance of survival and will rid itself of the hook in its own time. Messing about trying to unhook a deeply hooked eel will almost certainly lead to its death even if it swims off strongly after release.

If you prefer, the eel can be removed from the net for unhooking but you will need a slightly different technique to calm it down. If possible lay the eel down in a straight line on its back or side, cover its eyes with one hand, then wet the other hand and gently keep stroking from its head down to its tail until it goes limp. It then shouldn't be too long before the eel is lying quietly and you can remove the hook. If the fish starts to struggle, don't panic, just repeat the stroking process. Always handle eels gently; the more you pull and tug at the fish, the harder it will struggle and you will end up in a wrestling match, covered in slime. It won't do you or the eel any good at all. Laying an eel on its back has been a means of controlling eels for centuries. In fact, many years ago when eels were believed to be evil little fish, they were dealt with by scraping the shape of the cross in the dirt and then placing them on their backs in the cross where they would lie until they died. Just a little bit of folklore I thought you might be interested in knowing. I digress . . .

When it comes to handling big eels it also pays to try to avoid removing too much of the eel's protective slime as this can lead to possible infections at a later date. A damp cloth is another aid to anyone who is unfamiliar with handling eels as you can hold the eel quite firmly without applying too much pressure; as you gain confidence in handling them the cloth can be done away with. One thing to remember when using a cloth is always to make sure that it's kept damp as allowing the eel's skin to dry out will result in the death of the fish or at the very least it will cause illness.

If you wish to photograph your eel (the all important trophy shot) it may be best to allow it to recover for a while. The temporary retention of fish is another area that we need to consider carefully to ensure that we release the fish in tip-top condition. This can best be achieved by placing the eel in a well staked out keepnet or good quality carp sack. Whichever one you choose, make sure they are spacious enough and allow water to flow freely through the mesh. Never put a lot of eels in one sack as they quickly slime up the inside. This prevents water flow and they die of oxygen starvation. I learnt this through experience so I know it's true. They should be placed in deep water out of direct sunlight.

Before you take the photos make sure everything is at hand to save as much time as possible, then remove the eel and calm the fish down as you did before. When the eel is calm and you and the photographer are ready, lift the eel up carefully, supporting as much of its body as possible. You should have a good thirty seconds before it starts to come round. If the eel starts to struggle don't grip it tighter, just lie it down and start again.

The biggest killer of big eels is stress. Big eels are generally regarded as being very old fish, and as such they are extremely susceptible to stress and need the utmost care and attention when being handled. Another means of quietening down an un-cooperative eel is to use Tricaine Methanesulfonate, or MS-222 for short (Brand name 'Finquel') which is a mild anaesthetic. When an eel is placed in a bowl of water and MS-222 is added the eel quietens down and can then be handled comfortably for several minutes. This is the method used by fish biologists to study eels and other fish for routine scientific research without harming them. Anaesthetics work by reducing the metabolic activity of fish, which relaxes them and allows for increased handling when weighing or measuring. Our chief concern is the welfare of the fish so maybe if you get into eeling in a big way, this could be another very effective method of taking care of your hard won prize.

Night fishing is definitely not for the faint of heart but it is a magic time to be abroad. The total isolation of being by a neglected pool out in the wilds is an experience in itself. Sounds are magnified, the chittering of rodents seems to come from everywhere and the unexpected cry from a heron sends cold fingers coursing down my spine. It is a time when the imagination is free to run riot. It's also the time when you may come face to face with that long sought-after fish of a lifetime and forget all about whatever's crashing through the bushes behind the bivvy. And the runs, when they finally come, can be so exciting as to make one almost keel over and expire. The solitude night fishing affords me, the sense of seclusion, of being the last person in the world, are the reasons I love night fishing. Add to that I'm probably nocturnal anyway, my job requires me to work nights and I'm often more awake at night than I am in daylight hours. So how could I write a book on eel fishing and not explore all the possibilities night fishing has to offer? It's synonymous with big fish hunting especially when pursing eels. Those hot balmy nights in July, sat behind the rods wearing a t-shirt and being eaten alive by insects is what night fishing is all about, and so very much more.

For those seasoned anglers with hundreds of nights under their belts who may have forgotten that feeling, that excitement, remembering it only from days long past, I feel sorry. Mention night fishing to a youngster and you won't get a moment's rest until you're there, by the water. To them it is a great adventure whether they catch fish or not and their first night's fishing will be remembered far longer than the small silver fish they caught during daylight trips. Night fishing will always carry its dangers as well as its pleasures and is something that anglers should consider carefully before undertaking, especially our younger anglers. There are too many creeps lurking about in waterways open to the general public at night and these places should never be fished by young anglers on their own; if this is where you fish make sure there is a responsible adult present. This is a sad reflection on modern day life and is something you need to consider seriously when deciding on a water to wage your campaign.

The first excursion to a new water still gets my blood flowing and I may spend many days preparing for it. Knowing that I will be fishing hard, at night, preparation is everything. The first and foremost requirement is to 'know your water'. Do not turn up at the lake in the dead of night and expect everything to run smoothly, it very rarely will. It is imperative to arrive at the water long before darkness descends and if this is not possible then at least visit the lake before your session and decide on a swim beforehand. Getting in position before dark enables you to locate any features you may wish to fish to and any snags that may present you with problems when playing a fish. If you are going to be there for several days it also makes bivvy erection an awful lot easier. Also remember that the last hour or so of twilight can be very productive, another reason to arrive in plenty of time.

One of the biggest problems with night fishing is that you can't see. That statement seems obvious but you wouldn't believe the number of anglers I've met on the bank who have forgotten their torch or never thought to bring one in the first place.

Night fishing can be safe for youngsters in the right situations. Here a young Jolene Bulmer displays a nice eel taken on a club trip to Ardingly Reservoir.

Some means of light when night fishing is a must; it will be needed for bait-ing up, untangling tangles and more importantly, unhooking fish. There is a wide range of lights you could use - from head torches to flexible pocket torches to dedicated bivvy lights - so there is no real excuse for being without one, just avoid overly powerful lights, as this can be detrimental to your fishing. Keep the lights off when they are not required. Bright lights at night not only disturb the fish and annoy other anglers but also attract hundreds of flying insects which get everywhere. I can personally vouch for the fact that they don't taste very nice having eaten quite a few of those horrible flying critters (by accident before you ask) when using a head torch in the height of summer.

Make sure everything you need is easily at hand; a bivvy table is useful for keeping items off the floor and visible, as invariably anything lying about in the grass will be trodden on or lost. Be organised and night fishing can be a real pleasure. Take warm clothing; even in the summer the temperature can drop, the skies can clear and it can get very cold. A flask of hot tea or coffee helps keep the cold at bay, and if you are there for several days you can always re-fill your flask - just boil the water on the stove, pour it into the flask and use the hot water to make your drink as and when you're ready.

Eels are regarded as being primarily nocturnal in their habits although there's always the exception to the rule that makes you think again. The heavily coloured waters, for instance, often produce better fish in daylight than at night, a phenomena I have personally experienced. Eels are also believed to have poor vision, yet they are far from blind. Searching out their prey with an astonish-ing ability to smell and sense food at great distances, they glide effortlessly through the water aware of everything happening around them. Eels basically rely on their ability to sense or smell food rather than sight to hunt down their prey, senses that are far more effective at night or in poor visibility. So to stand a good chance of being consistently successful you will normally be required to fish a lot of night sessions. Daytime eeling can still be an option so don't rule it out, but this will usually be later on in the year, during the winter months, or as I have already mentioned, those lakes where the water is heavily coloured. Also, waters that have little in the way of other predators besides eels can be very good daytime fisheries. Here the eel becomes top of the food chain and has little competition, nor is it threatened by other predators larger than itself.

The weather represents the greatest threat to disrupting a good night's eel fishing; in fact it can really put the mockers on what should be an enjoyable part of our sport. At the pits I now frequent, wind and rain have caused havoc with my fishing, and at times I've hardly ventured out of the bivvy door because of the foul conditions. It's times like these you wonder what you're doing there in the first place! Getting soaked through, dried out, then soaked through again is a perfect way to make yourself ill. And just as bad is the chore of hanging out all the wet gear when arriving home - a job I could well do without. Still, you do eventually learn from these experiences and suffering a bad trip is the best way to avoid repeating the experience. A far better way, though, than going through all the suffering yourself, is to learn from the mistakes of others and go prepared for the worst.

Weather does have a big impact on eel fishing although I have taken eels in every type of weather condition going. The biggest impact of weather, in my view, is on the angler, not the fish. So my genuine opinion is that weather conditions are of no great consequence: if eels are hungry they will feed. There's no point trying to generalise about the best conditions as it would all be speculative anyway. Few people will bother to get out of bed if there is heavy rain or wind predicted. There have been times when I've been guilty of this too, having looked out of the window and thought, 'No way am I going out in that'. On the whole though, bad weather has never really bothered me if I have already become well established in a swim prior to its arrival. In that scenario I will stay to the end of my session and only hell or high water will cut it short. A little knowledge can also be a dangerous thing and it's very easy to over-think a situation especially when the weather's involved. If we read too much into the fishing conditions before we go, we can seriously knock our confidence. And confidence is what's really needed to be successful. Of course self-confidence will take a nosedive in adverse weather, this is only natural, but if each time we went fishing we believed that the weather, water temperature or air temperature was wrong and we'd blank, would we go at all? I've been fishing in atrocious conditions and because of this have not put 100% into my fishing when maybe I should have tried harder. After all, the worst that can happen is that you blank and that can happen under the best of circumstances. So if you feel like going, go, give it your best shot and see what happens. Wind, rain or cold affects anglers far more than we think in that we never try as hard in these conditions, and because of that the only reason that I set out in foul weather nowadays is if it has been sustained over several weeks and I've been grounded from fishing as a result.

The warm humid nights of summer, when it's overcast and muggy, do offer some of the best chances of catching big eels, as it supposedly sends them into an uncontrollable frenzy, but don't discount the days when it's warmer to be indoors wrapped up in a quilt with the missus. There are a great many other factors influencing 'when' eels will feed, and I'm pretty sure we are only scraping the surface with what we know of the subject, so go and enjoy the fishing for there will always be some fish that don't abide by the rules we assume they follow. One thought to bear in mind, in foul weather fish are more likely to be on the prowl as food is washed and blown into the water from the trees and banks; common sense really.

Water and air temperature can play an important part in eel fishing. With water temperatures, the higher the better is presumed the best and the same often applies to air temperature. Water temperature should be as warm as possible; below 49°F eels are believed to be quite torpid, burying themselves in the mud and weed on the bottom of the lake, only occasionally sticking their heads out to grab passing food items. Above this temperature, right up into the 70s and 80s, the eels become far livelier and actively hunt down their food. This is when the use of livebaits becomes particularly effective.

Right: Graham Wilkes with his personal best of 6lb 9oz. (Photo courtesy of NAC.)

Below: 7lb 10oz of Brummie magic for Paul Davies who was actually fishing for eels. (Photo courtesy of NAC.)

Moon phases are also supposed to have an effect on eel fishing. There is little doubt that periods of full moon represent one of the worst periods to be eel fishing. But there is a chain of thought amongst many thinking eel anglers that on nights with a full moon the eel comes off the bottom to feed where once it was believed it didn't feed at all. My own thoughts on this behaviour is that prey items are silhouetted against the surface of the water by the light of the moon making them easy pickings for the hunting eels. New moon periods are believed to be the best, yet things are never as clear-cut as that. Eel fishing on a clear, cold night with no moon can be just as bad as fishing on a night with a full moon; and fishing a full moon with heavy cloud cover can be as good as it gets. My own opinion is that eels prefer the dark, whether it's because it's night time or because of overhanging trees or dense weed-beds. Eels will feed in these places irrespective of the time of day. It's in the dark that they feel safest and their own instincts function the best. Feeding times will vary from water to water but the proven hot feeding times are as the evening sets in until a couple of hours into dark and one or two hours before light, just before the sun comes up. Eels can be caught all through the night yet these few hours in the morning and evening can definitely be some of the best. It may be because at the start of the evening the eels are coming out of their daytime retreats and are hungry, and possibly in the morning they try to grab a last meal before retreating back into their hideaways.

May to August is the presumed peak feeding months for the eel but these parameters are being stretched all the time by forward thinking anglers. There are quite a few anglers who now pursue eels the full twelve months of the year. For me, a full twelve-month campaign is now a little too much as I'm going soft in my old age. I plan out my serious eel fishing from March to the end of November. This gives me a full nine months of hard fishing. The remainder of the year I may go only if the right weather conditions present themselves and then just short sessions at that. I don't slog on any more in the face of astronomical odds so by the time March has arrived I am chomping at the bit to get down to the lake for a good session.

CHAPTER SEVEN

RIGS, WIRE TRACES AND ALTERNATIVES

Many years ago, when eel fishing for sport was still in its infancy, nearly all the rigs used to catch eels were designed to present baits either ledgered or free-lined on the bottom. Little thought was given to rig design as very little was known about the eel or its feeding habits, yet these methods have produced a wealth of specimen fish from many different waters and from all over the country. It would therefore be very easy to assume that these early rig designs just happened to be the most successful and that we do not need to vary our tactics if these rigs already catch plenty of fish. In truth I think we have become so accustomed to fishing in one particular style that the idea of changing is greeted with horror. Only rarely are we swayed away from bottom fishing. Many eels up to and around the 6lb mark are taken each year in this manner but what of the bigger fish, the elusive 8-, 9- and 10-pounders? Many eel anglers seriously believe these fish exist and quite often fish waters that are known to contain fish of this size and yet all attempts to land them seem to run smack bang into a brick wall.

My own style of fishing has been to fish baits on the bottom, something I have done for a very long time, and I have taken lots of very good eels by doing so. Yet, in fishing this way, have I been restricting my own catches? Who is to say that I wouldn't have caught more eels by popping my baits up from the bottom or by fishing surface rigs more regularly? The biggest of eels may have encountered baits on the bottom that have caused it problems in the past so it may only take baits that are fished off the bottom or in the safety of dense weed-beds. We have all experienced the problem of not being able to hit runs, and usually we put this down to small fish being unable to swallow the bait. But could some of the big fish just be toying with the bait before deciding whether to eat it? If so, we would probably have struck long before the eel had made up its mind. Baits that are fished hard on the lake bed with a heavy ledger and wire trace often become buried in silt, but although eels love to hide in silt, do they avidly feed in it? Have you ever watched wildlife programmes on TV that feature underwater scenes? On those rare occasions when eels are shown they always appear to be swimming off the bottom, never along it. The only time they are seen on the bottom is when they are at rest. The use of popping up baits has become an accepted method for producing big fish of most other bottom-dwelling species and there is no reason to think this shouldn't also apply to big eels. Perhaps this area could be the best place to present a bait; it's certainly worth thinking about as the perfect rig for eel fishing has yet to evolve.

Much of what I have just said is merely conjecture but those really big eels do fail to come to traditional methods with any consistency and therefore we must be doing something wrong. Either that or they don't exist in the numbers we honestly believe; we can't have it both ways. A lot of questions have been asked in this chapter to which I do not have all the answers, but I strongly believe that it's only a matter of time before some forward thinking angler gets lucky and solves some of these problems, and biggies start to come to the bank with more regularity. For it must be stressed that the more conversant an angler is with his approach, the more versatile he is, and the more successful he must inevitably be.

If there has been one particular style of fishing that has shown any progress in the field of eel fishing rig design it has to be the use of off-bottom and sub-surface rigs. These rigs were often discussed and occasionally dabbled with, yet only in the last few years have they been used successfully and extensively with any real confidence. It was once presumed that all eels feed on the bottom, and given the catches made on the bottom with the likes of the JS rig this was a safe bet. In the last decade or so eel anglers have come to realise this is not the case and eels have been caught on baits suspended off the bottom, mid-water and just under the surface. Again we must remember that what works on one water may not necessarily work on another, only trial and error will find the answers, but what we do now accept is that off-bottom rigs are definitely effective.

When it comes to constructing rigs for eel fishing the problem is that there are no hard and fast rules. At first, baits were only fished off-bottom in periods of full moon when it was discovered that eels came to the surface - whether to feed or just to have a look no one is quite sure. However, it has now been established that eels can be caught with this method at any time of night or moon phase and that the depth of water has made very little difference; eels have been taken just under the surface in thirty feet of water or from the surface in just a couple of feet of water. In the next few pages I will cover some of the different rigs you can use in the hunt for big eels. From bottom fishing to surface rigs they should all be considered as part of your armoury. But you will have to experiment on your own waters to find out which rig works best and where, as what works on some of my venues might not apply to your own.

Do not be frightened to experiment with new ideas or altering the old ones, for as I have said there are no easy answers, eels can have feeding habits peculiar to each individual water. The easy option is to copy the rigs that I have included as these have proved successful in the past and you might hope for results similar to those produced by the anglers who originally designed them. They will catch fish but relying on them full time would be a big mistake. Copycat tactics can only really be regarded as a starting point in your own development as a specimen hunter. Anyone can copy but the most successful anglers adapt and vary their tactics in accordance to the situations in which they find themselves. There have been times when I've racked my brains and fished every rig in my box and failed to get a run; it hasn't mattered whether I fished them short range, long range or even free range, those big eels have remained elusive. By continually chopping and changing rigs you try to eliminate the possibility that the failure to catch fish is your fault. But sometimes, if all else fails, you will just have to accept that the eels are just not having it this time.

John Sidley's link ledger rig : This rig was designed, as the name suggests, by the late John Sidley and is probably the most frequently used and well-known rig in eel fishing, with many big fish to its name. Many rigs and ideas have come and gone but this rig has now stood the test of time and has proved to be extremely efficient, as many good eel anglers will vouch. It is basically an improvement on the standard link ledger rig and offers several advantages: if assembled properly the rig is 95% tangle free compared to the basic link ledger rig, plus it will give improved bait presentation.

To assemble the rig take a length of line and tie a normal swivel to one end and a snap swivel to the other end; ideally when tied it should be about six inches long. This is the link part of the rig. The snap link takes your weight and you then pass your main line through the eye of the plain swivel, followed by a bead, then tie on another plain swivel to stop the link sliding off the line. Next is the part that makes it different from the standard link ledger. Take another length of line and attach it to the swivel tied on the main line. The most important thing now is to make sure this piece of line is longer than the link, then tie a swivel to the end. This swivel should be at least one inch below where the weight attaches on to the link, and then attach the hooklength to this swivel. This is the rig as originally designed but over the time I have been using it I have made a few modifications to suit my own style of fishing.

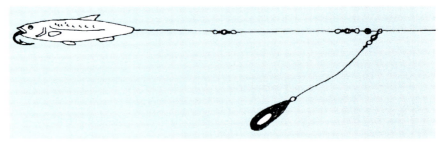

Diagram 1. The basic JS rig.

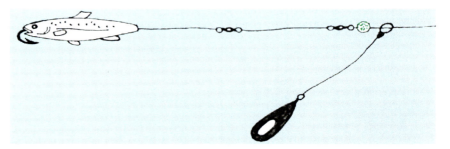

Diagram 2. Modified JS Rig.

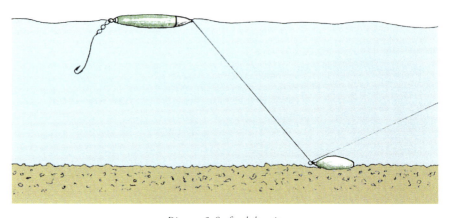

Diagram 3. Surface ledger rig.

How do you decide on the line that makes up the link? If I happen to be fishing areas with a snaggy bottom I will make the link up with a piece of line half the breaking strain of the main reel line so, if I do have the misfortune to get snagged, I increase my chances of getting a big fish back. The lighter line of the link will break, leaving me free to play the fish if the weight gets caught up. In areas where the bottom is relatively clean I will make the link up with a line called Amnesia as this is relatively stiff compared to normal monofilament and has very little memory. I also tie the length of line between the two plain swivels out of Amnesia as well; this improves bait presentation even more and decreases any chance of tangling on long casts. The other alteration I make is to replace the plain swivel on the link with a half-inch buoyant ring that I get from curtain shops. I don't think they were designed with fishermen in mind but being hollow plastic they are ideal. (If you can find it, the Free Spirit Marker and Run Ring Kit is a pretty cool item, comprising basically converted rod eyes, which means grooving of the ring is a thing of the past.) Next I replace the bead between the link and first swivel with a half to one-inch polyball or cork ball. The polyball has a small hole drilled through it and then a short length of rig tube is glued in the hole. Having made these alterations the rig now offers no more resistance to a taking fish than free lining and instances of dropped runs are further reduced.

Of course there are quite a few other alterations that can be made to this rig, like attaching a cigar-shaped bung on the link line to keep it clear of weeds or exchanging the weight for a swimfeeder. But if you remember that the most important thing is to maintain the basic principle of the rig and to keep the length of line between the two swivels longer than that of the link then you shouldn't have any trouble.

Sub surface ledger rigs : These, as the name suggest, are for fishing baits just below the surface but in a fixed position. First slide your weight on to the main line, then run the line through a cigar float or polyball (the choice is yours but try to use one that only just supports the hook and bait), next pass the line through a bead and tie on a swivel, then attach the hooklength; the rig is then ready to cast once you've baited up. When the rig has been cast out and the line has been sunk, you can then pay out line until the float appears on the surface. A stop knot and bead behind the float can be used to control the depth at which the bait is fished. I prefer not to fix the bait like this unless it is windy, instead controlling the depth by playing out a little bit more line once the float has surfaced; the weight of the bait then pulls the line through the float to the depth I want it to fish at. Once the line is clipped lightly into an elastic band that has been placed on the butt of the rod near the reel, the depth will be maintained. This rig will not drift around as the weight holds it in position. This method like most eel rigs should be fished with an open bale-arm - the elastic band will prevent line falling off the spool. See Diagram 3.

Another version of the sub-surface rig, Diagram 4, shows the Colin Dyson rig, known simply as the Dyson rig. I think this rig was originally designed for perch fishing but has adapted itself very nicely for use in eel fishing. It's best use is in conjunction with livebaits but any bait can be used. It may also look like a complicated rig but it is relatively easy to assemble and is tangle free when used at close to medium range. Note that the length of the trace between the stop knot and the Roberts' boom should be no shorter than twenty-two inches to keep the rig tangle free.

Surface rigs : These are variations on simple float rigs used for surface eel fishing in areas where bottom fishing is impossible or difficult because of snags or heavy weedbeds. See Diagram 5. Run a small bead followed by a cigar-shaped deadbait float on to your main line (the deadbait floats that have a swivel on the bottom or the ones where you pass the line through the middle are fine provided they are not too bulky), next slide a small bullet lead on to the line followed by a bead, then tie on a swivel. In some situations I replace the bullet lead with swan shots as using different baits will alter how much weight is required to

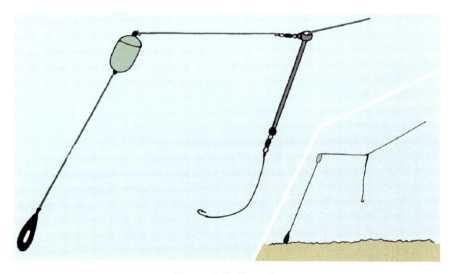

Diagram 4. The Dyson Rig.

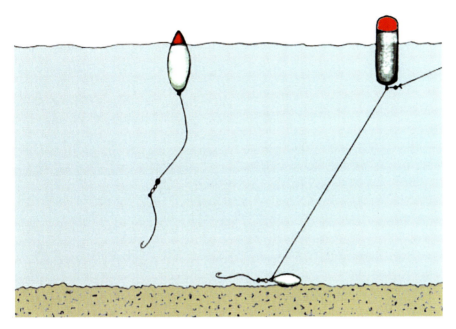

Diagram 5. Surface rig and float ledger rig.

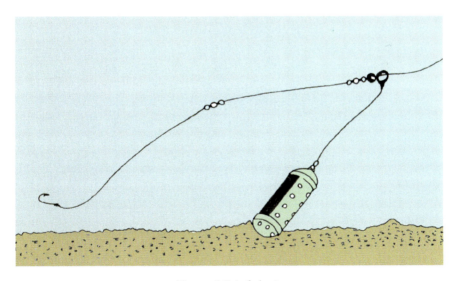

Diagram 6. Swimfeeder rig.

cock the float and with swan shots I do not have to break the rig down to alter the weight, I just add or subtract a few shot. With the swivel tied on, you can then attach the hooklength and the rig is almost ready to go. Finally, to set the float at the depth you wish to fish, tie on a sliding knot above the float. When using this rig at night an isotope or the brilliant chemical Starlights can be attached to the float. I wouldn't consider using this rig very far out, maybe thirty yards max., because watching a night float for any length of time makes your eyes go wonky after a while. Also, fishing this rig at distance you tend to have too much slack line between float and rod for successful striking. You can float ledger as a means of keeping your main line up in the water away from snags. This rig allows the sensitivity of float fishing and the attached ledger weight keeps the bait in a fixed area.

Semi-fixed self-hooking rig : This is a rig for using smaller baits and like many of today's carp rigs it's designed to hook the fish on the run. To begin, slide a bead on to the line followed by a swivel, attach the hooklength to this and then put on another bead, then attach the weight. The weight can be tied directly to the main line or you can attach a swivel and a short length of weak line, then the weight; this is for snaggy situations as the weak link will break off in the event you become snagged. Either side of the beads tie a stop knot; this will fix the hooklength and hopefully the fish will hook itself against the weight of the lead; it also means that if you become snagged and lose the trace a hooked fish can still pull itself free.

Swimfeeder rigs : These are a very good way of introducing small quantities of bait or flavours to a swim without overfeeding it. Groundbaits can be used to attract small fish, which in turn attracts eels. I try to avoid using worms as hook bait when using a feeder rig, as many other fish will home in on the bait before the eels can get a look in. When using a feeder rig I much prefer to use it as a means of introducing flavours or smells rather than items of food. This is a relatively simple matter of selecting a feeder and stuffing it with cotton wool, then dropping it into a pot of flavour for a few minutes prior to casting. Alternatively you could inject the flavour directly into the cotton wool; either method is suitable. This is a method I would prefer to use on a low density water as it does have some drawbacks; for example, as the cotton wool expands in the water it has an annoying habit of working its way out of the holes in the feeder. Small eels will attack the swimfeeder and run with it, often just holding on to the bits of cotton wool poking out. On striking, the run is missed, and presumably the eel is left looking like Santa Claus. To try and avoid this you can wrap the cotton wool in fine gauze or some people use a Tampax. As yet I haven't tried one of these as I don't now how I would explain away a box of these in my tackle box to the Missus and come up with a suitably convincing story. When using fish oils it can also be helpful to use an emulsifier as this prevents it all from floating to the surface. Nutrabaits do a sweetened one which is far better than the ones made with sodium lauryl acetate which is a detergent. Effective flavours are monster crab, freshwater mussel, prime scad and ace worm extract. I don't think the latter is available any more but there are similar products on the market that are just as good.

Pop-up rig : This isn't really a rig; it's a way of making the bait stand proud of the bottom while using any standard bottom rig. It can be a deadly method at times and for that reason I think it deserves a mention. Popping up a bait is simply a matter of getting the bait to float by the use of foam or air, injecting it with a syringe. Worms are the easiest item to pop-up; just inject air into the tail sections of several lobworms that have already been placed on the hook. You can inject a fair amount of air so that they float clear of the bottom or a smaller amount to neutralise the weight of the hook and wire trace; the bait then hovers about, enticingly, only just touching the bottom. When popping up deadbaits the easiest method is to stuff a small piece of foam down its throat before hooking the bait on. Again, you can vary the amount of foam to attain the buoyancy that you want. That's all there is to popping up baits - a very simple yet highly effective method.

Weed rig : One of the many lakes I fish suffers badly from very heavy weed growth during the latter part of the season. This represents a serious problem, not least in extracting fish from a jungle like this but in presenting a bait that the eels can find in the first place. The bulk of a weed-bed tends to be near the surface; underneath it can be relatively clear. So I needed to get a bait through the surface layers without the hook fouling up and staying near the surface as the lead sank. Knowing eels were in these areas I was baffled as to how to offer them a bait until I watched some carp anglers catching fish from similar terrain. The answer was clear PVA bags, not the mesh type. A straightforward ledger rig baited with worms or deadbait is dropped into one of these bags and cast into the weed. The whole lot sinks through the weed and after a few minutes the PVA bag dissolves leaving a perfectly presented bait lying on the bottom. Problem solved. Thanks to Mister Carper on the Radar Pit. PVA bags have proved to be a brilliant method for combatting heavy weed and have been applied to more and more of my eel rigs as time has moved on. PVA in all its guises has a multitude of other uses we eel anglers can take advantage of. For instance, if you have to cast a delicate bait a long distance you can bait up and drop it in a bag with some fish oils and other attractors along with the weight. Wrap the whole thing with PVA tape and whack it out. Wait a few minutes for the PVA to dissolve, then tighten down to the rig, moving it a few feet so it's nicely straightened out. A perfectly presented bait is achieved lying amidst a pile of attractors without the concerns of what condition the bait is in after a good chuck and also it's highly unlikely to tangle the rig either. They are also excellent for presenting halibut pellets, a bait I am using more and more for eels on heavily fished commercial lakes.

Wire Traces and Alternatives

The modern day eel specialist requires a trace material to perform several basic tasks. It must be strong enough to land the fish being sought as well as being thin and supple enough to prevent dropped runs. It must also be abrasion resistant in order to prevent broad headed eels from biting through it. All these requirements can be met with modern trace materials - wires, braid or some other new state of the art material.

So what governs your choice of hooklength? A straightforward answer is the type of eel that occupies the water you intend to fish. The large headed variety has teeth, lots of them, not great big pointed ones, just lots of little diamond shaped teeth and with the eel's habit of shaking its head from side to side it can manage to saw through nylon in no time at all. It can also break wire the same way,

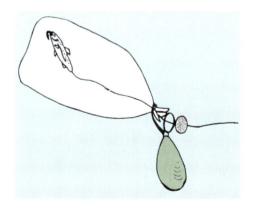

PVA bag rig.

chaffing through it strand by strand until it snaps. Small headed eels, on the other hand, have very little in the way of teeth, just hard pads that resemble wet and dry sanding paper, allowing nylon to be used with some degree of confidence. Anglers with these eels in their waters cannot comprehend what a broad headed eel can do to a nylon hooklength, hence the long running debate over wire versus nylon.

Wire versus nylon is a subject that has caused untold controversy amongst eel anglers for as long as I can remember. Whilst one side advocates wire, the other side says it's totally unnecessary. Without taking sides, as I believe both sides have a just argument, I would always prefer to use wire traces as opposed to a nylon hooklength as that's what I have confidence in. There will be times, however, when eels will not accept a bait presented on wire so an alternative is required, but I would still decline the use of nylon. There are products on the market now called braids, or even wires coated in Kevlar and other new materials which are far better than nylon. These new materials are extremely supple with very high abrasion resistance and are even difficult to cut with scissors. There are also methods of disguising wire so that fish cannot feel it when taking the bait.

There's another consideration too before choosing a trace material - 'bait'. If you are using deadbaits you need to remember that it will not only be eels that pick up the bait. Pike can be very active at night, contrary to most people's beliefs, and will readily take your deadbaits; and without a wire trace it's doubtful you would ever land such a fish without a large slice of good fortune. Some of these night pike are big fish and well worth catching. This has to be a consideration when choosing a trace material. Some of the waters I fish insist on wire if fish baits are being used, simply to protect the pike.

On a large percentage of the waters I fish the broad headed, predatory eel is the most regularly encountered so the use of wire is necessary to prevent bite offs. As wire is then my preferred trace material I will concentrate on its usage first before moving on to the alternatives. One of the first good quality wires I used to make traces from was called Marlin Strand. This was a very thin wire and came in a nice pale green colour. It was easily workable and being relatively supple I could obtain neat traces without crimps for the first time.

In fact this wire has still remained a firm favourite of mine, proving to be a reliable, good quality product. It's a wire I still use with confidence when making traces up with smaller than normal hooks, ie, sizes 6 or 8. Prior to discovering Marlin Strand I used the thick, nylon coated stuff, which needed to be crimped to attach hooks and swivels. The downside of this material was that crimps had a nasty habit of becoming clogged with weed and the thickness of the wire meant dropped runs were all too common. This stuff was banished to the bin when I discovered Marlin Strand. One of the features I liked most about Marlin Strand was the very small coil of wire that was created when a trace was spun. This meant the wire stayed supple right down to the hook and there was virtually nothing to get caught on the weeds; plus, being sold in 300-foot spools, it would last for ages, in fact I'm sure I'm on only my second spool in ten years.

PDQ and Drennen seven-strand wire have been used to make the bulk of my traces over the last few years. Used in 20 to 28lb breaking strain I have had little complaint with these wires although some of the new wires have been plastic coated of which I am not overly fond. I was shown one of these new wires by some friends on a trip to Birmingham. On my first trip to the canal with them a good eel was hooked, not by me I hasten to add, and within a matter of seconds the trace material was bitten through. I can't say I was impressed and come to think of it, neither was my friend.

Recently there have been several new additions to my wire collection. These are made from microfilament stainless steel and are incredibly soft for wire lines. The only drawback I can see is that they need to be crimped, but a small piece of silicone tubing can be used to cover the crimp after assembly. It has been stated that you can even tie regular knots in these wires but as yet I haven't succeeded in doing this without the trace resembling a spring around the knot. The only trace material that I have come across that I have successfully knotted is fibre-flex made by Cannelle of France. This is a 15lb b.s. wire that is covered by a Kevlar braid type material. Fibre-flex has proved very useful and instances of carp and tench picking up my lobworms and other baits have increased tenfold since using it. This may seem like a disadvantage but if carp and tench have no inhibitions about taking bait presented on fibre-flex, eels certainly won't and I have yet to have a trace bitten through by eels or pike whilst using it. I think these new trace materials look the business and may very well be a step in the right direction.

With nearly all the traces I construct small lengths of silicone tubing are used to cover any areas where the trace has been spun, crimped or knotted as this prevents weed becoming clogged on the line in these areas. Wires like the Drennan 28lb are quite thick and with these I use enough silicone so that it shows proud of the bait by at least an inch. In situations where the fish have wised up to normal presentation I'd swear blind this induces the fish to bite in a more positive manner. The lengths of silicone tubing are slid down over the wire trace prior to assembly and this is then pulled over the eye of the hook to keep it in place. When a taking fish picks up the deadbait it doesn't feel the wire as the silicone tubing has the same texture as the bait. It is also just as effective when

A 22lb pike taken whilst fishing for eels.
Would I have landed it if I hadn't been using a wire trace?

Who says you have to have designer bait and rigs to catch carp? This 28lb fish was one of over
twenty taken this year on baits fished specifically for eels with wire traces.

using worm. This method does work and nowadays I never construct a wire trace without it. I can also use it with confidence on waters with the small headed variety of eels and I'm sure you're going to ask why as they haven't got the dentistry to bite through a wire trace. The answer is pike. If the water has a large head of these predators I will use wire prepared in this manner; if it doesn't then I will use an alternative. I am 100% confident in the use and construction of my hooklengths and have yet to lose a fish due to a failed trace, although I have been bitten off by eels even when using wire and not necessarily by big fish. Before I move on to the alternatives to wire I will run through how to go about making a wire trace, either crimped or spun. Providing you have the correct tools for the job, it's not that difficult once you know how.

Items for making wire traces : Your chosen wire, a selection of swivels, hooks, a pair of locking artery forceps, a pair of crimping pliers and the finest gauge crimps you can get away with. And last, but not least, a pair of wire cutters - the type that cut at the front like pincers, are the best from my experience.

Making a trace : The first thing to do when spinning a wire trace is to select the pattern of hook you will be using, then, taking one end of a length of wire, pass it through the eye of the hook twice, keeping the loops of wire tight round the eye. You should have a minimum of one inch of wire left hanging free. Next attach the forceps to the one-inch length of wire, then hold the hook and the main piece of wire reasonably tight. The hook should be in your right hand with the forceps dangling straight down in front of you, the longer piece of wire is in your left hand. If you are left-handed then just reverse the instructions.

Now spin the forceps away from you, wrapping the short length of wire around the longer length, make sure it wraps around the wire evenly without any kinking or bunching. As the short length of wire is used up, the forceps will fall off. If, however, they don't then unclip them and trim the end with the wire cutters. Repeat this procedure with the swivel but always remember to go through the eye twice as this prevents any chance of slippage when the trace is under pressure and, remember, spin the forceps away from you; having them smack you on the bridge of the nose or in the eye is an unpleasant way of finding out that you're spinning them the wrong way. Now with the trace complete, inspect it, make sure there are no kinks and confirm that you are 100% sure it's okay. If not, do it again until you are. Practice makes perfect.

Crimping a wire trace is the simplest way to construct one. Slide a crimp on to the wire, again passing the wire through the eye of the hook or swivel twice.

Then slide the crimp back up the wire, pass the short length of wire back through the crimp and using the crimping tool, crimp it and trim off any loose ends. It's as simple as that.

There are other means of attaching hooks and swivels to wire but the ones I have mentioned are ones I have found to be very reliable. Bear in mind you may only get one chance of a really big eel so don't let your trace making be the reason it gets away. An angler confident in his tackle will be a successful angler; don't ever be too lazy to construct your hooklengths properly, even if it's in the middle of the night.

Moving on to soft hooklengths can be pretty advanced stuff until you get familiar with the wide variety available. It is perhaps better to become more confident in locating the fish and tackling them at night and move on to a more refined approach when you have a few good fish under your belt. But as I'm attempting to cover every topic I'll explain the two options I would use instead of wire in situations where the small headed eels dominate. Both have a high degree of abrasion resistance and can be tied with traditional knots. First choice is Kryston Quicksilver, a highly abrasion-resistant braid used by carp anglers as a shock leader. Compared to a lot of other braids this one has a stiff, waxy feel to it. Quicksilver has been used to catch some of the country's biggest catfish so eels with hardly any teeth pose few problems for this material. I use this in 30lb breaking strain and it is suitable for use with worms or deadbaits. In my experiments using braided hooklengths the only problem I have so far encountered is that braid is more susceptible to tangles on long casts. Restrict its use to short range fishing and there is no problem whatsoever.

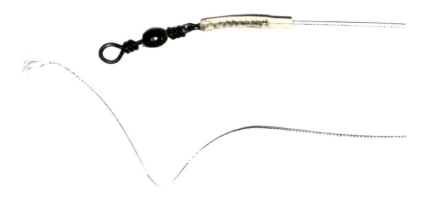

This trace ended up in this condition after a large-headed predatory eel of 3lb finally succeeded in spinning and biting through 20lb wire. Luckily enough the eel was in the net before the trace failed.

Kryston Multistrand is the other variety I use and again only where small headed eels are found. This material differs from braided lines by being made up from long, very thin individual fibres. The advantage of this is that when submersed in water it opens up into its individual fibres and becomes almost invisible. I know one or two anglers who use this on waters with large headed eels because they say the individual fibres lie between the eel's teeth, but personally I wouldn't want to gamble on it. Mutistrand is suitable for use with small deadbaits and protein baits but I would advise strongly against using worm. Worms have the habit of wriggling about on the hook and more often than not they will tie up the individual fibres in terrible knots. Both these varieties are available from good tackle shops.

There is a multitude of other hooklength materials out there and new inno-vative materials are coming on to the market all the time. Some of these may well be ideal for eel fishing and some may not so before using these products carefully weigh up your situation with regards to where you are fishing. Decide which type of eel is most prevalent and if are there any other large predators in the lake. It may even be a sensible idea to trial run these materials on waters that hold lots of small eels, preferably the predatory type, just to see how they stand up to abuse. No one wants to lose a fish through bite offs, especially a big fish. Wires are a proven safe bet whilst some of these new materials have yet to pass the test, so if you have any doubts, stick to what has a proven track record - wire.

Fred Gibby with a 6lb eel. (Photo courtesy of BEAC.)

Steve Ricketts with another lump.

Chapter Eight

Baits

Well what exactly do eels eat? Like most species of bottom-dwelling fish eels are opportunistic feeders and will, if the mood takes them, eat literally anything that comes their way. Taking a reflective look back through some of my old books and magazines I have found many accounts of them devouring all sorts of bizarre and curious foodstuffs, bird chicks, water voles, offal from slaughter houses, whole cooked sausages, leeches and even polo mints; in fact if it's seemed even remotely edible, eels have probably consumed it. These are exceptions to the rule but at least it proves they are not averse to trying something different, unlike many of us. Many eel fishermen are stubborn when it comes to choosing baits. They stick with familiar combinations for years on end reluctant to try anything new. If you are going to be brave and try a new bait, give it a fair trial before switching back. You might just discover a new bait that is destined to become a favourite with you and the fish. I am definitely not advocating the use of odd or bizarre baits on a regular basis unless you're allowed to fish with umpteen rods, it's just that most eel anglers would only ever consider using worms and dead fish. But as specialist anglers we should seriously be looking at using or at least experimenting with alternatives such as slugs, snails, shrimps, sea fish, paste baits and boilies etc, etc. Someone once said 'familiarity breeds contempt' and I'm sure many of the big fish out there show a healthy contempt for some of our baits or at least the way in which we present them.

Alternative baits are occasionally experimented with but very few are given a really good outing on a 'hot' fishery where you are already catching fish. They tend to be used as a last resort when the fishing gets slow and we are not catching anything anyway. And often baits are begrudgingly switched about the time the fish have stopped feeding altogether; a crime I'm often guilty of. This is never going to portray an accurate picture of a bait's potential. Is it, therefore, any wonder that worms and dead fish always manage to come back out on top if other baits fail to receive a fair crack of the whip? Eels do learn to associate baits with danger; this is a proven fact as far as I'm concerned. They may become aware of their mates disappearing into the sky after eating that juicy looking worm and this could be just one of many reasons making the remaining eels and those returned to the water very suspicious and difficult to catch. Therefore I think we should have a look at having at least one alternative tucked up our sleeve. Experimenting with baits will be perplexing so it comes as no surprise that so many anglers seem to think it's not worth the effort. Perhaps they know something I don't.

I am not the most patient of anglers and age has not tempered my will to achieve, in fact quite the opposite. I cannot sit waiting behind my rods reading crummy paperbacks for days on end just hoping that an eel will take the bait. If I am not getting runs, rigs will be changed, new baits tried and I will up and move swims as I think the conditions dictate.

Sometimes, just a small variation in bait presentation, or baits repositioned into a different area, can change a dull fishless session into an action packed encounter with the quarry. Playing around like this you occasionally get lucky, as I was to find out on one Sussex water. The lake in question was becoming a killer to say the least. I had failed to coax any runs on the last half dozen trips on what I knew was a prolific fishery. A friend returning from a bass fishing trip gave me two dozen peeler crabs saying that eels in the estuary found them irresistible. With nothing to lose I gave them a bash, and shock horror I caught. Yet surely these eels had never encountered crabs before! This water was many miles from the sea so what drew them to the bait? No pre-baiting was done with crabs but the eels obviously recognised them as a nutritious food item and scoffed them down with total confidence. Many were deep hooked, even hitting the runs as fast as I could get to them. This was a good example of not sitting back on your laurels and doing nothing. Experimenting with crab had given me several fish I know I would not otherwise have caught.

Eels' dietary requirements can also change with the onset of different seasons so a bait that works one month may be useless the next. The famed German biologist Tesch in the book *The Eel: Biology and Management of Anguillid Eels* (1977) noted that on one lake in early spring and summer the eels had a marked preference for fish, also that as the eels became larger, the instances of fish in their stomachs increased. As the season progressed to late summer and autumn the instances of fish found in the eels' stomachs reduced and larva and water snails, especially the nymphs and midge larva (chironomid), played a much more significant role in the eels' diet. Stomach surveys carried out on eels taken from several small Irish lakes showed that over a hundred different items of invertebrate were regularly consumed, and out of the fish species that had been eaten the most commonly found were baby eels and small perch, two baits eel anglers detest using. This actually comes as no surprise to me. Eels often become harder to catch as the season progresses. As the water temperature increases so does the abundance of weed growth, which in turn encourages fish, water snails and a profusion of insect life to multiply very rapidly. With the eels' larder fully stocked they become more discerning as to what they will eat. Come autumn, as the weed dies down and the insect life decreases, they become easier to catch again; something I've observed time and time again.

The typical natural diet of the European eel

Studies of the choice of foods that looked at body size showed that eels preferred items of food which were not too big and could easily be managed. In tests, small and large food items were placed in a tank. The eels first took the food items they could swallow the quickest, these were downed on the spot, normally in one gulp. With the larger items the eels attempted to rip pieces off by running backwards with the bait and making quick side to side head shakes until a bite-sized piece had been removed. In other cases the eel was seen to spin many times around its own axis to tear pieces off, very similar to the way you see crocodiles feeding on those nature programmes. Listed here are the results of the stomach surveys carried out in Ireland cataloguing the items of food in relation to size, something I found very interesting for as you can see the bigger the eels became, the more fish they consumed as opposed to larva.

| Eel length | Percentage of total stomach contents: | |
	Fish	Larva etc.
30-40cm	7%	60%
40-50cm	19%	44%
50-72cm	71%	14%

Further studies into this subject were carried out by V. R. P. Sinha and J. W. Jones. Their surveys into the stomach contents showed very little consumption of fish, which seemed to contradict my earlier findings until I discovered that no large eels were included in their research. This is a problem I regularly encounter as most studies survey fish in the 1-2lb bracket, not the size of fish we're after. These studies give an interesting insight nevertheless.

Before I run through the range of baits available and the ways the eel angler can use them to their best effect, there is one other finding that came from this research that may have an influence on the way we fish for eels. Eels can only be taken in fyke nets if they are on the prowl for food or returning after a night's hunting, a seemingly obvious statement. Of the eels that were netted for these studies the large majority had empty stomachs. Eels need a minimum of three days to digest their last meal so does this mean that they hadn't eaten for at least three days? If this is the case, do they lie dormant after each meal, only eating when the last meal is fully digested? Or maybe they just don't eat very much. If this is indeed a true reflection of their habits then we may have to spend much longer camped in each swim hoping that an eel picks up our bait in preference to something else.

A loveley sinuous eel. (Slava Stochl)

Many years have slipped by in my pursuit of eels but if I have learnt one thing it's that experimenting with different baits is effective. They don't have to be space age specials; simple things like flavoured worms used on a deadbait water may give results. Advancement in any sport is only achieved through trial and error. Playing around with baits, whether successful or not, is possibly the only way we are going to find a consistently effective bait in the search for a big eel, if of course, such a bait really exists. From deadbaits to specialist mixes, they will all have their moments of glory so don't be afraid to try anything, no matter how absurd it seems; just take time to mull over the options and see what happens.

As this book is for the beginner as well as the more experienced angler it may be wiser on my part to introduce you to the basic baits first and then progress to the alternatives. From the studies carried out on the eel's diets we know that fish features very high on the 'A' list. And not surprisingly fish baits are one of the oldest and most successfully used baits for eel fishing; baits that have accounted for hundreds, if not thousands, of this country's biggest fish. So what better way to start a section on baits?

Fish baits

In this piece I will refer to fish baits as deadbaits as that's how they are most often described. This will include cut baits, frozen baits and preserved naturals; I will discuss the subject of livebaiting a little further on. The eel's great love of dead fish is legendary but is there a species of fish that eels prefer eating in preference to all others? It's possible but in reality I don't think so, I think they just take advantage of whatever is the most plentiful in their surrounding environment. Each lake has its own ecosystem that enables certain fish to be more successful than others. On your lake it may be those suicidal, stunted little rudd; on another water close by it may well be perch. These are the fish you should be considering as your prime eel baits whether you like using them or not. Other fish such as roach and skimmer bream will still catch fish, but our aim is to present the most natural bait in the most natural way.

You should be able to answer this question yourself: if the water you are fishing is stuffed to overflowing with small rudd yet contains a few roach and perch, which species of fish is the eel more likely to come into contact with and therefore most likely to prey on? It's not really that hard to figure out. So in theory this is how I would arrive at the preferred deadbait for a particular water.

On waters that do not have a large head of small fish or where the cormorants have decimated them, a good all-round bait fish is the gudgeon. Even if it's not present in the water you are fishing it does seem to have the uncanny knack of attracting eels no matter where you use it. As most small streams and rivers contain shoals of gudgeon, they are fairly easy to obtain. It's possible the eels' love of gudgeon has more to do with the fact that their bodies are very narrow allowing the eels to swallow them much more easily than, say, a bream. It could also be possible that, actually, they are no better than any other deadbait but rather it's just that anglers using a bait shaped like the gudgeon are able to convert more runs into hooked fish.

A visit to the local fishmonger can also yield some effective eel baits. Sprats, sardines and many other sea fish are excellent baits yet many eel anglers are reluctant to use them. It's true they do not perform very well in the summer months but try them as the season progresses into the late autumn/winter fishing period and it's a whole new ball game. They will out-perform coarse fish deadbaits easily. The higher oil content present in sea fish permeates the water far more effectively in the lower temperatures enabling any feeding eels to home in on the bait that much quicker. Those big eels the pike anglers catch are normally taken on sea baits so do not dismiss them out of hand because someone else says so; give them a go and make up your own mind. Below is a list of the fish baits that I use in order of preference for summer and late autumn/winter fishing.

Summer	*Winter*
Bleak	Sprat
Roach	Sardine
Perch	Sand eel
Gudgeon	Whitebait
Bream	Herring
Rudd	Mackerel

This is not an exhaustive list and availability is very much dependent upon your own venue but these baits are proven to be effective, bearing in mind which species you find to be the most prevalent and the time of year. Deadbaiting is one of the most effective and in a lot of situations the most selective method of targeting large eels, whether you use sections, whole fish or just pieces. One of the first methods used was to thread your line through the mouth of a small fish with a baiting needle; the needle was pushed out through the root of the tail and you then pulled your line through until the fish's mouth was sitting in the bend of the hook. A small piece of cotton or elastic was then tied around the tail to prevent the bait from slipping back down the line and obscuring the hook point. This was known as the gorge method and as the name suggests it resulted in a very high percentage of gut hooked fish. This tactic did put a lot of eels on the banks and deep hooking was accepted as an unavoidable fact of life when using fish baits in this manner.

The theory behind this method was that eels always swallowed a fish head-first. When a run occurred you let the eel take line until it stopped to turn and swallow the bait, you then waited for the second run to commence before striking. If the eel was chewing on the bait anywhere but the head, the run was missed. If it had successfully swallowed the bait, you then had one deep hooked eel to contend with. For the specialist the emphasis is now more on the welfare of the eel rather than just catching them at any cost. So eel anglers have been looking for a means to improve 'runs to landed fish' ratios and cut back on gut hooked eels. With the use of section baits with different hooking arrangements this has improved the results but is some way off solving these problems.

Head section deadbait : Eels will nearly always swallow a fish bait head first as the fins and scales will all fold back allowing easy entry to the gullet so by placing a hook not in the mouth but in the cut section of the bait the hook nearly always catches the eel's jaw on the strike. This technique also presents a bait in a more natural position as the bait lies straight whereas the fully threaded bait often curls into the bend of the hook, not the way a cautious eel would expect to find a dead fish. The strike can be made as soon as a run occurs resulting in a higher proportion of lip hooked fish, a big plus point in anyone's book. The reason I began using this arrangement was because I started questioning the amount of runs I was missing when fishing with the hook protruding from the bait's mouth. Taking a close inspection of my bait after a missed or aborted run, on many occasions I noticed that the cut section was crushed or marked where it had been clamped in the eel's jaws. Moving the hook into this damaged area was an obvious solution.

When it comes to using a head section as bait my preferred method is to pass a baiting needle through the cut fish, pushing it through from the cut section or just behind it, so that the point of the needle comes out of the mouth area. When the trace and hook is drawn through the bait, the hook is left in the vicinity of the cut, the area that is leaking those attractive juices into the water.

Tail section deadbait : This would be my second choice as a hook bait. As with most of my baits I position the hook about one inch behind the cut, depending on the size of bait, running the hook through the body and then pulling the trace out through the root of the tail. This is an instant strike method of baiting up, but you can also put the hook in the root of the tail and I would then wait for the second run before striking. Another little tip when fishing tail sections is to cut the fins off the tail; this makes the bait more aerodynamic, making it less likely to spin and twist on the cast.

A whole perch rigged for eeling, twenty-first century style.

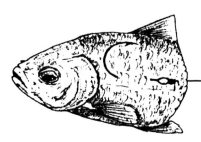

Head section deadbait.

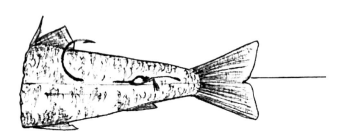

Tail section deadbait.

The middle sections have to be my least favourite parts of a fish to use and I will only use them if I fail to catch enough small fish for the night. With these, the eel has too many choices on where to seize the bait and, knowing my luck, it will grab them in a place where I haven't positioned the hook, so I do not recommend using them although in the end it will come down to personal choice and availability of bait. However, although the middle sections may be my least favourite bait, if the tail is left on so only the head is missing it becomes one of my top baits. This three-quarter bait with the head removed just behind the gills and the guts left exposed is an excellent way of presenting a bait. Depending on where you put the hook, it's a 'strike on the second run' method.

Another variation on this method is one I took from sea anglers fishing for congers and that is to remove the backbone and tail from a whole fish bait, which they then call a flapper. To do this you need a sharp knife. You lie the fish on its side and run the blade, starting at the tail, along the fish's backbone, until you reach the head. Then turn the fish over and repeat on the other side. This leaves two fillets either side of the backbone. You cut through the backbone, removing it and the tail in one go, and this leaves the head and two fillets either side of the guts. This makes a wonderfully soft bait and probably leaves more scent trail than any other method of deadbaiting. And the hooking is simple. You just pass the hook through the mouth and out of the V where the two fillets meet, but make sure the hook stands proud as being a soft bait the hook point is easily masked. This method does produce very confident runs; the only downside is that the eels tend to rip the fillets off when you miss a run leaving you with just the stripped head section. Deadbaiting is not an exact science and you will find different methods work better on different waters so keep changing the hooking pattern and baits until you achieve a satisfactory catch rate (with deadbaits I would class hitting 50% of your runs as successful).

One bait I haven't discussed as yet is the use of eels themselves. Yes you did read that correctly, eels as bait, very contentious and I'm sure some people will view that statement with horror! Yet eels preying on other eels is a fact and that's all the justification I need to advocate their use, but only under certain situations. There are some waters where the effectiveness of using eel section cannot be denied. Especially waters that contain a large population of small bootlace eels. The bigger, older fish often have to face stiff competition for food from their younger, more agile counterparts so as a solution to the problem they turn cannibalistic. This is especially true of the broad headed variety of eel, a strain that is definitely not averse to eating its smaller brethren. Using a section from a small eel in the 4-8oz range, you have a bait that is selective in as far as the small fish will ignore it and only the bigger fish will find it appealing. I have no compunction in dispatching a small eel for use as bait but I would never consider buying them from a retailer. For one, I require my bait to be fresh and bloody, not frozen and withered, and two, it encourages the netters and bait suppliers to trade in them; a personal stance.

In fact, I'd like to draw to your attention one piece of research that proves just how cannibalistic eels can be. It was an experiment carried out in 1938 by two well known biologists, Pellegrin and Spillmann, as part of a study to establish the cannibalistic tendencies of the European eel. The experiment was to be conducted over several years at an aquarium in the Jardin des Plantes in Paris. It began on 7th July, 1937, with the introduction of approximately 1,000 small eels into a large tank of water. The tank was without sand, gravel, stones or any vegetation but did have ample room for the young eels to move around. On the 5th July, 1938, just under a year later, there remained only 71 eels. Where had the other 929 gone? Despite being regularly fed with meat and other foods these remaining eels had devoured them. From this date events moved quickly. There were daily scenes of cannibalism; eels that had swallowed other eels whole had the tails protruding from their mouths or had distended abdomens. By the 8th of September there was only 12 survivors left. A month after that their number

4lb 10oz of eel taken in cold weather on sprat by locating a 20-foot deep hole.

was reduced to three and on the 17th of October the final battle commenced. The biggest eel killed both its rivals and devoured one almost immediately. There was no shortage of food in the tank so the question is, was the cannibalism caused by territorial disputes or by pure predatory instinct to be top dog? I guess we'll never know but what this test has shown is how aggressive eels can be in the right environment.

A great example of an eel section water is Westbere Lake in Kent, with the average eel weighing in the region of 1lb to 1lb 8oz. These smaller eels will hit fresh deadbaits and worms within minutes of them settling on the bottom. Using eel section the run rate reduces markedly but the fish you do catch then average 2 to 3lb with a smattering of 4-pounders. This may not be typical eel water but situations like this do exist, so you adjust your methods to suit; it's the only way to keep improving your catches.

On some of those waters that have been heavily pressured (with the amount of eel anglers about today that's not many waters), eels have been known to wise up to fish baits and become nigh on impossible to tempt. This is not the end of the world; if the eels on your water no longer appear to be interested in fish baits you still have the option of flavouring them, in much the same way that pike anglers extend the life of their fish baits.

How about injecting a bait with strawberry essence or some of the thousands of other flavours available? Now I bet I know what you're thinking and it's probably not very nice, so bear with me. A lot of today's fisheries receive pressure from carp anglers who introduce thousands of little, hard designer baits flavoured with all sorts of exotic ingredients. As I said before, eels are opportunistic feeders and presented with this nutritious food supply they won't turn their back on it. These designer baits are hard to hook eels on so using a strawberry flavoured roach may sound ridiculous but it may very well work when all else fails.

The size of bait is also worth considering. Normally baits will be between 3 and 5 inches long but keep an open mind if pike anglers are getting runs on big baits and you are not getting a touch on yours. It makes sense to use similar size baits but hitting runs can be almost impossible. Better to have the chance of hitting a run than to sit there all day twiddling your thumbs. Then you have the shoals of small fry during the summer; these too should not be overlooked, as they are a staple part of the eel's diet. One of my best eel catches came on 2-inch long bream fry that had been herded into the margins by hundreds of small perch, but I'll say a little bit more about that trip later on. So use 3 to 5 inches as a guide but do be prepared to experiment, as no size should be ruled out. Whole herrings have taken fish and so has the tiny minnow. It will all depend on individual waters.

The timing of strikes when using different size baits will vary and for this reason I have compiled a rough guide that may be of help to those of you just starting out in eel fishing.

Guidelines on when to strike a run

Method	*Strike*
Whole fish (hook in mouth)	When second run starts
Whole fish (hook in side)	When first run stops
Whole fish (hook in tail)	During the second run
Head section (small)	Soon as possible
Head section (large)	During second run
Middle section	During first run
Tail section (small)	During first run
Tail section (large)	During second run
Eel section	During second run
Small piece of fish	Instant strike
Large fish bait (ie, herring)	Your guess is as good as mine!

Livebaiting

There are few subjects that will promote as much controversy amidst anglers and outside parties as the use of live fish as bait. Many dedicated anglers who pursue predatory fish for the mainstay of their sport will insist that livebaiting is a necessary and worthwhile means of catching large fish; whilst others, even from within our own ranks, say it's a barbaric method of fishing. However the overriding fact here is that eels are predators and live fish are a staple part of their diet. Very few anglers like to use livebaits and this is understandable, whether on account of ethical reasons or any others, but you need to make this choice for yourself. Bear in mind that if you support the banning of livebaits this may also include worms and maggots - a ridiculous state of affairs, to put it mildly. If you can lay your objections to one side, livebaiting is an excellent method for catching eels; in fact, it is an excellent method for catching any of Britain's predatory species of fish. Of the different types of eel we may encounter, the broad headed variety is the most active fish hunter and has no problem in catching live fish and therefore livebaiting should be given serious consideration where this variety resides. In some instances this may be the only way to entice a run from the broad headed eels. Live fish are going to be far more numerous than dead fish on any water and as such will play an important part in the eel's diet. For me, this justifies their use as I can see no reason to equip eels with strong lithe bodies if they are not required to hunt actively for their food.

Fishing with livebaits does not require the same attention to detail and finesse as fishing with static deadbaits or naturals. But a lack of finesse doesn't mean we can get away with being crude. A big eel has more time to inspect a bait ledgered on the bottom whereas a livebait is more likely to be attacked instinctually by an eel without thought for its own safety.

The natural life cycle of coarse fish populations has a significant impact on whether fishing for eels with livebait will be a success or not. Most of our coarse fish spawn in and around the spring months and the tiny fry are generally too small to rouse the interest of a hunting eel until a month or two after hatching. Also at this time of year, the number of small fish from the previous year's spawning are at their lowest level, having been subjected to a year's predation by fish, birds and a host of other predators. Those that have survived the winter months have grown on and are generally too big for eels to handle. Therefore the big eels are more likely to seek out spawn-bound fish and others

Filming The Compleat Angler *for Sky TV. The author (right) with Geoffrey Palmer and Rae Borras.*

injured by over-enthusiastic antics in the shallow water. They will resort to scavenging for food and eating fish eggs.

By mid-summer things have changed, clouds of 2-inch fry mill about in the margins of most lakes and predators can gorge themselves in a matter of minutes. A lively fish presented on the correct tackle may still attract the attention of eels that have already eaten their fill. They may well ignore a shoal of small fish swimming right next to their head but strike out at a small fish wriggling on a hook. This is more instinctual behaviour driven by survival instincts rather than hunger. Therefore to improve your chances of a take, inspect the bait regularly. If it has stopped swimming vigorously, change it for a fresh one. It makes little sense to try to conserve bait at the expense of catching fish; it's far better to use all the bait and have a few fish under the belt than trying to eke it out so that it lasts the night.

By autumn the quantities of small fish have fallen again and with the onset of the colder months and reducing water temperatures eels spend more and more time feeding. As the water temperature drops still further, eels will then start to eat less and become much more difficult to catch.

The methods used for fishing livebaits are many and numerous but we still need to present the bait naturally so the overriding consideration must be to keep the livebait 'live' and fish it on balanced tackle. There is no point fishing a 2-inch roach under a large pike bung; eels will not tolerate this much resistance when seizing the bait and even the most appetising of meals will be rejected. A small livebait is a delicate creature so use small hooks (sizes 6 to 8 are ideal) and a small float if the livebait is to be float fished. If the livebait is to be ledgered use a gentle, underhanded cast. Remember you are livebaiting and that casting a fish any distance normally results in its death. You need the bait to stay healthy and active for as long as possible, otherwise you may as well fish with deadbaits. Small rudd or roach make excellent livebaits as they are tough, hardy little fish. Small perch or bream and some other species of fish do not take kindly to being fished in this manner so do not last that long. Livebaiting for eels should be strictly a night-time activity unless there are no other predatory fish in the water. If you use livebaits during the day perch and pike can become a real problem, but on some waters this can be a pleasurable interlude to while away the daytime hours in anticipation of those eels coming on the feed.

One last subject I feel I must say something about is the act of transferring fish from water to water. You can find yourself in deep trouble with the Water Authority over this if you're caught because of the now all too common instances of fish disease. If the water is notoriously hard to get bait sized fish from I have occasionally taken some fish with me. They are kept in a bucket and used as required. Just make sure you have permission to do so.

Worms

Lobworms : If I were given the choice of only using one bait to fish for eels for the rest of my life, the humble lobworm, without doubt, would be my Number One choice. They are more effective than deadbaits but not as selective, attracting eels of all sizes. Given a hard water with a low nuisance fish population, I would consider no other bait. The only drawback that I can see is that every other species of fish swimming in our lakes and rivers loves them so you can never be certain what you are going to catch. For example, there is one lake I fish where the eels will only accept worms (I've used deadbaits but have not had a run other than from small pike). The problem is that the water contains huge amounts of skimmer bream and I end up re-baiting and casting every ten minutes, and with four rods fishing at one time this can become very much like hard work. For the specialist eel angler, bream, the matchman's friend, are the eel angler's biggest curse. It has always intrigued me how these supposedly stupid fish seem to have the most uncanny ability of knowing when

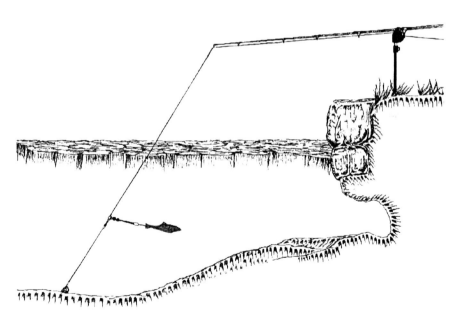

Fishing a livebait near an undercut bank. An excellent method for taking big eels.

you've just snuggled up into your sleeping bag to steal a bit of shut-eye. The second you get really comfortable, *bleep bleep,* they start pulling that worm to bits and nothing you do seems to discourage them. Words do not describe this event justly. Apart from this frustrating little drawback there is just one other problem. As I mentioned earlier, worms tend not to be selective as a bait; any size eel will readily take them, from bootlace to beast, but they do, without doubt, produce more runs than any other bait used in eeling that I can think of.

I doubt if there is any eel angler who wouldn't put worms at the top of his list of baits as the hitting of runs is much higher with worms than deadbaits and they are relatively easy to obtain. In fact, the gathering of worms can also be a sport on its own - trips to the golf course or the local park on warm wet nights with bucket and torch in hand can result in loads of bait (and quite often, the next day, a very stiff back). The only downside to collecting worms like this at night is, depending on where you live, the parks can be full of perverts and lager louts and the golf courses are often used by over zealous lovers with no homes to go to. It's also possible to attract the interest of the local constabulary and they will never believe you when you tell them you're collecting worms to go fishing. Nowadays I tend to avoid the stiff back and other nocturnal park users and take the easy option of buying them in bulk from a bait farm.

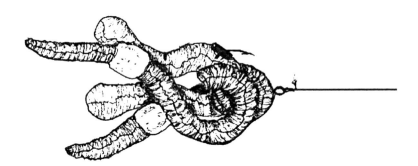

A nice bunch of irresistible lobs.

There are several types of worm available that you can use. The lobworm is the first choice, but there are also garden worms, dendrobena, brandlings and lugworms! No, that isn't a joke; lugworm is actually a very good bait especially on some of the coastal pits I fish. It has a very high blood content and does produce a lot of runs. The only downside is that they wash out quickly so need to be changed fairly often. They are also pretty expensive compared to the other baits we use, but they are readily available from tackle shops. When using lugworm bear in mind that they have to be kept cold, otherwise they blow. This will leave you with nothing but the most unattractive, foul smelling ball of slime you'd ever wish to encounter.

One tip that comes in handy when using worm is to condition them prior to fishing. It toughens them up and they can also nearly double in size. Take a medium sized plastic carton and fill it with worm bedding. Commercial beddings consist of finely ground paper mixed with soil but some are made from sphagnum moss and other plant fibres. You can make your own from torn strips of newspaper and dirt which can be just as effective. Be selective and choose about a dozen healthy looking worms, wash them and place them in the carton on top of the bedding. Add strips of wet newspaper to the carton on top of the worms and mound so that it's stacked well above the rim. Press the lid into place to create a pressure pack and place in the fridge or coolbox for a minimum of twenty-four hours. After that you should have some terrific worms for bait.

Other Baits

There are a few other baits that warrant trying from time to time, but it's better to experiment on waters with a large head of eels where it's easier to find out if they are enthusiastic about them or not.

Maggots : The Noddy's favourite. I did not consider this a serious big eel bait until recently but a few events on one water have made me rethink my options. (As yet, I have not been able to put thought into practice so I'll keep you in suspense as to what these events are!) Generally specimen hunters do not use maggots because they attract everything from bootlace eels to every coarse fish that swims so if you use them as bait for big fish they are very soon left sucked to death and skinned, rendering them useless as a bait. And that's the main reason I'm reluctant to use them as hook baits but that doesn't mean I would never consider using them. Maggots regularly fed into a water will induce eels to feed even in bright sunshine if there is cover near by. They will even wean the small headed eel off its diet of insects given a little pre-baiting.

One observation I've made is that eels seem to prefer picking them up off the bottom individually rather than in bunches on a hook so presentation can be a problem. Also, using finer hooklength and a smaller hook often results in getting smashed when a good fish comes along unless the water is snag free. To fish with maggots you need plenty to get the fish going and to keep a bed of bait on the bottom. The attentions of roach, bream etc. will soon wipe the bottom clean if a continuous stream of bait is not being fed in. At some of the places where I now use maggots I would not baulk at taking several gallons.

Do not discount maggots as bait; they can be useful but, personally, I use them as an attractor rather than a hook bait and fish small deadbaits in the vicinity. Maggots are an excellent attractor for eels and small fish and if you attract small fish into the swim you will in no time attract predators; so you can benefit from having both types of eel feeding in the swim. This can only improve your chances of a good fish.

Pouring hot water over the maggots or putting them in plastic bags and tying the top off kills and stretches them, and they can then be thrown into the margins without the fear of them burrowing into the bottom. Lying on the bottom in amongst the weed and bottom debris, they make an attractive carpet of bait that definitely attracts big eels. It is not unusual to have eels bubbling away in the silt in much the same way as tench feed, the clouds of tiny bubbles betraying their presence as they root around. The best combination I have come across is a mixture of dead maggot and squats (a tiny version of the maggot) mixed together with worm essence or some fish oils. This seems to do the business on several of my waters. When I started eeling the only reason I used to take maggots on my fishing trips was to catch the bait I required to catch the eels. I must have missed out on so many opportunities to increase my catches it doesn't bear thinking about.

Mussels / cockles : Mussels, either the freshwater variety or the ones you get from the seafood stall, are all worth a go. On a club trip to Ardingly Reservoir a few years ago, eels were being caught with the top of their snouts cut or marked. This coincided with dropping water levels which was causing fresh-water mussels to be cooked by the sun in the shallow water. The marks on the eels' heads were due to the eels taking advantage of the situation. They were using their heads to force a way into the dying mussel for an easy meal, cutting their snout in the process. This is where shellfish would have been a top bait to use except I didn't figure this out until it was too late. The moral from this story is to stay open minded. I had become preoccupied with using traditional baits and therefore missed an opportunity to bag up on eels that were avidly feeding on an alternative bait. We live and learn. Saltwater mussels and cockles can be a good alternative to the freshwater variety so long as they are not soaked in vinegar. With cockles now very popular amongst carp anglers I would expect this bait to be taken more readily by eels where they are being used.

Other more unusual baits : Peeler crab can be excellent in estuaries and some lakes, as can crayfish, brown shrimps and luncheon meat. In fact almost anything may be taken at times. Squid, sausage meat, cheese, sweetcorn, stinky paste type baits and boilies, the list is endless. All these baits account for big fish at one time or another. The eel is truly an opportunist feeder and will, by the looks of it, refuse nothing when it's hungry enough. All of these baits catch fish, but in the big scheme of things the percentage of eels caught on these baits is very low compared with the traditional baits like worms and deadbaits. So do unusual baits warrant serious attention or should you stick to the traditional? There is no easy answer to that question. If fish have been caught on one of these baits from your water then by all means try it, but I would only try it on one rod first to see what happens. Almost certainly there is a bait somewhere we have overlooked that is a wonder bait for eels. It could be a boilie or a natural water insect, anything in fact, so every now and then give something different a go, you just never know!

Preserved baits : Anglers can now buy almost every bait they can think of in preserved form: bottled, wet packed, tinned, dried and blast frozen. Although not the top baits to go fishing with, they are still handy for short-notice sessions where you haven't got time to collect your own bait.

Specials : These include boilies and paste type baits which must number in their thousands. But is there one that will catch eels, or should I say, is there one that will out-perform traditional baits? As far as I know the answer is no but maybe there is a carp angler out there who has developed a carp bait but was plagued with, or caught nothing but eels on it and crossed it off as a failure (if you are out there, can you give me a call with the recipe?). I do think that paste or boilie type baits have a place in specimen eel fishing, and it's likely that the breakthrough may come from the commercial sector where scientific research is a priority. The bait that may in the end prove the best will not necessarily be the one we expect. In the Kent area where I fish, boilies with milk and dairy based HNV ingredients out fish those with fishmeal based mixes. In fact, the carp anglers I know use fishmeals because they deter eels, something you would not expect knowing the eel's eating habits. Flavours, too, are endless nowadays but what works on one water may be useless on another. Here is a list of flavours and mixes that have proved successful in catching eels in the past:

Mix 1
  5oz soya isolate
  3oz casein
  1oz equivite
  1oz gluten

Mix 2
  4oz casein
  3oz lactalbumin
  2oz calcium caseinate
  1oz gluten
  1oz equivite

Mix 3
  5oz semolina
  3oz soya flour
  2oz gluten
  1oz vitamealo

The above recipes are simple base mixes that rely on flavourings as the main attractants.

Mix 4
  5oz sardine meal
  3oz salmon fry crumb
  1oz soya flour
  1oz wheat gluten

Mix 5
  2oz calcium caseinate
  3oz vitamealo
  5oz shrimp meal
  Fish oil flavouring

Mix 6
  2oz sardine meal
  2oz white fish meal
  2oz mackerel
  1oz sand eel meal
  2oz shrimp meal
  5oz casein
  2oz gluten

Mix 7
  4oz capelin
  2oz beef and hide
  2oz feather meal
  2oz calcium caseinate
  2oz meat and bone
  1oz wheat gluten
  2oz semolina

As you can see by the ingredients of the above mixes, adding flavours is not necessary, but the addition of some blended fish oils will enhance the baits. I also said I would give you a list of flavours that have been successful over the years in attracting eels and they are as follows:

Dandelion & Burdock *	Maple Cream ***
Smokey Bacon *	Maple **
Blue cheese ****	Liver (with extract) **
Cream **	Geranium oil ***
Roast beef *	Evaporated milk & ice cream *
Shrimp *	Dairy Cream **
Meat *	Strawberry ****
Salmon **	Sea food **

The * sign denotes how effective some baits are for eels, but remember they are effective because they are flavourings used on carp waters that contain eels. They may well not prove effective on your venue unless the flavours are currently in fashion. Other additives that may be of use are flavour enhancers and appetite stimulators; also amino acids, a list of which you will find in *Supersense* (Chapter 3). One thing to remember, when using amino acids is not to use tap water in your mix as drinking water contains chlorine. This kills the effectiveness of amino acids, instantly rendering them useless. It may be as well to make the bait up at the water's edge when you're fishing as, unlike carp fishing, you need only use a small amount of bait.

The eels I have seen caught on boilies have never appeared to have consumed that many prior to being hooked. This is quite easy to determine as very often you can feel the boilies lying in the eel's stomach; half a dozen is probably the most I've ever come across. By introducing large amounts of boilies or pastes you may only succeed in effectively feeding the fish off. A campaign of introducing a small amount of your chosen mix every time you visit the water may be a far more effective means of getting the fish accustomed to the bait. Like the flavours and bait mixes I've already mentioned, boilies have only become effective where the carp boys have been using them for long, sustained periods and as a result eels have become accustomed to finding them on a regular basis. A bait or flavour that has been heavily used on one water, when used elsewhere produces very little in the way of eels if the bait or flavour is unknown at the new venue. This seems to indicate that, with some baits, eels have to become familiar with them before they readily accept them as an alternative food source.

Your first attempt at a protein bait may be unsuccessful . . . and your next, and the one after that. This is a field that is still in its early, groundbreaking stages and success will not come easily. Remember there are thousands of carp anglers every week bombarding waters with protein baits so on waters like these a special may become a serious option for those eels that have become used to this rich, easily obtainable food source. This type of bait may also offer ways of hitting more runs and reducing the instances of gut hooked fish as instant strike methods and bolt rigs could be utilised. By using 10 or 12mm boiled baits and a fixed weight the eel is more likely to be lip hooked as it moves off.

These baits are still very much an unknown quantity and unless I'm fishing a carp water where eels are frequently taken on specials, I remain very much a sceptic, and stick to traditional worms and deadbaits for most of my fishing. You have to fish with the baits you believe in. At the moment I catch far more eels on the carp waters than the carp lads so my methods and rigs must be more successful than theirs for eels. But we should never be afraid to try something new; it's the only way we'll learn and improve our fishing methods. So to return to the question 'Are specials serious alternative baits to worms and deadbaits?' I would conclude that in the present climate, with very few serious eel anglers experimenting with them on a regular basis (myself included), I do not think so. However, they should not be overlooked. On the right water they may be as effective as anything else we have been using so do not dismiss them just like that, they do have a place on the list.

A recent special added to this list that I have been using with surprisingly good results has been halibut pellets in the 18-20mm range. They are big baits but are good for avoiding the roach and bream. Again, a lot of coarse anglers out there are using pellets as ground bait and the eels have discovered a taste for it. Pellets are not outfishing naturals but the one advantage I have noticed is that I haven't taken an eel under 3lb as yet. One of the ways of fishing with these little oblong type compressed fish thingies is either in PVA bags or stockings. Both have started to prove successful in tackling big eels on hard pressured waters. It can be an absolutely deadly method of catching eels if you are prepared to catch carp, bream and tench as a by-catch. In fact, you will catch far more of these than eels as the bait was specifically designed to target these fish. Eels have cottoned on to this rich source of protein and hoover them up along with the other fish in the lake. I use a large 20mm pellet in a PVA bag of smaller offerings that dissolve faster, leaving my hook bait sitting on top of a very attractive pile of bait. Because of the size of the pellet a small fish is unable to swallow it so it's left for the biggies. It can be cast a long distance when the rig is assembled correctly and presents a type of offering that is unfamiliar to most of the lake's fish. They are normally used to finding large areas of bait spodded out to form a carpet, whereas your offering will create a small compact pile that will not attract hordes of silver fish. The method is easier and less messy than some of our other methods but does take a bit of practice to perfect. PVA bags can be made up on the bank but PVA stockings filled with pellet can be made at home well in advance. Filling a bag is easy although I find a cut down shampoo bottle helps used as a funnel. Hold the bag around the nozzle of the funnel and half fill with pellet, drop the rig in the bag, add a few more pellets and drop the baited hook on top. Add a few more pellets, then lightly dampen the top of the bag and wrap it tightly around the trace line. This should stick it down but don't wet it too much as the bag will dissolve. And remember, you need to puncture the bag in several places so that the trapped air can escape, otherwise your rig will drift off somewhere else before the bag dissolves. PVA stockings are filled similarly but the rig is left outside. You just hook the hook on to the stocking, twist once and hook again. Is this method seriously worth a go? I have seen anglers around me take eels to over 8lb while I've stuck to traditional techniques and bait. I caught more eels than them but the ones I would love to have caught were the ones that succumbed to their baits. There could be a few interesting seasons to come.

Whatever kind of bait you choose, the one thing they should all have in common is that they must be fresh. Baits that have been in the sun or lying around since the previous day's fishing may very well act as deterrents. Some people also believe that smoking affects baits and that the scent of tobacco gets on to the bait through handling it after a fag. As I mentioned in *Supersense* (Chapter 3), tobacco acts as a deterrent to eels but not in its raw state; it was the smell of tobacco and tobacco smoke combined that the eels disliked. Many eel anglers I know smoke and I couldn't honestly say they'd catch more fish if they stopped as some of them have caught far better fish than me. Certainly it is a good idea to wash your hands regularly whilst fishing, usually in the margins of the lake. I doubt very much whether smoking or washing your hands in the lake makes the slightest difference to the eels, or any other fish for that matter, but there will always be someone to prove me wrong. That about concludes all the waffle on baits, a subject that can be as complicated or as simple as you wish to make it. Traditional or advanced, the choice is yours.

Chapter Nine

Pre-Baiting

How about trying a technique that improves your chances of catching eels without over exerting yourself either mentally or physically. Sounds attractive? It certainly does to me. Trying to create a super bait or rig for eels is fine if you've got plenty of time on your hands to put them through their paces. If time is at a premium you need something that gives you a leg up without all the hard work; something that encourages eels to venture forth in search of a meal. So what is this magic formula for success? A very simple, very under-utilised system called pre-baiting or groundbaiting; a method that can be so ridiculously effective in encouraging them to feed in earnest that I'm surprised how few people actually bother to use it. I have no doubt in my mind that most eel anglers would be very pleasantly surprised, even shocked by the results if they got off their backsides and gave it a go. How many anglers can say they have ever seriously pre-baited for eels? Very few I imagine. Most just turn up at the water and fish, and by doing this they are certainly missing out on a golden opportunity to improve their catches. It's a proven fact that large eels are territorial and only move home when regularly disturbed, when their food source runs out or they are presented with an easier opportunity to find food. With a regular pre-baiting campaign you give the eels an opportunity to locate an easier food source. Eels will soon find that going to a quiet, secluded part of the lake with a regular food supply is healthier than searching continuously for individual offerings elsewhere. They will often stay in the vicinity of the baited area until they are either disturbed away or caught. So the longer you can leave an area undisturbed, in theory, the better the fishing should be. I owe almost half of all my big fish catches to pre-baiting so sharing my different approaches should offer some very useful ideas to the would be eel hunter.

Well known eel specialists such as John Sidley and Dave Holman have regularly employed pre-baiting campaigns as part of their eel fishing and have used them successfully to take some very big fish. In fact I'm sure John Sidley's best ever eel of 8lb 3oz came after a sustained pre-baiting session. John Sidley's method was to bait up with sardines and sprats well in advance of his trips whilst Dave Holman used maggots and chopped lobworms both prior to and during his sessions. Both these methods have their good and bad points yet the excellent catches these two anglers shared were proof enough that preparing a swim before actually fishing it worked. Obviously if you want to be consistently successful in catching eels you have to locate them, but failing that you have to attract them to your swim. Locating them is fraught with problems because they never show themselves so attracting them is the next obvious choice. This is especially true if you are fishing one of those waters where eels are known to be notoriously difficult to catch and time is at a premium.

Every water you come across will respond differently to a pre-baiting campaign. On waters with low eel stocks but big fish it can be a definite advantage, attracting fish from far and wide but it can cause the water to blow extremely quickly. My own experience of having a water blow on me so to speak, was when I was fishing a Hertfordshire lake that was known for being a very challenging place to fish. I initiated a pre-baiting campaign prior to my trip and during the session the results spoke for themselves. I had the best catch of my life on a water that normally produced one or two runs on a good weekend. Since then the fishing has taken a dramatic turn for the worse. I can still coax runs from the water but have only connected with eleven more fish in the last eight years, a total of a hundred and sixty nights' fishing. Not a record I am overly proud of. So what conclusions can be drawn from this experience? As a result of my baiting up tactics I obviously concentrated the lake's smallish population of eels into the one area and put them under heavy fishing pressure if only for a few days. This resulted in an excellent catch of eels in a very short space of time but was detrimental to my continued success on this fishery. For all intents and purposes the fishery has now blown as an eel water leaving me no alternative but to find somewhere else to fish. This lake is nearly two hundred acres in size so any chance of me having caught all of the fish is pretty remote. The question is, have all the eels just moved elsewhere because of the angling pressure or have they abandoned the lake? This I doubt very much, I think they are now very wary and cunning fish. Not one eel after that trip has fallen to a bait fished on a wire trace. They have all been taken on braided hook-lengths and the use of any attractants now seems to repels the few eels that still feed. You don't have to be Einstein to see pre-baiting had its advantages by giving me that one good catch of eels. The disadvantage is that I shortened the fishable life of the water considerably.

At the other end of the scale, on waters that contain a large population of small to medium sized eels, pre-baiting has no positive benefits; in fact sometimes it can be a real disadvantage, attracting hordes of bootlace eels into the swim which attack anything and everything edible that lands in the baited area. This is fine if you just want runs, but wading through the small stuff while you wait for a big fish can be an absolute nightmare. If you're fortunate enough to have this kind of water then pre-baiting is definitely not necessary. You are far better off fishing the water just as it is.

6lb1oz of eel taken after a bag of fish guts was suspended in a swim that had previously produced only the occasional small eel. It was accompanied by others of 5lb 1oz and 4lb 7oz.

Baiting a swim weeks, even months in advance if we are to be totally realistic, is only feasible if the water is just around the corner. With the rocketing price of petrol, pre-baiting a venue many miles from home can work out a very expensive operation both in time and money. If you are one of the fortunate few who have a promising local water then make the most of it. Try and bait up at least twice a week with chopped sardines mixed with breadcrumbs, sardine meal and fish oils, the whole concoction rolled up into small balls. These can even be frozen if small fish are a pest. Deposit this lot into the chosen swim, preferably in the evening to

European eel anglers. (Slava Stochl)

discourage pike from picking up the baits before the eels get a look in. Scatter it about as well; piles of bait in one spot do not seem to have the desired effect. The slick this concoction makes as the balls break up and the fish oils spread out on the surface has to be seen to be believed; you could easily be fooled into thinking the *Exxon Valdez* had sunk in your swim when you weren't looking. This approach to pre-baiting is best suited to a water with a respectable head of eels, not necessarily small fish, just a larger population. Also if the swim you are fishing holds little in the way of attractive features for an eel this is a very effective way of drawing fish into an area that otherwise holds little temptation for them.

Even though pre-baiting is acknowledged as being a successful method there will always be a few anglers who turn their noses up at the idea of fishing in this manner. Basically they believe it feeds the fish too well and takes away their appetite. Another thought is that when large amounts of bait settle on the bottom during hot weather it will, in a very short time, start to go off which in turn releases foul smelling odours; whilst some of the bait will have been eaten there may be a considerable amount left over to decompose and rot. This area would then act as a deterrent to eels rather than attract them. These arguments are plausible but in my experience untrue as I have taken many good fish by pre-baiting.

The only real problem I have experienced whilst pre-baiting is that the eel's feeding habits are prone to change. The normal vicious line-stripping takes seem to be replaced by more gentle affairs - slow lifts of the bobbin more associated with a confidently feeding fish. John Sidley once summed it up quite well by describing this feeding behaviour as being similar to that in a cage of chickens: if you throw in the odd titbit a mad scramble ensues and the successful bird runs off with its prize to eat it in seclusion; throw in handfuls of seed and the chickens will peck away in the vicinity all day without a squabble.

If you do decide to pre-bait a water have a trial run first to see how effective it is. Visit the lake a couple of days prior to your trip with a box of blanched maggots and a hundred or so chopped worms. Depositing this lot into the margins each evening can get a lot of hungry fish grubbing about in double quick time. This is an excellent short-term baiting method and once fishing has commenced only a limited amount of baiting up is needed to maintain the eel's interest. The downside to this method can, on some waters, also work to your advantage, as the bait you are using to attract eels is also very attractive to other fish. This is fine if they are small roach and the like, as these will also represent food to the eels. If bream are in the water in any quantity they can take over the swim and even deadbaits offer no protection, as they move in and devour everything they can find that's edible.

If, like me, you have no good eel fishing on your doorstep, then intensive pre-baiting trips are out of the window so other devious methods have to be employed to get the fish going and there are several different methods I use. Check out a good tackle shop that stocks fish meals - capelin, sardine, and shrimp are all excellent. These are normally used in the making of carp baits and are the basis for one of the groundbaits I use to attract eels. Mix the fish meal with a small amount of sand or mud from the water you are fishing then add some finely ground breadcrumb, fish oils and emulsifier. Make into balls and then chuck them in to the swim. The devious part is that there is nothing for the fish to eat, just the scent of food, so with luck your baits should be readily taken. With many years of experience behind me on the matter of pre-baiting or baiting up I have come to the firm conclusion that introducing smells and flavours are far more effective on a short-term basis than any other method of attracting eels. The idea of pre-baiting with chopped fish, chicken guts or any other concoction you can come up with works fine if it's done well in advance of your trip. But the methods I will describe here to introduce smells and minimal amounts of food can be used right up to your trip and during it with no detrimental effect on the fishing.

Several years ago Essex eeler Harry Gordon gave me a metal tube made from perforated steel, sealed at one end and a flip lid with a catch at the other. This was ideal for introducing smells into the swim without introducing actual food items. A very simple idea, the tube is filled with your groundbait mix but not packed tightly as you want water to circulate through the holes. The can with holes in (that's what it looks like) is then placed in the swim, either on the end of a cord tied to the bank or it can be thrown into the swim with a marker float attached to show its position. The great thing about the can is that it can be removed easily from the water and the contents can be changed daily to keep the scents fresh. This has proved to be a very useful little item, thanks Harry.

If boats can be used on the water you are fishing then by far the most effective method is to suspend a bag of fish guts several feet off the bottom in an onion sack or any other similar sort of netting bag. A heavy weight is tied to one end of a length of nylon cord with a loop tied at the depth you want the bag suspended at. The cord is then tied beneath a large float, a few feet over depth - I use an old toilet ballcock but an empty plastic drinks bottle would be fine. The whole lot is then rowed out and placed in the swim. When using this method I try to place it as far downwind as possible so that any undertow draws the scent along the bottom, through the swim. If there is little or no wind I will place the bag of fish in the centre of the swim and fish to either side of it.

Larger waters are more suited to this type of pre-baiting as you really need wind or wave action on the float to maximise its effectiveness. If the float is made to move about in the wind then the bag of fish, suspended below, is also made to jig about. This releases more scents into the water as well as small particles of fish, making this one of the most effective methods I've used. In fact sometimes I think it's been too effective as I've had fish attack the suspended bag, either pike or eels I'm not sure, but it's not unusual to see the float bobbing on the surface as something attacks from below. This idea was poached from the sea anglers' use of a rubby-dubby bag for shark fishing. Many other species of fish followed the scent trail in the ocean and it has proved just as effective in fresh water.

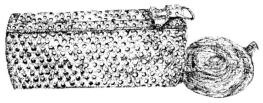

Harry's can, a useful little item.

In small lakes or confined areas the methods I've just mentioned can sometimes be a little overpowering but there are still several ways to go about attracting eels on smaller waters, you just have to refine the baiting up process. As with the previous methods, I tend to prefer introducing smells rather than large quantities of bait as I have found in the short term this is far more effective. If the pre-baiting is done for any length of time prior to the actual trip then small amounts of the hook bait will also be placed in the swim but I do emphasise, *small* amounts. And finally here are my two favourite recipes for use on smaller waters, fish pops and smelly jelly.

Recipe One - Fish Pops : Acquire yourself a pack of disposable plastic or paper cups, several pounds of oily fish (sardines, herrings etc.), some fish oils and anything else you would like to include. Blend this lot up in the mixer and empty into the cups, then simply freeze. Fish pops can be prepared in bulk, ages in advance. They can be thrown or catapulted a long way and take a few hours to disperse in water. You can also freeze chopped worms and maggots the same way, just add some water and sand (the sand makes it sink as ice floats) and 'voila!' you have fish pops.

Recipe Two - Smelly Jelly : Take a baking tray with a depth of at least one inch. Mix together 1lb of liquidized fish, 30ml carpmino and 30ml fish oils. (Blood can be added too but not your own as this can be painful.) Add this concoction to a pan of heated gelatine (one leaf should do) and leave to set for several hours. The solid bait, once set, can then be cut into cubes and introduced into the swim. The smelly jelly takes at least eight hours to break down so is ideal for longer pre-baiting. This concoction can also be used as a hook bait if you're into trying alternative baits.

Pre-baiting and groundbaiting does increase the chance of success when fishing for big eels. Their use as a method for attracting other species is widely accepted in specimen hunting yet it is under-utilised in our branch of the sport. Maybe if eel anglers used it more, a lot more good fish would grace our nets and it might make some of those impossible waters, possible.

Chapter Ten

Winter Eeling

Winter eeling, now there's a challenge for the hardened eel angler. Catching big eels is tricky enough during the warm summer months so considering a campaign to fish for them during the depths of winter, you would have to be plain crazy, or I suppose just fishing mad. Fishing during the winter is going to be a stark contrast to those hot, sultry nights in summer, spent under a brolly wearing just a t-shirt and batting away mozzies. Gazing out from your bivvy across a bleak windswept lake padded out to the nines in warm clothing; you'd have to constantly question your sanity.

Winter eeling is a relatively new approach to catching eels and is very much still in its pioneering stage. Until recently it was commonly believed that eels hibernated for the entire duration of the winter. We now realise that this is not necessarily the case and that given the right conditions, they can be tempted to take a bait. Following this discovery a few die-hard anglers have set out to attempt to catch eels for twelve months of the year. To give credit where it's due, some anglers are attaining these goals although it can be mind-numbingly slow unless the right weather does present itself and unless, of course, you have found the right water.

The months of October and November herald the start of the cold weather, with longer nights and shorter days, and this has the effect of signalling to the eels that winter is well on its way. It's also around this time that the vast majority of *Anguilla* hunters turn their attention to other species, chub or pike for example. By doing this they could be missing out on a very good opportunity to catch that bigger than average eel. With the ever-decreasing amounts of natural food items in the water the eels have to search much harder for what small amounts of food they do require. They may very well leave the safe havens of snags and weed-beds that they have been occupying all summer to do this. With the onset of autumn eels need to feed harder to acquire the

Right: A 2lb 10oz eel caught on a night in January when temperatures dropped to -8° and snow covered the banks. It was the biggest of a five-fish haul.

This is what we should be catching. Chris Price with a 9lb 13oz eel taken in March whilst pike fishing. 48 x 10¾ inches. (Photo courtesy of BEAC.)

body fats they need to see them through the bleak winter months. If the weather remains mild eels will continue to feed and over the last few years we have experienced some very mild winters. Whatever the causes, be it global warming or the greenhouse effect, it provides eel anglers with an opportunity they should be aware of, and as such should be in a position to take advantage of.

I feel many of us stop eeling and change over to catching other species of fish far too early and almost certainly miss out on a prime time for big eels. We should at least carry on eeling until pike anglers stop getting false runs and having their baits torn to pieces or until the weather turns so cold that eeling is not a viable option. When we are faced with periods of severe cold weather it may very well be worth turning our attention to something else until there's a sustained mild spell when it may well be worth giving eels another go. Winter eeling, then, has to be acknowledged as a possibility, providing the weather is on your side. For me, the worst thing about winter eeling is the nights: twelve to fourteen hours of darkness, with no guarantee of action; it can be soul destroying. There is also the cold. If you are not warm and dry there's no way you can fish properly. Frankly I admire anyone who can put up with these conditions and fish religiously week in, week out whatever species of fish they're pursuing.

So what do we consider as a winter eel? Is it an eel caught in the winter months or one taken in winter weather; there are arguments for both points of view but to my mind it is one taken in winter weather, ie, heavy frost, snow and ice, yet any eel taken in the winter months is technically a winter eel.

Our winters (especially in southern England) seem to be increasingly mild; it is well past Christmas before we get any bad weather to speak of and by the end of March it's warming up again. For us anglers down south, fishing for eels during the winter *is* getting easier. The eel's feeding habits appear to be changing; they are continuing to feed much longer into the winter months than was generally considered possible. More of us need to get out there fishing at this time of year because unless more of us do, those really big eels, like Chris Price's, may continue to be caught only by pike anglers.

Pike anglers are, in fact, a very useful source of information when it comes to locating feeding winter eels. Their methods of using oily sea baits not only attract pike but also attract the occasional big eel. This is sometimes a curse to the pike angler as their baits can be destroyed by eels; they have runs they can't hit and the stomachs of the baits they are using are quite often ripped out. For eel anglers these instances are very good indicators that we should be down there fishing. As pike angling has grown in popularity so too have the instances of big eels being caught accidentally. Every year numerous big eels are taken by pike anglers, and some waters have even become infamous for their winter eel catches: lakes like Broadlands in Hampshire which has seen lots of big eels fall to fish baits, particularly trout livebaits; and Westbere Lake near Canterbury where the eels regularly take whole herrings. Catches of big eels from waters like these, and many others, seems to confirm that eels continue to feed when a lot of good eel anglers have packed their tackle away.

If you do decide to have a crack at winter eeling, try to locate a water that has a large population of eels as this will offer the best chances of success. If the water contains broad headed eels you increase your probability of success exponentially as this variety of eel tends to be more active and feeds for longer periods in the colder weather. The more eels the water contains, the longer they seem to feed into the winter and the better your chances are of catching one. This may very well be due to the lack of insect life in and around the lake in the colder months causing the eels to compete for the ever decreasing food supply and forcing them into searching for it over a much larger area. It may also account for the fact that fish baits, especially large oily baits, become far more attractive; baits they wouldn't look twice at during the summer. Waters such as these may be your best shot but don't write off the waters that only throw up the occasional big fish during the summer; again, with the reduction in water life and given the right conditions, these fish may well be easier to catch later in the season. Waters that contain the small headed variety of eel I would give a miss. Their diet consists mainly of water insects so they are the first to suffer in cold weather. This is the type of eel most commonly found buried in silt and dying weed-beds during the winter months, just picking for small food items, and are therefore nearly impossible to catch.

To stand the best chance of catching a winter eel you need to understand what a 'thermocline' is and how it works; not all the technical stuff, just the basic principles which should be enough to put you on the right trail. We said eels suffer from the cold more than most fishes - around 45° they are almost dormant and uncatchable (in some instances extreme temperature changes can kill them). This is where simple science comes to our aid, as only parts of the lake will be this cold. Water becomes heavier the more it's cooled until it reaches a temperature of around 39°, whereupon it proceeds to become lighter, hence the reason ice floats. So you find a set of guidelines appear. Above 39° the warmest water is on the surface and below that figure the reverse is true. This explains why, as water temperature drops, the summer hotspots change and deeper parts of the lake will become far more likely to produce runs. Water temperatures at these depths are far warmer and more stable, therefore encouraging eels to feed. They may feed less frequently and be reluctant to move far but they will feed, even in the worst weather. So you need to put the baits in the correct areas and make them as enticing as possible. Many other coarse fish follow the same pattern and will also hole up in the relative calm that this warm, deep water offers for much the same reasons. The predator sleeps with the prey, a strange situation.

This also explains the phenomenon of eels being taken from areas regarded as pike hotspots during daylight hours. During the summer eels and pike do not mix as pike enjoy a diet of eels. Hence the reason eels are only taken at night on waters with large pike stocks. Remove the pike or find a water without any and eels can be caught twenty-four hours a day. But they do seem to co-exist during the winter without any problems. Basically this is because they have to share the same areas of warmer water that are found on that specific lake. Also, the baits used by pike anglers during the winter represent an easy food source to both fish and as the water temperature is low the fish are too lethargic to get involved in any territorial disputes. This gives us rule one to fish by: avoid the shallow areas that produced many fish during the summer; these will be vacated until the weather warms up.

Another fine European eel. (Slava Stochl)

Rule two is to understand the effects wind has on a thermocline, as this will have a direct effect on your fishing. Imagine a thermocline as being perfectly flat, like a tabletop. The warm water is on the bottom, cold on the top. As the wind blows, it drags the cold water with it, pushing more of it to one end of the lake. This squashes the warm water to the sheltered end, almost like tilting the tabletop. Swim selection in breezy weather is therefore much easier than in cold, calm conditions. You just head for the deepest water at the sheltered end of the lake. The only reason that these guidelines may fail to work is if a stream runs into the lake or a spring. Either of these may upset the balance so look for areas well away from them or find another lake without those obstacles. Winter is also the time of year when daytime fishing can prove just as effective as fishing at night, especially on waters with well-coloured, deep water. Those cold nights when the temperature drops by many degrees may very well discourage eels from feeding or you may find that feeding patterns are condensed into very short periods. As a result, daytime eeling may be your best option. This is an advantage on those waters that have banned night fishing and you may well find that you have an opportunity as good as any to catch fish from a place like this.

There has always been an approximate benchmark for winter eeling of around 50°F. Above this temperature they begin to feed ravenously; below this temperature they either bury themselves into the bottom of the lake or feed only on the odd occasion. This is based on the fact that eels are cold blooded. As the water temperature drops so does the eel's body temperature. The eels become more lethargic and require less food; it also takes longer to digest what they have eaten. There is a lot of truth in this but it doesn't mean they don't feed at all. In all probability they are most likely to feed in shortened periods and without the aggressive feeding habits of summer. It's also possible that they lie up and only take food items that drift into their immediate vicinity.

Baits such as sprats, sardines and herrings come into their own at this time of year as the higher oil content of these baits appears to become more attractive to eels. Sea baits definitely have the edge but like most eel baits they must be fresh; baits frozen for long periods of time or left on the bank for a day or two will be next to useless. Rigs are basically the same but I would forget about using off-bottom rigs. I have used these on occasion and have, as yet, failed to get a run other than from pike.

There are other areas apart from the deep water that may offer the chance of a big snake. Areas that were covered in heavy weed growth during the summer months should not be overlooked. The rotting weed raises the water temperature in these areas by several degrees and many fish can be found buried deep within it. Fishing these places it may be possible to tempt one or two of them to take a small bait. Forget about those screaming runs of summer, most takes from winter eels are much more gentle affairs. I have sometimes wound the rod in just to check the bait and found myself attached to an eel that gave no indication whatsoever that it had taken the bait.

And that just about concludes all I know about fishing for eels during the winter. There has been little previously written on the subject and I know only a handful of anglers that fish all year for eels. I wish I could be more forthcoming and say this rig or specific bait will give you an advantage but I cannot. This branch of our sport is still very much in its infancy and many more rod hours will need to be spent on the bank to establish a pattern, if one exists; and even then it may only apply to certain waters rather than more generally. There are big eels to be caught at this time of year but do not underestimate the obstacles involved. It's going to be hard, so to anyone who gives it a go, I wish you luck - and lots of it.

CHAPTER ELEVEN

HEAD SHAPES

Eel fishermen and naturalists alike have always recognised that there are differences in the eels they catch. The colour variations of the big autumn fish - black backed, bronze flanked specimens - contrast with the brown and yellow eels of summer, the olive-green fish extracted from deep within weed-beds, and the silver fish preparing for the sea run. The other difference and the one we will now concern ourselves with, as this is the only physical feature that impacts on our fishing methods, is the peculiar variation in the shape of the eel's head. Very rarely will you come across variation in head length; rather the changes all seem to be in the head width, shape of the mouth and occasionally the eyes. This phenomenon intrigues not only the eel specialist but also the layman and the scientist, and all parties have been hard pushed to come up with an indisputable explanation. As so very often found with the eel, fact based information as to why occurrences like these happen is extremely hard to come by. Years of research have been carried out on the eel yet most of the information we have is based on supposition and this topic is not going to be very much different.

For many years people have been aware of differences in the head shapes of eels. As far back as 1836 W. Yarrell submitted a scientific paper to the Zoological Society distinguishing between three different types of eel occupying the waters in and around Great Britain: the sharp nosed eel, the broad nosed eel and one he refers to as a 'snig', which is considered a link to connect the other two more extreme forms. We know from anatomical studies, carried out as far back as 1858 when Heckel and Kner produced their research, that there is only one species of eel living in Europe - *Anguilla vulgaris* an early name for the fish we know as *Anguilla anguilla*. This was discovered by dissection of a large amount of European and American eels. All European eels, whatever their size or shape have between 113 and 115 vertebrae. The American eel has a few less, and this is the only anatomical difference between the two. Therefore if all our eels are the same species the question that needs answering is what triggers or causes the variations in head shapes? And how does this impact on our fishing, if at all?

Many of the variations are thought to be caused by sexual maturation, age or local environmental conditions, ie, food availability in their surroundings. However, if, as is widely believed, it is the eel's diet that is responsible, this would go against all the laws of evolution as we currently understand them: physical changes due to diet should take generations to achieve, not years. If a young fish entering a new environment had the ability to adapt its head shape relative to the most prolific food source this would be a very neat trick indeed. It's widely acknowledged that the eel undergoes numerous physiological changes during its migration but these alterations occur because of fluctuating hormonal levels in the eel and are a separate matter altogether. Many fish, such as the salmon, undergo metamorphoses during spawning. But for the eel to change its head shape to accommodate eating fish or insects - that can't be right, can it? If we as humans could do this, can you imagine what some of us would look like? I, for one, would resemble an egg and bacon butty!

At present no one knows for sure whether eels enter the waterways of Britain with a pre-determined head shape inherited from their parents or whether they adapt to their environment as they mature. The most generally accepted theory, and the one to which I subscribe, is that eels enter a water as young fish and adapt themselves to the most easily available food source. The broad nosed, large mouthed eels, appear as a result of large quantities of small fish being present. The pointed headed variety survives by eating small water insects. The 'inbetweenie' is a combination of both. It is also a common belief that once an eel's head shape has been determined, there is no going back if its food supply changes; it's stuck with that shape for the duration of its life. This theory could well be the most plausible as cultured European eels are exclusively narrow headed, their diet consisting only of small pellet-based food items. It is only wild eels that display an array of head shapes. Eels are capable of many amazing things, and changing its head and mouth shape, I believe, is just another extraordinary characteristic in a list of many. It does make sense if you think about it logically: a small eel entering a water and finding that it's full of fish will take maximum advantage of the situation and the same goes for the water that is full of insect life. On many occasions eels are the first fish to colonise new waters and therefore must make the best use of whatever food is available. There's an old saying, 'adapt and survive', to which I think the eel subscribes admirably.

During my pursuit of big eels I have encountered these variations in the shape of the head and have identified different characteristics that distinguish them. There are hundreds of slight variations in head shape and colour but, by and large, they can be divided into three different categories. The small headed eel, as the name suggests, has a small head and mouth in comparison to its body; its head can be exceptionally pointed and its mouth contains very few teeth. In fact it effectively has no teeth, its mouth often nothing more than tough pads that bear a resemblance to fine sandpaper. This eel does not warrant the use of a wire trace when fishing for it, as its dental array hasn't the capability of damaging braided or nylon hooklengths.

The large headed eel, or broad nosed (it's commonly known by both names), has a large thick head and wide mouth with a pronounced lower lip, almost resembling a frog's head at times. These eels can have a formidable array of small diamond shaped teeth called cardiform teeth. Eels like this will make short work of nylon hooklengths, biting through them with relative ease and leaving you hookless and, even more distressing, fishless. You can be sure when one of these has been encountered that it is a true predator; an eel whose diet will consist almost exclusively of fish, and will definitely require the use of a wire trace.

Here we can see the difference between two eels of similar weights.
The one on the left is a fish eater, the one on the right is an invertebrate feeder.

The snig or 'inbetweenie', a peculiar looking fish.

John Sidley with 6lb 10oz of bull headed, predatory eel - a perfect example. (Photo courtesy of BEAC.)

The 'inbetweenie' is a cross between the two varieties. These eels are adapted to take full advantage of all the available food sources - aquatic life, worms and fish. Hence the inbetweenie can reach a large size in an extremely short space of time. This type of eel will generally be the biggest in most lakes as its diet is so varied it has no problem locating food; it can therefore be a difficult beast to tempt with a hook bait. It is also believed that the inbetweenie is probably the first shape adopted by eels when entering a newly formed water. Long before a lake is stocked with any sort of fish life, this type of eel may well have been in residence for many years.

When you set out to catch eels it will become more than evident that feeding habits are very much predetermined by the type of head shape the eels in your water possess. The resident eel populations on any given water are normally 80% of one type, 20% of the other, with a few inbetweenies thrown in. If you have just started fishing a new water you will obviously have little idea as to which type of eel is occupying the water until you have landed some, so the best idea is to start off by using worm. Deadbait feeders will take worms but worm feeders will rarely take deadbaits, so it's in your best interests to start with the most readily acceptable bait irrespective of the size of eels you expect to catch. Once the dominant head shape has been established your tackle and bait can then be adapted to suit. If they are of the large headed variety you should concentrate on deadbaits, if the small headed variety you should concentrate on worm, it's as simple as that. During a survey carried out on the stomach contents of eels from an Irish lake, the resulting data found that thirteen out of sixteen broad headed eels examined had fish remains in their stomachs whereas just three out of nineteen narrow headed eels from the same place had consumed fish. This is a very good pointer as to what baits to use for each type of eel.

As I said, 80% will be of one kind, but what of the other 20%? These eels can, along with the inbetweenie, reasonably be expected to be big fish, as they do not have to compete so much for their main source of food. Therefore if your main line of attack is going to be worms because the eels are small headed, take the gamble and put one rod out with a deadbait; it may take a long time to get a run but it may be worth the wait.

CHAPTER TWELVE

SOME MEMORABLE SESSIONS

This section includes tales of the most memorable or successful trips written by some of our most experienced eel anglers. The stories told are not necessarily of the biggest fish caught by these individuals; they are of occasions that have imprinted themselves on the minds of their authors as being enjoyable or well deserved. The hard work some of these anglers have put into not only catching eels but also in promoting eel fishing as a serious big fish pursuit is immeasurable, and I feel privileged that they have chosen to be included in this book.

A NIGHT TO REMEMBER
John Sidley

During my pike and eeling exploits over the years I have had one or two stints that have been, what I can only describe as mind blowing, for the fish landed have been out of this world: over ten double-figure pike landed in one day, four 20s in less than five hours' fishing, and many big hauls of eels in one stint - for size the best haul coming from Westwood Park, a twenty-three fish haul, the best going 5lb for a total weight of 68lb.

Reading the above one would think that this would be the limit of my success for a single night haul, yet on an August night in 1988 fishing my Birmingham lake I was to smash that target out of sight, and put together one of the biggest single hauls of eels for the size in one stint by an eel angler in many years, if not ever. It was a fishing stint and a night to remember.

This was in the height of the summer months and believe it or not no heavy rain had fallen in Birmingham for quite a few weeks. The main holidays of the factory workers had just started and, to boot, the good old British Waterways

Board had opened the valve of the lake I was fishing, the water being used to top up our canals for the boat traffic.

At full level my lake is just over ninety acres but after the valve was opened the lake began dropping at an amazing rate. During one night stint I measured that six inches of water had been taken off, and on a ninety acre lake that's one hell of a lot of water. I fear they may have taken the *Queen Mary* down the cut.

The swim I had chosen to fish had, in the past, according to one or two of the club members, only ever produced small eels, and the same was said about the pike; only small jacks and the odd double ever being taken from this area. Yet at the tail end of the previous season I had taken a 25lb 8oz pike from the swim. The conditions at that time were very different to what they were now, the lake having been full, but this swim seemed to be telling me that it held big fish - my watercraft knowledge or perhaps just gut feeling paying off again.

Even with over six foot of water taken out of the lake, this area as I looked at it kept saying to me 'snakes'; it just looked the part even though there were no real features to look at. All it was, was a bay off the main lake and for thirty yards or more from where the water level used to be, there was nothing but hard sand and gravel. But I knew in the centre of the bay there must be some sort of channel, and after plumbing the area found its deepest point to be just over four feet. I also found out about two very important factors which to me spelt snakes. Firstly, the channel was thick with heavy silt-mud, the perfect lie for any big snake for they love to bury themselves in such mud. Past experience of watching my pet eel Rover in my tank at home proved that point. Secondly, the bay was full of this season's fry. On a flat calm one could see thousands of these little fry scatter across the surface as the resident perch and pike smashed into them; even the grebes were coming into this bay to feed on the harvest. If ever a place and time spelt big snakes then this was the place and the time, and that old gut feeling inside me said, 'Sidley Snakes!'

I arrived at the swim at about 5.30 in the afternoon. This gave me enough time to set up my gear and nod out a few fish baits in the form of small roach and skimmers. These would be fished in sections, the only way, I feel, to fish any dead fish, for section baits will out-score full dead fish hands down because an eel finds its food 99% by smell rather than by sight or vibration. A head section on one rod and a tail section on the other was my plan and they would both be fished in the centre of the bay, smack bang in all that silt-mud. I felt that the eels, if present, would not wander far from that channel. There was no need for them to move on to the margins for food because that channel held all the food they wanted, with the bonus of two other free meals - my hook baits.

Rods being used were my own design - the JS eel rod, 11-foot long with a test curve of 2lb 6oz, with a good through-action. When those rods put the hook home, the action could be felt right down in the handle, a feeling which I think gives you full control over the hooked fish, for the action felt through the rod enables you to know what the eel is doing. Reels were the ones I have grown up with - the Mitchell 300 (the model I now use being the M300s). Main line 12lb Platil, a robust line that will handle any size of eel or pike regardless of the terrain being fished. A size 4 Z10 Partridge hook, coupled to a 12-inch 15lb PDQ wire trace made up my end rig, with a 1½oz ledger fished on a 6-inch link and set up in the well known JS eel rig.

This, I told myself, saw me ready, hopefully, to give the snakes some stick, but unknown to me at the time, there had never been a truer word spoken. The time was 7.45pm. Enough fish baits had been caught and the light was now fading fast. For my rod rests I set up an optonic on the front rest and a monkey climber set just in front of the reel spool. I hooked up my first rod with a roach head and cast out to where I knew the centre of the channel was. With the first rod set up and cast out, I hooked up my second rod with a roach tail; this again was cast to the centre of the channel and set in its rest. With my monkey climber set up, I walked a few yards from the water's edge to where my deckchair was placed under my brolly.

I set about sorting my gear out in its right place, for there is nothing worse than trying to find one's bits and pieces in the dark. Forceps, wire cutters, weigh sling and Avon scales were all placed neat and tidy on some soft grass, all ready to help me unhook and weigh the snakes I was hoping to catch. With my torch shoved inside my welly, I was now ready. My rods were lying in their rests, my landing-net by their side. I looked across what little water there was left in the bay. By now the wind had dropped completely, a mist was already lifting off the water, and, going by my brolly, it was going to be a wet night, for even at just 8 o'clock my brolly was covered in a heavy damp dew. A No. 6 fag was taken from my fag packet, my lighter removed from the top pocket of my jacket. I went to light up my fag and as I took the first draw on it the roach head went off. The optonic gave a single bleep then just screamed out, the red light staying on as the eel took line at an amazing rate. My monkey climber was going up and down the needle like there was no tomorrow and within seconds I was closing the bale-arm and striking in to my first eel of the night. As my rod bent over, I knew I was into a good snake as I could feel the tell-tale thumps and the backing-off motion of a sizeable eel. For a few seconds I could not move the eel from the lake bottom, but with gentle pressure I eventually moved it. I have found that the more you try to bully a good eel, the more that eel will fight back, so take a tip: once hooked, refrain from trying to pull the eel's head off.

Take your time and let the rod do the work. Once it's removed from the bottom and away from any dangers, the more gently you play your eel, the more easily it will come to the landing-net; start bullying it and trying to pull its head off and, believe me, the more abuse it will give your end rig. That abuse will take the form of sudden surges backwards and severe head shaking and it's these two actions that can and will cause the knots in your main line to break, so remember - take your time.

Within only a few seconds of casting out my first rod, I was now looking at a good eel. On the Avons she went 3lb 6oz. I placed her in my keepnet, checked my end tackle for damage and was about to re-bait with another roach head when my second rod did an action-replay of the first - the optonic was screaming its head off and the monkey climber was going up and down the needle so fast it was becoming a blur. My second strike of the night gave me another eel of exactly 2lb. I had done less than half an hour of my night stint and already I had got two snakes in the net that any eel angler worth his salt would be proud of, yet there was better to come. What followed next was mind blowing. I cast out both my baits but it was no more than twenty seconds before both optonics began screaming at me that both rods had got a run.

As I struck into the first rod and a good snake, I again felt the thumping on the other end. I looked over to my second rod and saw my rod tip bouncing from side to side; the reel line on my spool was going down so low it couldn't run freely off the spool. The eel I was now playing was gently but quickly brought to the bank, and safely netted. I rushed over to the second rod, closed the bale-arm and wound down for all it was worth. There was no slack to take up for as soon as I wound down I felt a heavy weight at the other end; the eel rod just bent double as I set the hook home. I was speechless as I beached a short but very fat snake at my feet. Seeing its size I near on dropped on top of it to man-handle it up the bank and away from the water's edge.

Sadly the hook could not be seen; a few seconds more and I feel the eel could have passed the hook through its vent. My delay in getting to the rod while playing the other fish had given this snake time to swallow the bait out of sight. There was no time to mess about; I had to remove the hook quickly, for I knew from past experience that trying to remove a deep-set hook in any size of eel causes more damage than good. My wire cutters were brought into action and the wire trace cut just inside the mouth. On the scales she weighed 5lb 1oz. And I was speechless as I weighed the other eel I had just left covered in my landing-net, for she took my Avons round to 4lb 3oz. In less than an hour I had taken eels that would normally take another eel angler all season to catch.

After placing the eels in the keepnet and replacing my lost hooklength, I

A net of eels any eel angler would be proud of. (Photo courtesy of BEAC.)

John Sidley as we would like to remember him, holding a good eel for the camera. (Photo courtesy of BEAC.)

re-baited my two rods but did not cast them out straight away. I sat on my deckchair and lit a fag, and just sat there tingling all through my body with excitement - this was eeling at its best, it felt so great to be alive, old Sidley had done it again. I remember sitting there wondering why I should be so lucky in my angling, for at times it has scared me trying to work out why I have been blessed with some of the big fish or hauls of fish I have had, where on many occasions friends fishing with me have blanked. Are some of us gifted to catch where others are not? It cannot be luck all the time. Still, if I am gifted I only hope that gift stays with me as long as I can hold a rod in my hand.

My fag smoked, I walked down to my first rod and re-cast my bait. With the main line sunk, I placed the rod in its rest and went to open the bale-arm so as to give spare line to set up the monkey climber. However, as I opened the bale-arm my main line went rushing out through my fingers as another run developed. I could not believe it. I was fishing a tail section so waited for the second run, but on striking felt nothing. When I wound the bait in it showed the marks of a snake that had just held on to it, not looking too badly mashed up. I re-cast the same tail section and the line sank even before I could put the rod on the rest. I felt pressure at the rod tip, and could plainly see my main line rising out of the water as another eel took my bait. I opened the bale-arm as fast as I could, allowed line to be taken, awaited the second run and struck into another eel. This was truly eeling at its best, a moment most eel anglers dream of - to be on the water when they go mad. And go mad they did, they went bloody barmy, for it was action all night long.

By 7.30 in the morning there was one very wrecked eel angler on the bank. I was truly knackered, and covered in slime. How many runs I had that night I just cannot remember but if I said over eighty I would not be giving you a load of bull. There were no more baits to throw at those eels. I had completely run out and was so tired that I could not be bothered to catch any more. I dread to think how many snakes I would have caught or how long the action would have lasted had I caught more bait.

It was now time to do the David Bailey bit and to weigh these snakes landed, for in the net I knew one of the eels would reach the 6lb mark - it was a very long fish that held its girth all the way down past her vent. On the Avons she went bang on 6lb, her length was 48 inches, her girth some way past her vent was 8$\frac{1}{4}$ inches. All told I had put twenty-seven eels in the keepnet. There were quite a few 1- and upper 2-pounders. The total weight I will never know but the best six fish went 6lb, 5lb 1oz, 4lb 3oz, 4lb, 3lb 6oz and 3lb.

As I returned those eels none showed signs of ill effects, and even the five that had been deep hooked swam away strongly. As I looked across the bay I had been fishing I thanked the venue for giving me such a great moment. It was then I noticed my second rod, the rod tip pointing to the sky as I had left it, resting on the back rest. The action had been so great that I had not been able to get back to re-baiting and re-casting my second rod; in fact I had forgotten all about it. You must agree, it was a night to remember.

To Capture an Eight
Mick Bowles

After months of waiting and anticipation, July 4th/5th arrived - the first weekend of the BEAC Weirwood Reservoir fish-in. I don't think anyone really knew what to expect, as during all its years as a coarse fishery, not one eel had ever been reported and furthermore, unlike Bewl Bridge and Ardingly, no eels had ever been taken in the perch traps. SWA bailiffs had never claimed to have seen any eels taken this way at Weirwood Reservoir.

However, there had to be eels in the reservoir; it was dammed up over the old river Medway bed, and its inlet was jammed open to the river for three months in 1976. No eels had ever been taken in either electro-fishing or netting, but they had been seen during these activities and were described by one bailiff 'as thick as moped tyres' and by another 'as thick as motor bike tyres'. The bailiffs said that not many eels would be caught, but if any of our lads hooked one, it would be a monster.

So it was a journey into the unknown. I had almost resigned myself to the fact that probably not many eels would be caught, if any, but I had the feeling that if someone did catch an eel it would be a biggy. Obviously I hoped it would be me, but even if I didn't catch it, it would give us all a lot of confidence if someone did.

Well the 4th arrived. A desperate attempt to try to catch myself baits prior to the trip saw me catch just two bait-sized roach, not a good start. Arriving at John Calverley's house, I was well cheesed off; not that John has that effect on you, it's just that having two fresh deadbaits, eight sardines and one hundred worms is not my idea of being well prepared for an all-out weekend stint for eels, so frankly I didn't feel like going.

Anyway, John Calverley speaking of monsters got my enthusiasm up and off we set. Another reason I was cheesed off was because, deep down, I was worried sick that we'd catch loads of trout, and perhaps not be able to fish there again; a whole host of worries played on my mind. En route we met up with Matt Johnson, on his C5. Hooking a piece of string to my car bumper we dragged Matt to Weirwood, where he nearly wet himself when he saw the size of the water. I worked it out that at one yard apart I could have 6,660 rods out around the water! We checked in at the fishing lodge and had a look at the trout catch returns for the week - nil, nil, nil, nil, only four trout taken all week.

Anyway, we filled out our fish forms, posted the money and list of names through the letterbox, and set off to the swims we had chosen to fish. After humping my gear up the dam wall I was flaming knackered and as I arrived at my chosen swim, in the dam wall corner, a strong wind was blowing right down the reservoir into it. It also had dead roach in it (spawning victims, some well over two pounds) and, I noticed, a concrete bottom, so I decided to give it a miss. Instead I walked up the bank till I couldn't walk any further and said, "Sod it. I'll fish here" - an excellent way to choose a swim.

Actually, whilst the swim had no real apparent features, it did have loads of fry being attacked by trout, plus some small roach or rudd shoals, pinned right in, in the margins. Anyway, I decided to fish this spot. Trout anglers looked on in horror as we set up bivvies and rods but were quite friendly and wished us luck. When they left we started fishing - or blanking I should say, just the odd line bite. I had four rods out: two long-range worm and DB, and two in close, worm and DB. Then, between 1am and 1.30am, I had two DB runs on in-close half sardine which were dropped. Then Matthew had a few DB runs, which he missed. Then it went quiet again. At 3am I had a good steady run on worm in close. I hit it and hooked, well in all honesty I ain't sure, it could have been any-thing, but whatever it was it came off.

I wound in, re-baited and re-cast some twenty-five yards out, in approxi-mately four feet of water and just beyond what was giving us line bites. It had been out some ten minutes, and I was just starting to walk to Matthew's swim, when a slow steady run developed. I legged it to the rod, set the bale-arm and struck. The fish took off out into the reservoir, to my right, with me back-winding like mad. Matthew asked if I had it. "Yes," I said, "it feels like a bloody great trout." I backwound some more and decided to give it some stick. Sidestrain made it veer around to my left instead of my right, so then I really piled the pressure on and it stopped dead. "Damn," I thought, "it's weeded me up." So I hauled at the fish and started pumping at what seemed a dead weight. Then, suddenly, it all went slack. I shouted at Matt that whatever it was had come off, and being in a pretty bad temper, I wound in like mad. Suddenly the rod was wrenched right over again and I shouted to Matt that it was still there. He came running with the net and I told him it had swum towards me and was beginning to feel like a eel because it was banging like hell and was coming in a straight line. "If it's an eel, it's heavy," I said.

Matthew came and stood at the water's edge with the net, and two yards out and thumping like a good 'un the eel broke surface. What followed next would be something my now good friend Matthew Johnson would never be allowed to forget. "Yes, Mick, it's an eel," he said, "looks like a nice fish, Mick. Oh yes, Mick, it's a good eel . . . Take care, Mick!" Then . . . "*!*!*!* hell it's a monster!"

The eel, on seeing the net, shot straight into it, surely the easiest eel netting ever. Matthew by this time was having a fit. He ran up the bank with my net and eel shouting, "It's a monster, it's huge, I ain't seen an eel like it." By this time I wanted to see it myself, and when we were safely fifty yards up the bank we stopped and opened the net. Matt put on his torch and we looked inside. "Bloody hell!" we both said together. I then proceeded to do a hop, skip and a dance.

The legendary John Sidley rig - wire trace, three lobs, size 2 hook, 11lb Sylcast - had done it again. I was stunned, and was doing handstands, and generally leaping about like a prat. When we unhooked the eel we could see she was hooked on the rim of the top lip, but had a nasty fresh tear in the rim of the bottom lip. Was this the eel that I lost earlier? We couldn't estimate the weight very well because she wasn't very long, but very thick. We quickly placed her on unchecked scales in a weigh sling. She weighed 7lb 11oz.

Eight pounds of muscle-packed Weirwood eel. (Photo courtesy of BEAC.)

We'll weigh her properly in the morning when it gets light, we thought. So into the carp sack she went, with seven turns of the cord around the top, and a whole host of knots to make sure she didn't escape. We took the precaution of two bank sticks and further knots to ensure the sack would not go adrift and with this done, I re-baited, re-cast, sat down, had a fag and a cup of tea, and re-lived the experience again.

When it got light the moment of truth had arrived - it was time for the weighing. Three sets of scales were used and after a bit of organisation, all three were zeroed with the weigh sling. All three scales went to 8lb. To say I was over the moon was an understatement. In all honesty I was stunned more than anything else, for in the space of some eight minutes my whole eeling career had changed. My ambition was a 6 and I thought I had a fair chance of catching one of these, bearing in mind the restrictive waters I fish in Kent. To be honest, I don't think I ever thought I would crack an 8, well especially down this way. Obviously, every time you put a bait in a water you hope to catch something big - but in reality, you just do as much research as possible, try hard and basically hope; there's no certainty.

Our photography was done in appalling light conditions with heavy rain moving down the reservoir almost a mile away.

I took one more admiring glance at my eel and then released her to her home. She moved slowly and gracefully out of the shallows and then disappeared into the deep. I waved goodbye, said thanks and wished her well.

MY FIRST 4LB EEL
Brian Crawford

I have caught many hundreds of eels over the years, from a great variety of waters all over England, Wales and more recently Brittany in north-west France. My first eel of any size, at about eight ounces, was as a young teenager, from the yachting pool on the seafront at Fleetwood in Lancashire. I remember the event most clearly, mainly because I 'discovered' that eels are coated with slime when out of water. However, following several chance encounters with eels from farm ponds, I had my first deliberate eel session at about sixteen years of age on a pond on a recreation field, one warm summer evening in 1958. I was successful and landed two 'monster' eels of about two pounds. I was most impressed with the fight on my float rod. I had not heard of ledgering at that stage but decided I needed a stronger rod if I wished to catch bigger eels, knowing that the record at the time was $8^1/_2$lb.

Unfortunately, my plans for bigger eels had to be put on hold while I went into the army, serving as navigator on small tugs and landing craft, firstly at Southampton, and then for fifteen months in the Persian Gulf, based on the island of Bahrain, where the sea temperature got into the 90s and air temperatures into the 140s in the summer. I left the army in December 1964 and moved back to Fleetwood in early 1965 with my new wife Jill. I began working for my father in his shop. It sold just about everything and was open 9am until 8pm every day of the year except Christmas Day. I worked every other morning or afternoon and every evening for £10.00 per week (out of this I paid a mortgage, ran a car and our housekeeping!).

In the summer of 1965 I began fishing the local reservoir that served the railway sheds where I once worked as a steam engine boilerwasher. I'd go in the afternoons when I was free, 2pm until 5pm, tackled up for eels. My tackle at that time was a single eel rod, a solid fibreglass 7-foot spinning rod, Mitchell 300 reel, 10lb nylon line and a long-shanked Aberdeen size 2 sea hook. I used a running pierced bullet ledger of 1oz, stopped with a swivel and the hook tied direct to the 10lb line with a trace length of about two foot. The bait was two or three lobworms collected from pulling back tufts of grass from the edge of the reservoir. The rod was placed in a single rod rest pushed into a gap between large stone blocks and the butt placed level on the sloping bank. The bite indicator was a plastic clothes peg clipped on to the line between the first two bottom rings, about two yards of line pulled from the spool and the peg laid on to a concrete block. Obviously when I got a bite the line would tighten and I would hear the peg rattle on the stone blocks. It always worked. As soon as the line tightened and the rod tip began to bend round I would strike.

The rest of my gear was just as simple. I took a plastic sheet to sit on if the grass was damp, and if it rained it was big enough to put over my head. I sometimes took along a built cane float rod as well, to fish for the bream and tench until the eels decided to bite.

Even though at that time I was only able to fish in the afternoons, I still caught eels, quite a few between one and two pounds. The reservoir was square in shape, with sloping stone block banks and a vertical two-foot wall at the top - impossible for eels to migrate from, a 'prison water'. Each bank was about a hundred and fifty yards with peg numbers painted on the wall every three or four yards. The reservoir water was very murky and about sixteen feet deep in the middle, which was towards where I cast. The bottom was deep silt.

As I was doing quite well with eels most afternoons, my brother-in-law, Terry Lomax, decided to try the action for himself, so during the first week in July 1965 we had our first session together. I tackled up in my usual way and cast out, then as he was fishing the next peg, helped him set up also. "How long do you wait for a bite?" he said. I replied, "Sometimes I get a bite instantly but, if not, I reel in about two yards of line every ten minutes until either I have to re-cast or I do get a bite."

As I had not had a bite, I reeled in about two yards and re-set my plastic peg. Just as I released the peg it shot off towards the rod. This is usual - getting a run just after moving the bait. As the line tightened right up, I lifted the rod and swung it over my head to strike into the eel. At least, I pulled the butt of my rod over my head; the rest of the rod was still pointing at the water and the rod almost in a circle. "Funny!" I said. "This has not happened before. Perhaps it's a bigger one!" A bit of an understatement. The rod obviously could not cope with the eel, which continued to try to swim away, taking line off the clutch. This was the first big fish I had ever had on so was not too sure what to do. Eventually I was able to slowly gain line and bring the eel towards the bank. We could just about see this gigantic fat snake-like monster writhing about just below the surface - the biggest fish either of us had ever seen! I then thought of a new problem. I only had a small landing-net - as had everyone else who was fishing the reservoir that afternoon. "Get hold of it when I get it to the bank!" I told Terry. "BUGGER OFF!" said Terry, moving away. "YOU HOOKED IT - YOU BLOODY LAND IT!" Great! I desperately scanned the Crawford memory bank to see if I could log on to useful information to enable me to get the beast safely on to the sloping bank. *Bing!* Out of the murky depths of my consciousness I recalled an article by Dick Walker or some such writer advising that the best way to deal with eels was to wrap them in newspaper. Terry had brought a paper with him to read! "Quick!" I yelled to Terry, "throw me your newspaper." "But I haven't finished reading it yet!" he replied, a bit bemused at my unknown intentions for his daily read, but he still threw it at me.

Delicately, while hanging on to the bucking, bending rod with one hand, I used the other hand and my feet to spread the paper near the water's edge and eased the eel nearer and nearer the bank. "You're not going to put that ******* eel in my paper are you?" Terry shouted in his loud scouse accent. "It's all right," I replied "I don't think it can read." And just then the eel shot out of the water, up the bank and on to the newspaper. I dropped the rod, grabbed the pile of thrashing eel, newspaper and several tufts of grass and threw everything up the bank, over the top of the wall and on to the level grass. I followed immediately and threw myself on top to secure it. The eel, however, was having none of this. It strongly objected to being wrapped in newspaper and being manhandled by Brian Crawford. I had experienced nothing like it before, not even Jill on our wedding night. "Hold still, you bugger!" I said - to the eel not Jill!

Brian Crawford with a 4lb 8oz eel from Colemere in Shropshire. (Photo courtesy of Brian Crawford.)

Terry had almost fallen into the water screaming with laughter. Eventually I had it tamed. I was covered in slime and bits of newspaper - as was the eel - but I had it. One of the other anglers had a set of scales. There were about ten anglers grouped round - none had seen an eel so big. After deducting an ounce to allow for the newspaper and grass and other rubbish stuck to the eel - it scaled just 4lb - nearly 50% of the British record. Nobody had a camera so the capture just had witnesses although it was filed in my memory forever. An hour later I had an eel of 2lb. Two weeks later at the same time in the afternoon I had another 4lb eel but this time I was better prepared - I had a large hessian sack to capture it in.

Since that summer of 1965 I have enjoyed many, many eel angling sessions, most on my own but lots with a multitude of eel angling characters. Of course my tackle became more appropriate and sophisticated. Many sessions were memorable, many were not - but that's eel fishing and, of course, my mind often travels back to that summer of 1965 and my encounter with my first 4lb eel.

A DIFFICULT SWIM TO FISH
Barry McConnell

Big eels like to seek refuge. Due to its shape and manoeuvrability the eel can slip through a small gap to enter a lair that other fish and predators can't gain access to. It will be able to rest here safely. Sometimes, eels bury themselves beneath the silt or in a weed-bed, other times they can be found in a crevice, amongst debris or boulders on the bottom. One of the most consistent places to locate eels is amongst piles of sunken branches particularly big, old branches, which will have the most established eel lairs, for the biggest and oldest eels.

A few years ago I came across a typical eel holding area, in a shallow bay full of sunken branches. The bay lies in a quiet, sheltered corner of a large natural mere that has existed since the ice age. This scenic water is fringed by ancient woodlands, which have, over the years, deposited many old trees and branches into the water. An angling club has removed lots of snags to clear some swims for fishing but many parts of the lake remain too choked with fallen trees. The main body of the lake is open to the wind, which pushes any fallen timbers towards the bowl of the shallow bay at one end, where they gather, become waterlogged, and then sink. The bed of this bay is an intermesh of sunken branches lying in, on and under the silt. Two or three huge trees have fallen into the marginal lily pads on one side of the bay. In the middle, many yards from either shore, some branches rise from the water to cast a reflection on the surface, adding to the picturesque setting which seems so extremely eely. This is more than a gut feeling or a hunch.

There is no sixth sense needed here - this swim absolutely screams out big eels! Unfortunately, because the log strewn shallows of the bay looked absolutely impossible to fish, I didn't try there - initially.

I first fished this lake in 1996 with Pete Drabble. We didn't know if it held any eels but the water had that look about it so we just had to give it a go. This paid off in a big way as we found the water held some massive eels. The first night was spent fishing some relatively snag free swims in open water. By a stroke of luck, we had set up on a hotspot where Peter caught two massive eels at dawn - 6lb 12oz and 5lb 4oz. Local anglers told us that is was a very hard water for eels and reckoned our catch had been a lucky one. They told of others that had tried for eels before us and fished hard all season for one big blank. However, our luck in this swim continued as I went on to add eels of 3lb, 3lb, 4lb 7oz and did eleven blanks. Pete caught three more eels - two 4s and a 3 - and blanked nine more times that season. We caught all the eels from the same hotspot.

Explorations of the lake with a plummet revealed the hotspot to be a shallower area that runs out in to the middle of the lake. This shallow bar is flanked either side with deeper water and a very soft layer of decaying leaves and silt which is several feet thick. The silt is so soft that even a small ledger sinks deep down into it. It was here, right amongst the silt, that we caught all the eels by pulling a big bunch of worms back to the bottom of the shelf from the side of the bar. It seemed that the eels were going under the silt for the baits, which must surely have been buried beneath. Furthermore, all the eels taken from this swim came between dawn and sunrise. I've got two different lines of thought on this. Firstly, the eels were there to feed - bubbling amongst the silt-bed for bloodworms and other food items. Secondly, the eels were there to hide away and rest - and they stumbled on the baits as they made their way to the silt-beds where they intended to bury themselves away from the increasing daylight. Anyway that's a topic for another time.

We fished the hotspot a lot the following season and caught quite a few more eels. This put the swim under heavy fishing pressure, which started to tell as catches became less and less frequent. In 1997 I caught eels of 5lb 1oz, 4lb 12oz, 4lb 5oz, 4lb 2oz and 3lb 14oz from the hotspot and did nineteen blanks. Pete managed eels of 4lb 2oz, 3lb 10oz, 3lb, 2lb 8oz and did thirteen blanks. In 1998 Pete caught a 5lb eel on the first night and hasn't fished there since. I also caught on the first night - a 4lb 9oz and then went on to do twelve blanks in the same swim. In 1999, once again the hotspot produced an eel on the first night – 5lb 6oz and then nothing but blank after blank.

As catches from the swim gradually decreased it became very hard going, so hard that Pete, who couldn't spare enough fishing time, gave up on the water.

There was only one - Only the Lonely (a name given to me by Dale Robson, a leading zander angler from the Fens). I tried different swims around the lake - nothing, nothing, nothing - the pattern became predicable; I couldn't locate any eels despite fishing every cleared area where it is possible to fish. Even the hotspot cooled off. Between us we had caught twenty eels and spent over seventy nights on the swim. This had fished it out. Eventually, no matter how many days and nights were spent fishing there, it didn't seem possible to catch another eel. It seemed that my luck had run out and now, like others that had tried before me, I was to suffer continuous blanks; perhaps I would never catch another eel from this water. Eventually desperation and dreams of monster eels drove me to try to fish amongst the log-strewn bay. Impossible? Or just a difficult swim to fish?

I set the bivvy up in a clearing amongst some large trees that overlooked the bay at the lake's end. From here, it is nearly a hundred yards across to the far bank, where angling is not permitted. From the branch of a tree it could be seen that the depth gradually increased from less than a foot under the rod tip to no more than three feet, seventy yards across the lake. At this point, the water deepened into a darker area where a deep trough ran roughly twenty yards along and about ten yards across before it shallowed off again just short of the far bank some ninety yards away.

Several exploratory casts, with a 3oz bomb, were bounced back through the swim to help get a feel of the layout. The right-hand side of the deep area was full of snags. Towards the other side there were two branches protruding from the water. These appeared to be attached to a large tree lying embedded into one side of the deep hole. There was just one small patch on the lake's bed where it was possible to bounce the ledger on the bottom without getting snagged amongst the sunken logs. Long-range plumbing revealed the depth of this clear zone to be around seven feet.

I was later to learn that a diving club, which used chains and winches to remove some massive tree stumps, had created the hole. But some of the stumps proved impossible to move. The clear zone to which the cast must be aimed was a very small area of about ten square yards. Even here the occasional attempt at opening up the swim to angling wasn't too successful and they had eventually given up. Rigs had got caught up on pieces of rotting logs and branches that littered the bottom. All casts that had gone off target resulted in disaster. Even plumbing the swim resulted in the ledger snagging up and the line pulling against sunken branches. Then, when the line was pulled it would cut a groove through the branches' softened exterior until it came against the harder inner wood, damaging the line.

The problem increased when you added a hook because its sharp point so easily pricked into and became embedded in the wood. What I was up against here was a lakebed made up predominately of wood. When pulling into a snag a mass of bubbles would spread over quite an area as one became connected to an intermesh of petrified wood. With strong tackle it was possible to rip some of the thinner branches and I went on to collect quite a pile of these as I gradually dug my way into the swim using 3lb Armalites, 15lb Berkeley Big Game, 25lb wire trace and 3oz Arlesey Bombs.

The first night on the swim was a nightmare. It isn't easy trying to accurately taper the cast down and get it on target at this range. Things are even more difficult in the dark when the rod must be aligned with silhouettes on the far skyline, after which it is down to guess work and luck - or bad luck, as the case often was; most casts became snagged solid and I spent nearly all my time tying rigs rather than fishing. I made things worse for myself because I often use more rods than there seems to be room for. To add to the stress, nuisance fish soon whittled down any baits that were successfully cast to a snag free patch; this increased the frequency of re-casting and stretched the patience. During the first day and night I managed to catch bream, perch, pike, tench, lots of pieces of wood and absolutely no eels. The second night proceeded to be just as tortuous until dawn, when suddenly, in the middle of the nightmare, I managed to hook a big eel. During the fight I could feel some scary twangs and bumps being transmitted up the line as the eel writhed backwards and managed to bump its snaking tail amongst snags. Somehow I managed to win the tussle and get a superb 5lb 13oz eel into the net.

The following night I caught no eels and ran short of terminal tackle after getting hooked up on snags a trillion times. Spirits ran low until it became easy to put the previous night's capture down as a fluke and I decided that it just wouldn't be possible to land another big eel in such a ridiculously snaggy swim. I went home after the second night and declared the swim impossible.

Next season, on the spur of the moment, I braved the swim again and hooked something heavy at dusk. It managed to kite off to the right and snag around an emerging branch and the line was heavy enough to apply brute force. The branch snapped with a loud crack after which I wound in a 7lb bream with the tip of a waterlogged branch attached to the line. Eels don't kite to one side so readily and are usually easier to steer. Although eels can pull harder than any other species, they tend to swim backwards and fight out their tug of war in straight lines, making it easier to choose a line of play with no snags.

After this bream it took me ages to get a line back in. Every cast went solid as soon as I moved the lead in order to check that the rig was on a clean bottom. I lost so many rigs that I got quite fed up and decided I would give up at dawn.

Just as it was getting light I hooked a big eel. It fought the same as the eel I had caught from the swim the year before. The weight was exactly the same too - 5lb 13oz. Last year's eel measured 42 inches by 9, this time 41.5 inches by 9. How accurate are my measurements of length? Was it the same fish? I've got photographs of each but they aren't close-ups and it's difficult to tell. While I was weighing the eel I got a screaming run on the other rod. I struck into another big eel, which I managed to raise to the surface and haul rapidly across the lake. Then, in a careless moment, I lost it when I eased off slightly to stoop for the landing-net. I had misjudged the position of a large branch that lay just below the surface only a few feet away to the right of the net. I was demoralised by the loss of this eel, even more so, when, a few minutes later, I lost what felt like another eel as something powerful got around a snag within seconds of being hooked. I moved swim that morning and vowed never to fish there again. This time it had taken just the one night before I lost the plot as once again the swim had proved too hard for me.

The following season I once again targeted this water but this time I intended to fish more manageable snag free swims. A lucky 5.6 on the first night was followed by many blanks on snag free swims. Twelve consecutive blank days and nights on the old hotspot had my thoughts straying to the 5.13 swim. Impossible had become too strong a word for the swim since I had caught there. Instead I started to think of it as a swim requiring extreme patience, a real bastard or just a very difficult swim. I thought about the best approach when playing an eel there - it's simply a matter of raising a hooked eel on to the surface, then keeping it there and hauling it in hell for leather on a tight line without pausing to give it an inch. Of course this isn't entirely possible in practice but so far I had somehow managed to land two big eels and get another one close to the net. I decided that a more determined assault, requiring extreme patience, on this swim seemed a better prospect than totting up endless blanks on other swims.

This time I was better prepared, with stacks of home made ledgers. I tried some sea anglers' lead lift vanes, which fit just above the ledger and speed up its ascent to the surface on retrieval. These lift vanes work, but they are better employed in deeper water and I often found myself attached to a snag before I could raise the ledger to the surface. Since first fishing this swim I had been experimenting with different ledger rigs to use amongst the snags. I normally use a link ledger with a long link but in this swim the link tended to cut into the wooden snags and get trapped or damaged. I tried an inline ledger with no link but I wasn't happy with this as I kept thinking of it lying amongst the silt and wooden debris, which would restrict free movement of line through the centre hole of the ledger. This time I opted for a very short link, just long enough to fit a plastic ledger lift vane on before tying a large run ring on the end of the link. Later in the season I dispensed with the ledger lift vane and replaced it with a lift ledger - a flat-bottomed vaned ledger. This did away with the need to put a plastic vane on the line and meant I could replace the line link with a sturdy snap swivel link, which didn't cut into the wooden snags when the rig was ripped back through the swim.

During the first night I caught a 1lb eel, the smallest I have ever seen from this water, followed a couple of hours later by a 5-pounder. This was a good result but it was very hard going; in fact, it was positively tortuous at times. A string of big tench up to 6lb 12oz kept me on my toes, caused a few false eel alerts and generally caused havoc as I brought them through the shallows. The pile of wood beside my bivvy got bigger and bigger as I continued to extract bits of log from the 'clear zone' that I was casting to.

The following day I was visited by Eric Brown, a fanatical carp angler with an interest in eels that had recently led him to join the NAC [National Anguilla Club]. The 5-pounder I had in the sack was the biggest eel he had ever seen so he thoroughly enjoyed taking some photos for me. Later, after he had gone a strong breeze chilled the waters and activity from nuisance fish ceased as they went right off the feed. I only got one run that night, at 11.45pm, when I hooked into what was obviously an even bigger eel. The rod arched fiercely round as I struggled to control the eel for a few minutes before getting the upper hand and managing to raise it to the surface, over deeper water in the middle of the clear zone! Now came the tricky bit, the eel had to be brought across the lake for seventy yards through shallow water full of snags. I'd been here before - it was shit or bust time. Maximum pressure had to be applied in order to keep the eel on the surface and keep it moving. If it was brought in fast enough it would never be able to gain its composure enough to start backing off.

My familiarity with the swim enabled me to pinpoint the snags and form a pretty good idea which route to negotiate with the big eel. It's hard to recall exactly how I did it. The adrenalin kicked in and I brutalised the tackle. In other words, I held my breath and applied more pressure than the rod was really built to take. Somehow the tackle held up and I ended up with a personal best in the net.

I weighed it in at 7lb 4oz, sacked it up, and then made a quick call to Eric. It didn't seem long till dawn when he came to photo the eel on his way to work. We weighed it again to find it had lost an ounce and a half but agreed on the original weight after noticing the sack was full of pale yellow coloured excrement, which was oozing from the eel even as we photographed it. The eel was very fat and it had obviously been gorging on something that comes out the other end a kind of yellow colour. We measured it - 43 inches long with a

Top: 7lb 4oz of hard-earned eel.

Bottom: 5lb 7oz - another excellent fish from a difficult swim. (Photos courtesy of Barry McConnell.)

girth of $11^{1}/_{8}$ inches. One big chunk of eel, making me happy, very happy.

A week later I was back again for a six-day session. This time I was using lift ledgers rather than plastic vanes. I also threaded a hollow wine-makers' cork on the line above the ledger where it could pop up to the surface and help to raise the line above the snags. These additions, though far from perfect, definitely assisted me but only when the cast was landed within the 'clear zone'. As usual, many casts went astray and I lost a lot of tackle amongst the snags. Once again all the hardship seemed worthwhile when I landed a 4.14 first night. The following five nights produced no eels, only stacks of nuisance bream.

I had now sorted out the ledger as best I could but the point of the hook was still catching in the wooden snags far too often to make for enjoyable fishing. The next step was an obvious progression; the point of the hook must be masked. A quick phone call to Pete had his inventive mind rising to the quest for a hook guard. Within a few days he had made progress. Trying various household objects that were to hand he had found one that did the job satisfactorily. A washing-up liquid bottle top, with the stopper bit cut off, was threaded on the line, then a small bead was threaded on before tying on the hook. He then reeled off a list of other objects he intended to try, such as half a plastic Kinder egg or anything cone-shaped. However, he reckoned on being happy enough with the prototype bottle top because a size 8 hook, matched to the appropriate size of bead, would retract into the hollow inner until the bead

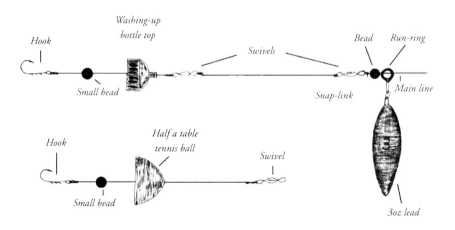

The two rigs used by Barry to beat a difficult swim. (Courtesy of Barry McConnell.)

butted up against the small holes at the top, and the point of the hook would be shielded within.

He told me the best bit at the end of the phone call. To put the rig through a proper test he had gone into the back garden to engage in guerrilla warfare. A cast right over the top of a fully-grown sycamore tree had been successfully retrieved through the branches. His last words were, "Is that good enough for you, Baz?"

The next session of five days saw me trying a new snag-beater rig with a cut-down washing-up bottle top and a bead threaded up the line where it could slide down over the hook to shield the point (I don't know where I get these ideas from). I tested it in the margins and found that I could bounce the lead and hook guard against underwater branches, then scrape the whole rig over the top of a sunken log without catching the hook or losing the bait. Hence the name 'sunken log rig'.

The first night saw the swim full of skimmers, which were constantly attacking my massive bunch of lobworms. Generally they moved my bobbin between an inch and a couple of feet before finding the bait too big and dropping it. I didn't mind this activity for two reasons: firstly, it provided a good test for the rig which definitely didn't deter the skimmers; and secondly, once the bobbin had moved several feet I knew that both swivels of my rig had been pulled clear through the small hole in the centre of the hook guard. I hadn't been too sure about this part of the rig - would the swivels catch on the hole and provide resistance causing the eel to drop the bait?

If the bobbin activity ceases this is a sign that nuisance fish have pinched all the bait off the hook. This is not a problem as the hook will retract into the guard and can be retrieved without snagging up. So long as the bobbin keeps dancing there must be some worm still attached to the hook and it can be left there until an eel happens along. This is exactly how it went on the second night when eels of 5lb 7oz and 3lb 8oz were caught, along with countless bream. I felt quite smug after that. I had scored. The rig worked.

The following day I got hold of two whole, large king prawns and tried them as bait to avoid the bream. I never found out if the bream would eat them because the first one was picked up off the bottom by a 9lb pike within minutes of casting and the other one, first cast, went astray only to be taken by a pike as it was dragged back across the surface. A miracle pike bait? I ran out of washing-up bottle tops so I improvised with pop bottle tops punched through the centre. These did help guard the hook but were less effective. The following day, a visit to a sports shop armed me with some table tennis balls, which I cut down to suit the preferred hook sizes - 2s and 4s.

I developed sufficient confidence with the rig to be better able to carry out and enjoy my fishing so I spent a few more nights fishing the swim during which time I was able to put my favourite improvement - the cut down table tennis ball - through a lengthy test. It passed the test, as I caught pike, perch, bream, tench and roach but no more eels came from this swim, not even during perfect weather conditions on nights with no moon.

Since first fishing the swim I have amassed a total of nineteen night sessions there (thirteen blanks) and caught eels of 7.04, 5.13, 5.13, 5.07, 5, 4.14, 3.08 and 1.00. As I write this, during the depths of winter, I wonder if I've caught the biggest, if not all the eels from this area. Yet there is still a gut feeling that something even bigger is lurking there. This gut feeling makes me think that I will fish there again, probably as soon as the water is warm enough next spring. One thing is for sure; this swim was conquered the hard way. The exercise was a learning curve from which I developed a rig for fishing over a wooden bottom. This rig has helped turn an impossible nightmare swim into just a very difficult swim to fish.

BROADWATER
Steve Ricketts

Getting prepared for another trip to Broadwater was not a thought I relished. Fighting my way through London's hellish traffic jams to complete a thirty-five-mile journey often took in excess of two hours, with most of this being done at a frustratingly slow crawl. In fact, I had come to the conclusion that in London the term 'rush hour' was now a redundant phrase and that 'rush day' was more appropriate.

Arriving at the lake, totally stressed, the thought of the impending half dozen trips to the top of the lake with the tackle loaded on to a wheelbarrow seemed just too much to cope with, especially in the blistering summer heat of midday. Pulling into the car park, I pulled the car over into the shade of some trees, grabbed a cold drink from the cool box and flopped on to the grass and tried to unwind.

Broadwater and the two other lakes on the site are set in some of the prettiest surroundings I have ever fished. The river Colne, flowing bright and clear behind the lakes, plus the area being classified as an SSSI site, means the whole area is mostly left to its own devices. But more importantly as far as I was concerned was the fact that the lakes contained big wrigglers. The lakes on this site had the potential to throw up some biggies, the bailiff having already taken fish to seven pounds. Yet I was struggling. This season I had already clocked up nineteen blanks without so much as a twitch on the bobbins, and the prospect of this continuing looked all too good.

Sitting on the grass I heard the gates to the site rattle and shortly afterwards another car pulled into the car park. This turned out to be Dougal, the local bailiff, and what a godsend he turned out to be, for on this occasion I was granted a rare privilege: he unlocked the chain across the path and allowed me to drive my gear to the top of the lake on the proviso that I brought the car straight back. Carefully manoeuvring the car along the heavily overgrown path, stinging nettles and grasses reaching over door height, I wondered if I would ever get the car turned around but by the time I had reached the end of the islands the path had cleared and I was able to view the large, daunting expanse of water on my right that was known as Broadwater.

Stepping out of the car into a swim that was near the end of the islands, I surveyed the lake trying to decide where to fish. Swim selection here is never an easy task. Every swim contains lots of likely looking features: numerous gravel bars that nearly breach the surface then plummet into depths of fifteen to twenty foot; margins that drop straight down to twelve foot of water only feet from the bank; and countless large weed-beds. So, understandably, locating fish involved as much luck as it did skill and judgement. Yet this time was to be different, I was given a sign no predator angler in his right mind could ignore. To my left, maybe another hundred yards further up, there was a commotion going on that was obscured by bushes and the curve of the lake. I couldn't accurately see what was going on but I could hear splashing. Walking along the path, the disturbance soon became visible - black-headed terns were bombing the water and perch were exploding on to the surface in every direction. It was a feeding frenzy caused by the shoals of perch who had cornered bream fry, thousands of them, in this small bay. To say I was gob-smacked would be an understatement, for I had never caught a bait-sized fish from this lake before, nor had I ever seen signs of small fish. Yet here I was, confronted by several feet of water that was black with fry, so many in fact that they were beaching themselves in an attempt to evade their attackers. To this day I have never witnessed such an occurrence again, on this lake or any other. I can only liken it to the way mackerel shoals herd small fish against piers or beaches in their feeding frenzies. Choice of swim was therefore decided for me. The tackle was deposited in the swim and the car was swiftly driven back to the car park.

By approximately 4pm, my bivvy and everything else had been assembled and I could now relax and wait for the arrival of dusk. End tackle was to be standard JS rigs coupled with Richworth flavour bombs; wire traces with size 6 hooks. Bait was to be double lobs and bream fry. A quickly assembled landing-net when I first arrived had given me enough bream fry to last a life-time, let alone the coming session. As the perch were still harrying the bream fry, I attached a small red and white Mepps spinner to the line of my float rod and spent the next few hours happily extracting perch to nearly two pounds.

As the afternoon wore on into evening I inflated my small dinghy and set about exploring the contours of the swim with a newly acquired fish finder. This experience I found almost as exciting as the fishing itself, and as I watched the black clouds of small fish surrounded by larger fish drift past I wondered what was going on in the depths below. But I wasn't out here to fish spot, I was out here to locate any underwater features and deposit my rubby-dubby bag in a likely looking position. Forty yards out the water shelved up to reveal the presence of a good-sized gravel bar. The rubby-dubby bag was positioned half way up its inner slope. The bright orange ballcock marked its position and I rowed back to shore feeling confident in the knowledge that everything was in the right place, including me. And, believe me, confidence is something you need on this lake.

By 8 o'clock all four rods had been baited, cast into position and set on their individual rests, primed for action. Everything that should be at hand was. I then put up the mozzie net and retired to the bivvy to cook dinner. Lying on the bed-chair, allowing the large chicken curry and several slices of bread to settle, I was disturbed from reading my latest Shaun Hutson novel by several bleeps from one of the optonics. Curious as to why it bleeped (it's so rare to get a run here, you forget what they sound like), I went outside to take a look. Nothing seemed to have moved so I presumed it had been a bat brushing the line or some other night critter dashing about on its nocturnal business. Looking up I noticed that the sky had silently filled with ominous-looking black clouds, which definitely looked like they contained rain. I decided to cover up some of the gear I had strewn about outside, and as I did so the optonic sounded again. I spun round and caught sight of the bobbin lifting several inches from the floor and then stopping. Walking over to the rod, I crouched down beside it and squinted to see the line where it entered the water. The line was twitching, sending off little circles around it so I picked up the rod, wound down and struck. Shock! There was an eel on the end. Not a great deal bigger than the bait, but an eel all the same. Weighed at 1lb 4oz, I placed the little fellow in the keepnet to have another look in the morning. I know it seems sad weighing and retaining such a little fish but eels seemed so hard to come by from this lake that catching an eel of any size at this moment in time I regarded as an achievement. A fish from my own water! I was chuffed and settled back down with my book, content in the knowledge that my run of nineteen blanks was finally over.

At five to eleven the deadbait rod screamed into life. I pinched myself to make sure I wasn't dreaming, then rushed outside. Line was steadily being taken so without hesitation I closed the bale-arm and struck. This time the strike connected with something that pulled back. Several thumps were felt through the rod, then nothing except a ponderous weight that began kiting slowly to my left, leaving me to believe I might have connected with a pike. As the fish drew closer, the lead became visible, then a large black head appeared which shook from side to side before sliding easily into the folds of the big net. The fish and net were hurriedly carried up the bank and the torchlight revealed a big fish. The scales registered 4lb 6oz; I'd equalled my p.b. after so long. The eel was placed in the net along with the other fish, then the rod was re-baited and cast back into position. I'd equalled my personal best and caught two eels in one night, in a place where one run a weekend was the norm; maybe my luck was changing. Now I was up for it, the chair was positioned by the rods. I'd donned a waterproof jacket to ward off the very fine rain that had started to fall and sat myself in the chair and watched those bobbins with a new found intensity!

I must have dozed off for I awoke at 3.45am to the sound of two optonics screaming one-toners. I grabbed the nearest rod, struck, engaged the bait runner and placed the rod back on its rest. Then I picked up the second rod, felt resistance and struck into that fish as well. Quickly I pumped the fish towards me, netted it, unclipped the trace and moved the rod out of the way, then grabbed the first rod. Line was still being taken with the bait runner engaged. Flicking the bait runner off, the rod bucked over and I found myself connected to a very good fish. Trying to pump this fish towards me was more difficult; the fish didn't appear to want any of it. Eventually it came within range and was netted, with the other eel still in the landing-net. Again the trace was unclipped and both fish were carried up the bank away from the water's edge. Pulling back the folds of the landing-net, two eels were exposed to my torchlight and by my standards one of them looked huge. The smaller of the two weighed 2lb 9oz, the bigger fish pulled the scales round to 5lb 1oz. To say I was chuffed was an understatement for I had equalled and beaten my personal best in one night. No more runs came that night, probably due to me hopping around the bank shouting "Yes! Yes! Yes!" but at that point I couldn't have cared less.

As daylight slowly broke through the thick grey clouds it brought more rain with it, this time persistent and heavy, accompanied by gale-force winds. The strong winds and wave action had now created such an undertow that the bobbins were pulled up to the rod within seconds of them being attached, making open bale-arm fishing all but impossible. I then had no choice but to fish with the bait runners engaged. This done, I retired into the dry and warmth of the bivvy and decided to get my head down for a few hours. Some time later I awoke and decided to try to find someone who could take some photos for me.

Luck was definitely on my side as Eric Hodgson from the British Carp Study Group and a couple of mates had arrived to do a trial fish-in in the hope of discovering the water's carp potential. Photos taken, everyone retired to their respective bivvies to get out of the rain.

Daylight fishing on this lake is very rarely worth it, nothing appears to feed except perch and the large waterfowl population but the rods are left out just in case. Evening couldn't come quick enough; by then the rain had stopped although the sky still looked dark and angry. The wind had died away leaving the lake flat calm, patches of oil rising up from my rubby-dubby bag the only disturbance on a lake that now resembled a sheet of black glass. I had butterflies in my stomach; I had that feeling that something was going to happen tonight. A sixth sense or maybe the atmospherics but I believed and felt that the eels were going to have a serious grub-up and that for once I was in the right place at the right time.

By 8pm all the rods had been armed with fresh baits - small perch, bream fry and worms, with sardine oil in the flavour capsules placed on the leads. Bale-arms had been opened and bottle tops placed on the line. I was ready! I brewed myself a cuppa, placed the chair by the rods and sat back to await the action I was expecting. And I didn't have to wait long: 8.31pm signalled the first run, resulting in an eel of 2lb 8oz. Four more runs were missed until 9.02pm when I connected with another fish. This eel weighed 3lb 3oz and went absolutely ballistic, shooting out of the water and up the bank as it approached the net. There was no netting required as the fish was already half way up the bank, buried in the grass. By 9.34pm two more eels had been netted - 1lb 6oz and 2lb 14oz - with several more runs missed. This was crazy. I was having more fish and runs in one night than I had had in the combined trips of the last two years.

I brewed myself another drink and at 11.02pm the margin-fished perch dead-bait was taken. By now the rain had returned, blanketing everything in a fine mist-like drizzle, yet I hardly noticed it. I picked the rod up, felt the line steadily being pulled through my fingers and waited. The line stopped as the fish turned, then swallowed the bait, then moved off again. I felt the line move again and struck. This time the strike met something solid.

For the first time I experienced the raw power of a big fish throwing a tantrum. The rod keeled over as the eel tried to back off, taking several yards of line before I managed to lock the drag up. Then it just held there, shaking its head in defiance. An eternity seemed to pass before I had the fish moving towards me but in reality it was probably only a matter of twenty seconds or more. With steady pressure the fish was begrudgingly drawn forward until its head appeared in the V of the landing-net; one good pull, lift and she was mine.

I'd done it again. At 5lb 12oz I'd smashed my personal best again. This was

Eels of 5lb 12oz, 5lb 8oz and 4lb 11oz.

Eels weighing 3lb 3oz, 3lb 5oz, 3lb 8oz, 3lb 10oz.

unreal. With shaking hands I re-baited and cast back out. By 4am seven more runs had been missed and three more eels had graced the net - 2lb 12oz, 3lb 6oz and 3lb 10oz. I was beginning to think every eel in the lake must be in this swim, feeding. As if to prove me wrong, the bobbins hung motionless as the early morning light tried to filter through the fine rain that had been falling most of the night. Once light, any chance of an eel run has usually gone. Whether it was the heavy cloud cover and the rain, this morning was going to prove different.

It had just turned 6.30am when the margin rod signalled another take. The strike met something that just powered off before coming unattached. I didn't have time to contemplate whether it was an eel or a big pike as the optonic on the next rod burst into life and 4lb 11oz of angry *Anguilla* came writhing to the bank. With two rods now out of the water, I started to bait up but the third rod now took off. This also resulted in the landing of another biggie of 5lb 8oz. No more runs were to follow that day but I don't think it really mattered. I was soaked to the skin, absolutely knackered.

That morning you couldn't have found a happier angler anywhere in the country. I had a net full of big eels and a big soppy grin that wouldn't leave my face for many a day to come. Later that morning the bailiff came round after hearing about the previous night's catch and was just as surprised at what I had caught the second night as I had been in catching it. Many more photos were taken, the fish released back whence they had come, and the day was spent trying to catch more baits for the third and final night's fishing. Several small bleak were extracted from the river and combined with the bream fry I had left so I had enough bait for the final night. The weather had now reverted to bright sunshine and the clouds had all but dispersed but I was still hopeful of extracting a few fish.

Between eight and nine that night I caught two more eels - 4lb 14oz and 3lb 10oz - on two-day-old dead bream fry; the other baits never moved.

Since this catch of eels was taken in September '94 I have continued to fish this lake and have landed a total of eleven more eels in eight years of trying, beating my personal best two more times with two fish both weighing 6lb 2oz. The lake was a hard fishery when I started and still is, so why the eels behaved in such a manner over those few nights remains a mystery. I have since fished the lake in similar conditions and blanked consistently. Maybe the eels behave like this occasionally every year and you just need that bit of luck to be there when they do. I was there once and had a field day so I look forward to being there on the occasion that they do it again.

CHAPTER THIRTEEN

DO MONSTERS EXIST?

Do monster eels really exist? Now that's a leading question if ever there was one. Many well respected eel anglers believe that eels well in excess of the British record are waiting out there to be caught yet the vast majority of the angling world snorts at the idea; they believe fish like Steve Terry's 11lb 2oz record are flukes and will never be bettered. Here I hope to present you with some of the facts, stories and conjecture which might shed light on whether there just might be a leviathan existing in the depths of a lake, unknown and unfished for. Perhaps, though, as many anglers believe, they are just myths conjured up from our own fertile imaginations.

Over the years I have come across many reports of huge eels in books, newspapers and many other sources. The reported instances and stories detailed below are the more credible of the ones I have encountered. For instance, Christopher Moriarty in his book *Eels: a Natural and Unnatural History* records that in the 1840s Leonard Jenyns, in his notes on Cambridgeshire fishes, gives mention of two incredible fish that were taken from Wisbech near Cambridge after a dyke was drained. These eels weighed in at 22lb and 28lb, with the largest measuring 6-foot long. Jenyns was acknowledged as a very accurate and well-informed observer of wildlife and this lends credibility to his story. Scientifically these eels are within the limits that European eels are capable of attaining but they would be at the extreme upper limits and exceptionally old and rare. The measurements he provides for one of these fish also equates to an eel weighing between 20 and 30lb. Jenyns' records carry some authority as Alwyne Wheeler, the zoologist and author, published his notes on Cambridgeshire fishes in 1973.

Sitting on my shelf at home is a dusty old tattered book I picked up in a flea-market called *Birds, Fishes, and Insects,* written some time in the nineteenth century by Captain Thomas Brown, in which he devotes a rather interesting section to eels. Some of the writings are quite amusing now that much more is known about the eel and its life cycle. For instance, he believed that eels travelled to the sea via the network of rivers and canals and on entering the sea changed into congers - a reasonable assumption for him to make in the nineteenth century but one we now know to be quite false. However, this is not the reason why I mention the book; in the book he gives several mentions of eels attaining very large sizes. He speaks of Sir John Hawkins who had a small section of canal at the back of his property in Twickenham - this was around 1840 - where he regularly fed the ducks. During one hot summer he noticed that all the baby ducklings had disappeared. Fearing that a great pike had taken up residence, he decided to have the section drained and cleared and the offending fish removed. As the water disappeared, a great many large eels, some a yard and three-quarters in length, were discovered, yet no pike. When these eels were gutted and cleaned the remains of the ducklings were found in their stomachs.

Captain Brown also refers to an eel weighing 16lb taken in Peterborough in 1667, the earliest record of a big eel I have come across. He gives several accounts of similar eels yet what I find most amazing is that he shows no surprise for the size these fish are attaining; he refers to them as though they are a perfectly natural occurrence rather than an extraordinary phenomena.

Throughout history reports of eels in excess of double figures continue to crop up. There are numerous references in some of my early research material to an eel weighing 15lb that was supposedly trapped in the river Kennet at Newbury in 1835. The Reverend Richard Lubboch in 1839 recorded in the book *Fauna of Norfolk* an eel weighing over twenty pounds taken near Norwich. The *Manchester Guardian* in July 1926 reported the trapping of an eel in a salmon fisher's net weighing 16lb 8oz from Whiteadder Water near Berwick.

Some time during the 1960s the late, great, Richard Walker reported seeing an eel fall from a mass of weed being dragged from the river Avon and estimated its weight to be around sixteen pounds. J.W. Martin, the 'Trent Otter', an excellent angler of great standing, mentioned an eel of 25lb shot in the river Welland. Double-figure eels have been reported to have blocked the intake grids on a power station at Loch Ness, although Loch Ness is part salt water so these could have been congers, and Abberton Reservoir near Colchester supposedly had double-figure eels taken from it by commercial trappers. Hanningfield Reservoir has also claimed to have taken immense fish in nets as recently as the late Eighties; some of these fish were reputed to weigh as much as 18lb. And to top it all, there are three reports of eels exceeding 30lb, with one being put on show at the International Fisheries Exhibition at South Kensington in 1883.

One of the most recently reported monsters, although not in this country, was an eel weighing 28lb and measuring 7 feet 1 inch long taken in a fyke net in

Holland in 1994; an overseas member of the BEAC sent in a newspaper clipping from his local paper showing the captor holding the fish. This is the closest I have come to obtaining a photo of one of these large mythical eels but sadly newspaper copies are bad quality and I have been unable to track down the original photo, my Dutch not being what it should be! Maybe if this book is published, a kind Dutch person living near Amsterdam might be able to help me out here with this report.

Drawing of eels by H.G.C. Claypoole, from The Art of Angling, *1957.*

Undertaking the research for this book I was able to find many stories of eels surpassing double figures yet hardly any photographic evidence. During the advances of fishing in the twenty-first century reports of eels this size diminish and become very difficult to trace, yet rumours of these monsters stubbornly seem to persist, albeit less frequently. Even in 2005, reports of a 13lb fish were rife. The angling papers even carried the story that the eel record had been smashed yet no photos were forthcoming. So the existing record of 11lb 2oz still stands. You would think that with the amount of anglers fishing the banks nowadays, if one of these huge fish were still out there it would surely have put in an appearance on the bank at least once. It could therefore be argued that, in the past, monster eels probably did exist at these huge weights but that fish of this calibre no longer now survive in British waters. Having said that, reports still persist that anglers have been smashed by fish they claim would have broken the existing record by several pounds but until someone lands one of these fish and provides photographic, authenticated evidence we are left only with the intangible dream that monsters are indeed out there.

My own opinion is that an exceptionally big eel is not going to be an energetic hunter; it will be an old, smart fish that doesn't move around much, just hunts in its own little patch, hijacking prey from its lair, just like those big old congers in the deep sea wrecks. Maybe it just mooches about on the bottom, sucking in silt and syphoning off insect larvae, the theory that John Sidley believed. If this eel's territory is just a small area, let's say ten square yards in a lake of thirty acres or more, a fish of this size and age would not have a fast metabolic rate so might eat only every couple of days. How many nights' fishing would you need to put in to locate the area this fish may inhabit and then wait for it to feed? And for those reasons I think it's possible for a very large eel to go uncaught by rod and line almost indefinitely.

There are also numerous theories as to why, if they do exist, anglers don't catch them. These vary from the ridiculous to the absolutely bizarre, so let's have a look at some of them but stick to the more sensible ideas. One of the most common theories is that big eels don't eat dead fish. Bull! Many very big eels are taken accidentally by anglers fishing for pike with fish baits, for example, Chris Price's 9lb 13oz fish from Revesby Reservoir and D. Boyers' 8lb 1oz fish from Broadlands Lake in Hampshire, which took a sardine in December. The late John Sidley claimed to have seen an eel of exceptional proportions feeding on a dead four-pound tench; John had handled an eel of over twelve pounds taken in a netting so was in a good position to gauge this eel's size. This should throw doubt on the argument about eels not eating fish but are these exceptional fish we are talking about? At what weight does a fish become exceptional? For me it's just into double figures but as far as history reads I may be being a tad conservative.

Another theory is that the really big eels swim about sifting small food items from the silt; this one is possible yet I cannot imagine a big hungry eel, when presented with a juicy lobworm, swimming past and refusing this tasty morsel. There has been a lot of research done into the stomach contents of eels and some of this has shown large quantities of small food items to be present in larger eels. They have also shown a large quantity of fish so nothing in these studies is conclusive regarding the eel's diet. Again it comes down to size: the eels studied very rarely, if ever, exceed four pounds and these are not the mythical creatures we are trying to unearth. The stomach contents of eels also show huge variation in diet dependent on the areas they are taken from, so diet is unlikely to be the problem. John Sidley's eight-pound fish came on lobworms as did Mick Bowles' eight from Weirwood. Many other documented big fish have also been caught on worms. So therefore we know that big eels will consider eating worms and dead fish, our two prime baits.

If bait is not the problem, could it be the tackle we use to try and catch eels? For many years eel anglers have been going round in circles: small baits, light tackle, big eels smashing you up; big baits, strong tackle, eels avoiding you. It seems little progress has been made in this area since Noah built the Ark. When we use the standard eeling tackle and hook a good fish the initial response is to pull and wind as hard as possible to get the fish off the bottom. The eel's reaction is to pull back with equal force placing enormous stress on your tackle, so maybe we need stronger tackle but more refined. Richard Walker once stated, after seeing his eel fall from the weed on the river Avon, that if he was ever to fish for such a creature he would have to use 20lb line and a beach caster type rod; maybe this isn't too far from the truth. Most of the big eel anglers I know have reported being smashed by above-average sized eels. John Sidley and Gerry Rogers, to name but two, have lost battles to these leviathans through their tackle letting them down. I have not yet had the luck to connect with a fish with this sort of power. The rods I use, coupled with 15lb line, could stop a good swimmer doing a length in a swimming pool so I have little doubt that a big eel will not cause me any more problems than my stepson did.

Below is a list of record eels taken in the UK and Europe. Apart from the UK fish, all the other weights are not dissimilar. Some people may well take this as proof that eels can only just reach weights of low double figures and that these are very exceptional fish. Others might suggest that this represents the upper limits of fish that our tackle is capable of handling when one is hooked. Who really knows?

Record Eels

Wales	8lb	Rob Jones	1969
England	11lb 2oz	Steve Terry	1978
Germany	9lb 8oz	Unknown	1982
Norway	8lb 9oz	Unknown	1980
Sweden	8lb 1oz	Unknown	1982
Holland	8lb 13oz	Unknown	1980

*Gary Mason with the second biggest eel ever taken on rod and line,
weighing in at 10lb 7oz - a fish we all dream of catching; well I do anyway. (Photo courtesy of BEAC.)*

The American record for an eel is 10lb 3oz, taken in the Shetucket river, Connecticut. Although this fish is a slightly different species, *Anguilla Rostrata* (the difference being a couple of vertebra), it is still related closely enough to make little difference. Some people are even speculating that it may very well be the same species, but that's something for the scientists to debate not me.

So what do you think? Are we at the limits nature has imposed on the eel or are there still greater things to come? The eel record is generally believed to be one of the hardest records to break, but I don't agree with that. The eel record being broken by a dedicated eel angler would be a great achievement but it's against all the odds. There are not enough of us fishing on different venues to make an impact. True, we catch some good fish, but spread out across the country we probably fish less than 1% of all the water available, and with the problems posed by big eels a handful of specialists are going to struggle. If eel angling, just for one week, had the turn out of the carp angling fraternity across the country, I believe the record would go pretty quickly and with a bang. Until eel angling has reached those giddy heights of popularity the ability to separate fact from fantasy may never arrive.

We may never have all of the answers to all of the questions posed by the eel and perhaps that isn't a bad thing, for one of the attractions of eel fishing is the mystery that surrounds them. Perhaps if all the mysteries were solved, eeling would lose its attraction. From everything I have learned, eeling can be fun, exciting, frustrating and heart breaking. The fish you catch may be older than you, have travelled further in its life than you, and been in the water, undetected, for many more years than you could possibly imagine. And if those mythical fish are now just a dream, then dream; for without dreams like this, fishing would be no fun.

Chapter Fourteen

Conclusions

Where to start, how do you wrap up a book about eels when so many of the questions asked still remain unanswered? I don't know. Maybe what I have written will stimulate thought from within our own ranks or just maybe it will induce a few defectors from the throngs of other specialist anglers out there to give it a go and try to solve some of these mysteries for us. Surely with a little understanding of how to approach and catch all our fish species, whether large or small, you must in the end become a better, more knowledgeable brand of angler? For instance, you can pick up ideas used from other branches of angling that have applications you might never otherwise have considered if you single mindedly pursued one variety of fish. Some of my best angling companions, who by coincidence or just bad luck happen to be carp anglers, have given me rigs and baits to try that they have developed. Exchanging ideas, sitting by the lake discussing problems, just having a chat and being friendly is how we may, possibly, come up with some solutions to the many problems posed by eel fishing. Learning from the mistakes and experiences of others can considerably ease the task, almost an impossible one to some minds, of being a consistently successful big eel man.

It's taken a long time, far too long in fact, for eels to have gained any respect from the big fish world and I think it will take even longer before they are generally accepted as a worthwhile quarry by many of today's specialist anglers. It seems ponds and lakes stuffed with commercially bred fish are now the main reason to go fishing rather than the pioneering challenge of the unknown. There is no learning curve for young anglers, no chasing dace or roach in a small stream, but then cormorant predation has put paid to much of that anyway. New anglers come into the sport, buy the best gear, join the local syndicate and expect to catch 20lb-plus fish with no more experience than what they have read in the papers. And where can you go from there? Nowhere. Most of these anglers sell their gear, having 'been there, done it' as they say.

Over the last thirty years or so, in my branch of the sport we have been fortunate enough to have had a few special anglers in our midst, people who have campaigned vigorously to improve the image that eels have and to promote our sport with no thought of financial gain. To give credit where it's due, they have had some success but they are sadly a long way away from achieving their objectives. For my own part, I have never been much of a campaigner, I'm just your average Joe with a passion for fishing. This book is therefore intended as my token effort in supporting a sport I love; a sport that is under threat from anglers' ignorance, commercial activity and a myriad of other problems. Therefore I wholeheartedly support the actions of those who stand up and campaign for the protection of all fish, be it individuals or groups like the Angling Trust.

It would be great if all anglers could put their differences aside and stand together. Modern carp anglers seem to have little time for anyone else; trout anglers despise coarse anglers; pike anglers feud with eel anglers over using eel as baits, and so on and so on. A little more understanding and tolerance from each group could go a long way in helping to show a united front to the anti-angling brigade, and to the public in general for that matter. In my own sport of eel fishing I have been shocked many times by the ignorance of anglers towards the eel. The eel is a worthy sport fish and is not something that should be slung up the bank for swallowing tenpence-worth of hook.

There has always been a small band of dedicated specialists who have pursued the eel, knowing that to catch a 6lb eel is a far harder achievement than to land a 30lb carp. Many of these anglers have moved on to fish for other species but have still maintained a healthy respect for the eel; something some of our more single-minded anglers should think about. This following has never been huge but it's been consistent; there has always remained a small hardcore faction who pursue nothing else. It's a group I would like to think I have come to belong to, yet I still love catching other fish; if a big tench, carp or pike picks up my bait it can be just as enjoyable as catching that which I set out to catch - I bear them no malice.

For me, one of the most exciting things about eel fishing is when, in the dead of night, that buzzer bursts into life signalling a take. At that moment, until I feel the weight of the fish bucking through the rod, I am that young boy again dreaming of childhood monsters. As the years have crept on, in retrospect the one thing I was not prepared for was how hard big eel fishing has actually proved to be. I have fished many waters expecting blanks, but I have racked up many more blanks than I ever thought humanly possible. I have always pursued the dream of landing a double-figure eel, a fish I am still seeking after more than two decades of trying. Nowadays my patience isn't what it used to be and sometimes I ask myself if I am still cut out for this type of fishing as I seem to have less time to go and everything appears to be getting harder as I get older. Things could have worked out differently but they didn't. I have fished hard, tried everything I know on some soul-destroying waters for, yes some very good fish but not the one fish I have so desperately sought.

But then I suppose big eel fishing has to be hard; if it wasn't, everybody would do it. The hard is what makes it so attractive to me. I've experimented with new baits and blanked with new baits; I've tried traditional baits and blanked with traditional baits; I've popped baits up, bolted them down, floated them with rig foam, used small baits, big baits, bizarre baits and failed to get a run. Is it my fault I couldn't catch or is there some other reason? I certainly hope there is, for my sake. Trying your heart out for so long, you can forget that fishing is supposed to be relaxing and enjoyable, and it becomes hard work to get motivated even when a fish is caught. So what has made me so determined to continue in the face of all this disappointment? Why do I still spend far too many days and nights pitched up on the bankside in the foulest of British weather, wasting my hard-earned cash on the best tackle I can ill afford and risking the wrath of my beloved partner by leaving her sat in front of the TV? For me - and I guess many other specialist anglers would agree - all this is rewarded by the sense of achievement. After all the hard work, the planning, the selection of waters, the experimentation with rigs and various baits, surviving the tedium of fishing hard waters night after night, coping with the ever reliable British weather, when all this work comes to fruition and a ruddy great eel is cradled in the folds of the net, the sense of achievement is not easily put into words. Ecstatic would be summing it up lightly. So what else can I say? Eels are the final frontier of angling. They are one hell of a challenge, a challenge I cannot walk away from. So I guess that's why I do it.

When I first started eel fishing, the great thing I loved was the runs, screamers that happened regularly through the night, they were electrifying. By all means go after big snakes, for these are our fantasy, but don't forget the fun factor. Every now and then fish a water where you get plagued with runs. So what if the majority of fish struggle to make two pounds in weight; if they put a smile back on your face and remove that sourpuss look, it's a job well done. I once spent a whole season on one water pursuing rumours - my total result a 1lb fish, a fish I could have caught anywhere. As a result, I failed to fish the following season with any conviction, I just couldn't begin to get motivated. This is quitting and I am not a quitter, so fish those waters with smaller fish occasionally, if just to remind yourself what it's all about. Those hard waters with big fish are fine if you have one on your doorstep - in an ideal world this would be perfect - but many of us are not that privileged. If you are, you can come home from work, relax, have your dinner and go down in the evening, cast out and are almost guaranteed a good night's kip, only rarely being disturbed by a run, then go home in the morning. This is not the ideal way to fish for big eels but it is not as mind blowing as pitching up on a hard water, enduring sixteen hours of hot sun, unable to kip in the bivvy because of the heat and then trying to stay awake for the few hours of darkness when they may feed. These day and night sessions can take a lot out of you and I end up sleeping the sleep of the dead when I return home. Long hours camped on the bank do not automatically equate to bigger fish, although they undoubtedly help. Angling experience, accumulated knowledge and making the best use of the time available is the best recipe for success.

It has taken me many years to learn that you should mix your fishing between a large variety of different waters. Some I fish, eels have never been caught yet are believed to be present, so I try. Others fish their heads off with runs all night and have the possibility of throwing up a good fish or two, but most are in the 2-3lb bracket. Fishing like this I can now stay motivated. Having watched many a good friend fall by the wayside, either through lack of fish or loneliness, it seems they have simply burnt themselves out by fishing too much. I really don't want to end up in this situation myself; I love my fishing, but I have come close, too close in the past.

So what does the future of eel angling hold for me? I will still be out there fishing for eels whenever I get the chance, only now I have to remember I have the responsibility of a home and family (I was warned they get you in the end) so I may not always go as much as I would like to, and may never be as successful as I'd like to be, but with the help of an understanding wife who knows of my dreams I am allowed out enough to possibly make them come true. So at this moment in time the most important thing to me is that when I do go, I make the best use of my time and really enjoy what I'm doing. There will always be that excitement that big eel fishing offers; it's possibly the last great challenge of angling left to be surmounted and will probably remain so for many years to come. The repeat captures each season of known carp, bream and barbel virtually hand-fed on protein baits to bolster their weights to record levels, do not offer the challenge I seek in fishing. I would rather catch naff-all than pursue these fish. But each to their own. A lot of anglers cannot understand why I pursue eels, so I hope that in writing this book I have relayed that big eel fishing is not a chuck it and chance it affair. Give it a bash and see.

Over the years I have learnt much about the eel, yet in some ways I feel I know very little as they always seem to do something I don't expect. I dare say I'll die before I have half the answers. But that's eel fishing, a challenge that won't make your day, your week or even your year. A big eel will make your life.

I hope you have enjoyed reading this book and being subjected to the insane ramblings of an eel-angling fanatic. Good luck with your fishing, for the future of our sport lies in your hands.

S. J. Ricketts

Some Useful Contacts
and a Few Waters Well Worth a Go

The National Anguilla Club

The National Anguilla Club is the oldest single species group and has been established within specialist angling since 1962. The NAC is presently headed by Steve Richardson as President, Mike Brettle as Chairman, Mark Salt as General Secretary and Patricia Huish as Treasurer. The club produces two publications of its bulletin, *Anguilla*, each year. The bulletin is compiled from articles, photos, letters etc., etc. from the membership and all members are encouraged to contribute towards each issue. Each publication contains approx fifty-five pages of eel angling information. There are also at least two newsletters each year and these carry information regarding club fish-ins, regional activities and political information.

The NAC holds at least two national fish-ins per year and each region organises at least one fish-in as well. The club has a very active and social focus which helps to generate sharing of information and, along with the club reporting scheme, helps to build up an understanding of eels and eel angling. Every effort is made to make all new members welcome and the breakdown of the club into regions helps towards this goal.

An informative website and active forum can be found at:

www.thenationalanguillaclub.co.uk

The NAC also boasts a large merchandise base, which includes t-shirts, polo shirts, sweat tops, metal and cloth badges and hats. All products apart from the badges are available with personalised embroidery as an extra. In summary then, membership of the NAC is open to all anglers who have an interest in fishing for eels, whether large or small (the eels, not the prospective new members). The golden rule within the NAC is this: 'No one is bigger than the club'. Anyone who wishes to enquire for further information about the NAC should contact

The President of the National Anguilla Club, Steve Richardson
showing how it's done with a 4lb 10oz fish. (Photo courtesy of NAC.)

the General Secretary: Mark Salt, 2 Home Close, Marshalls Lane, High Cross, Herts SG11 1AJ or e-mail him at *secretary@nationalanguillaclub.co.uk*

Anyone wishing to join the NAC should contact the Membership Secretary via their website or email *membership@nationalanguillaclub.co.uk*

(And here's a personal message from the NAC: *The National Anguilla Club would like to offer their thanks to Steve Ricketts for allowing us the space to offer information on our organisation and wish him every success with this book. Steve is a valued member of the NAC and is a dedicated and successful eel angler in his own right. In having written this book, Steve has opened up the way for more anglers to enjoy and understand the fascinating species which is* Anguilla anguilla.)

Cemex Angling

Cemex Angling has been more than helpful in my pursuit of big eels and I owe them a big thanks for allowing me on to some of their more exclusive waters. They can be contacted at: Cemex Angling, Cemex House, Coldharbour Lane, Thorpe, Surrey TW20 8RA. Tel. 01932 583630. They are a helpful, well run organisation with many waters of interest to the specimen eel angler.

BW Bradley Baits

These are a great bunch of blokes who've generously backed my eeling campaigns over the last decade or so by supplying me with loads of fresh lobworms, saving my poor old back from all that hard work; also the tons of old manky maggots I use for my pre-baiting sessions. They supply all types of fresh and frozen baits that should more than cover the eeler's needs. They can be contacted at: Cottington Court Farm, Sholden, Deal, Kent CT14 0AR. Tel 01304 614049.

And Lastly There's Me

I can be contacted by email at *finalfrontier62@hotmail.com*. Just because I've finished writing the book does not mean my research into the eel has. If anyone has photos of big fish, stories, factual or otherwise, I am always interested. You may wish to voice your opinion on something I've written that you do not agree with. I am always open to hearing differing views whether I like them or not. You may wish to ask advice. I have never claimed to be an expert but I have many friends in the angling world and, between us, we should be able to solve most queries.

A FEW WATERS WELL WORTH A GO

Lake Bala, North Wales. This is certainly a big water to take on; being four miles long and half a mile wide in places, you have almost 1,200 acres of water to choose from. Bala Lake is not renowned for giving up its fish easily unless you count perch. With depths to a hundred foot and miles of banks, the specimen fish this place holds will require some work to winkle them out. Very big brown trout, including the ex Welsh record, and pike well into double figures exist in the depths, but what of the eels? I know of fish to over four pounds being caught so bigger fish must surely exist somewhere. Dave Holman, in his video, fishes Lake Bala and catches some small eels so if you're interested it may be worth acquiring his video. The water has big fish potential and is definitely worth a bash. Permits are available from local tackle shops in Bala and are reasonably priced.

Bayham Abbey, near Lamberhurst in Kent was once a very prolific coarse fishery until it closed its doors to become a trout fishery. After operating like this for some time the owners then trialled coarse fishing again which was a success. It's now open for coarse fishing again with proven 4lb-plus fish and reports of 5-pounders. River fed, with a good age to the water, it definitely has potential.

Johnson's Lakes, New Hythe, are famed big fish waters. They are famous for big carp, pike and tench, and also have some big eels to offer, but they are not easy. Basically a five-lake complex, the waters have got harder as the years pass by, and their lack of bootlaces prove small eels are not getting into the waters any more. You'll need a day-ticket or season-ticket, both of which can be obtained from the bailiff on the bank. You'll need a season-ticket to night fish. It's worth noting that you should never leave your tackle unattended here, day or night, and make sure your car contains no valuables. Unfortunately petty theft is a sure sign of the times.

Westbere Lake, now owned by Mid Kent Fisheries near Canterbury, is a season-ticket only water and in my view is one of the top eel waters in Kent. It's also a brilliant winter eel lake. Although all types of eel exist in here, most are huge mouthed, bull headed beasts and, as such, deadbaits produce the bigger fish, worms you stack up on small eels. On bottom, mid-water and sub-surface rigs blitz this water. There are eels virtually everywhere: it's produced 4s for Mick Bowles and I; also 6s have been taken by pike anglers on whole herrings. It's a fantastic starting water. Pike and big perch can also be caught in this 80-acre lake.

Piltdown Pond, Newick, East Sussex. A $1^1/_2$-acre water which is free fishing and has a car park. It's noted for bream, roach and tench but has produced eels to six pounds in weight. Quite a few eels over three pounds are caught each season. It's worth a go.

The Sedges, Bridgewater ,Somerset. Two ponds of $3^1/_2$ and $2^1/_2$ acres, noted for carp fishing, bream and decent tench. This old brickworks fishery also has a reputation for big eels. Night fishing is allowed and unhooking mats compulsory.

Chapmans Pond, York. A free fishing old clay pit, run by the council, has produced perch over four pounds in the past. This water was long neglected and was only tidied up a few years ago. No night fishing makes this a difficult eel venue, but a few big eels have been reported.

Markeaton Park Lake, Derby. Only 300 yards long, this lake is quite established and produced a surprise pike of 37lb 8oz some time ago. Night fishing is allowed but its eel fishing potential is largely unknown. However, if it can produce a pike of that size there could also be some very big eels.

Basingstoke Canal, Mytchett to Ash Vale. With day-tickets just a couple of pounds from local tackle shops, this stretch of canal opposite Mytchett Lake is worthy of attention. Eels to six pounds have been reported, though generally most are much smaller. Jack pike can be a pain on deadbaits. Day-tickets are dearer if purchased on the bank.

Lower Foulridge Reservoir, Colne, Lancashire. An all year round venue (no close season), this large water with depths to thirty feet, has a reputation for producing a few big eels each year. It's used as a match venue. Tickets are available on the bank.

Bolingey Lake, Perranporth, Cornwall. An unusual water, man-made and not yet twenty years old, this water has produced eels to eight pounds. Although the eels in this water are few and far between, they all seem to be very big fish, as are the carp and perch.

Connaught Water, Epping Forest, Chingford, Essex. An old Victorian gravel pit that has produced eels to over five pounds, some to well-known eel anglers. It has a silty bottom in places. Night fishing is allowed and at weekends a small café is opened beside the lake. Tickets on bankside.

The Chase, Dagenham, Essex. A water made famous for producing an eel of 9lb 2oz. Serious eeling is hampered by no night fishing. Tickets on the bank or from Bowlers Angling tackle shop in the town.

Homewood Trust Fisheries, Chertsey, Surrey. Tickets for this water are quite expensive and require booking in advance. This may explain why it's not fished more often by us hard-up eel anglers. At over four hundred years old, this water was only opened up to fishing in the early Nineties and has produced eels to over six pounds with lots of smaller fish being reported. Contact Botley Park Hospital.

Wraysbury No. 1, Berkshire. Famous for once holding the tench record and the home of Mary, a 50lb carp, the water is believed to hold some enormous eels, possibly double figure fish. The lake best is 7lb 8oz. Contact RMC Angling for permits. Four rods allowed, a sensible policy.

Nickolls Quarry, Kent. This is one of those big coastal gravel pits I tend to spend a lot of my time on nowadays. Some sixty acres in size with depths to twenty feet or more, its potential has hardly been scraped, yet two kosher 8s have been caught and there are the usual rumours of much bigger fish being present. Small eels can be a pain but time invested here may pay dividends. There are tremendous shoals of rudd everywhere you fish, many to specimen size. This makes catching little ones for bait a problem, good fun though. Contact Derek Weller for more details - 07970 704584.

These are just some waters that may be worth a go for the budding eel angler. Most of the details for these waters were correct when gathered in early 2009 but things change as time moves on so it's worth checking before visiting them. Although these waters have produced big fish or have big fish potential your best bet is still to try to locate a water of your own.

SOURCES

Barak, N. A. E. & Mason, C. F. 1992, 'Population density, growth and diet of eels *Anguilla anguilla* L., in two rivers in eastern England', *Aquaculture and Fisheries Management*, 23:59-97.

Bertin, Leon, 1956, *Eels a Biological Study*. Cleaver-Hume Press, London.

British Eel Anglers' Club, archive material and photos supplied by Mick Bowles, 2001.

Brown, Captain Thomas,1850, *Illustrative Anecdotes of Birds, Fishes and Insects*, James Blackwood & Co., London.

Cousteau, Jacques Yves. Estuarine Research Reserve, USA.

Dekker, W., 'Is the European eel overfished?' Paper presented at the 11th Session of the EIFAC/ICES Working Group on Eels, Silkeborg, Denmark, 20th-24th September, 1999.

Egusa, S., 1979, 'Notes on the culture of the European eel (*Anguilla anguilla L.*) in Japanese eel-farming ponds', *Rapports et Proces-Verbaux des Reunions, Conseil International pour l'Exploration de la Mer*, 174:51-58.

EIFAC, 'Report of the thirteenth session of the Joint EIFAC/ICES Working Group on Eels, Copenhagen, Denmark, 28th-31st August, 2001', EIFAC Occasional Paper No. 36

Environment Agency consultation document on a proposed National Eel Management Strategy, March 2000.

Environment Agency, 'Commercial netting of eels and elvers', June 2009

Kinder University, USA. 'A bibliography of the eels of the genus Anguilla'. Fisheries Research Board of Canada. Technical Report 28.

Knights, B. & White, E. M., 1997, 'An appraisal of stocking strategies for the European eel, *Anguilla anguilla L.*', in I.G. Cowx, ed., *Stocking and Introduction of Fish*, Oxford, Fishing News Books, pp 121-140.

Knights B. & White, E. M., 1998, 'Enhancing immigration and recruitment of eels: the use of passes and associated trapping systems', *Fisheries Management and Ecology*, 5:459-471.

ICES 9.3.2.6 EC request on the Draft EU Guidelines for Eel Management Plans (EC regulation no. 1100/2007)

Knights, G., Russell, I. & Hamilton, R. M., 1999, 'National report on eel stocks in England and Wales', ICES/EIFAC working group paper, Silkeborg, Denmark.

Lecomte-Finiger, R., 1994, 'The early life of the European eel', *Nature* 370:424.

Loefving, Stellan, 1999, 'Eel farming for oriental markets'.

Malaysia Koi Club (Internet site) 'Fish anesthesia'.

McCosker, J. E., 1989, 'Freshwater eels (Family Anguillidae) in California current conditions and future scenarios', California Fish and Game. 75.

Moriarty, C., 1973, 'A technique for examining eel otoliths', *Journal of Fish Biology 5*, 183-4.

Moriarty, C., 1978, *Eels, A Natural and Unnatural History*, David & Charles.

Pellegrin, J. and Spillmann, J., 1937, 'Inegalites de developpement et cannibalisme chez l'anguille', *Bull. Soc. Cent. Aquic. Peche*, Vol. XLV, Paris.

Poole, W. R. and Reynolds, J.D., 1996, 'Growth rate and age at migration of *Anguilla anguilla* (L.)'. *Journal of Fish Biology 48*, 633-42.

Sidley, John, 1990. *Eels*, Beekay's 'Successful Fishing' series.

Tamarkin, Dawn A., 2000, 'Olfaction', Springfield Technical Community College (STTC) Foundation Press, USA.

Tesch, F. W., *The Eel*, Chapman & Hall, London (revised UK edition 1977).

Vollestad, L. A., 1992, 'Geographic variation in age and length at metamorphosis of maturing European eel: environmental effects and phenotypic plasticity', Journal of Animal Ecology 61, 41-8.

Wirth, T. & Bernatchez, L., 2001, 'Genetic evidence against panmixia in the European eel', *Nature* 409, 1037-1040.

INDEX